Faustus and the Censor

For Hetta Empson

Faustus and the Censor

*The English Faust-book
and Marlowe's* Doctor Faustus

WILLIAM EMPSON

Recovered and edited
with an introduction and postscript
by
John Henry Jones

Basil Blackwell

First published 1987

Basil Blackwell Ltd
108 Cowley Road, Oxford, OX4 1JF, UK

Basil Blackwell Inc.
432 Park Avenue South, Suite 1503
New York, NY 10016, USA

British Library Cataloguing in Publication Data

Empson, William
  Faustus and the Censor: The English
  Faust-book and Marlowe's *Doctor Faustus*.
  1. Marlowe, Christopher, 1564–1593
  Doctor Faustus
  I. Title II. Jones, John Henry
  822'.3 PR2664
  ISBN 0-631-15675-5

Library of Congress Cataloging in Publication Data

Empson, William, 1906–
  Faustus and the censor.
  Bibliography: p.
  Includes index.
  1. Marlowe, Christopher, 1564–1593. Doctor
  Faustus. 2. Marlowe, Christopher, 1564–1593—
  Censorship. 3. Faust, d. ca. 1540, in fiction, drama,
  poetry, etc. 4. Censorship—Great Britain—History—
  16th century. I. Jones, John Henry. II. Title.
  PR2664.E47 1987 822'.3 87-11699
  ISBN 0-631-15675-5

Typeset in 11 on 12½ pt Baskerville
by Joshua Associates Limited, Oxford
Printed in Great Britain by
T. J. Press Ltd., Padstow

Contents

Preface

In presenting this essay, Empson's last major study, before the public, I feel the need for an advance defence against those who will criticize the undertaking as an unwarranted exposure of material not fully prepared for publication by the author. Their cries will be even louder in the present case owing to the highly controversial nature of Empson's thesis and the difficulties in recovering a unified text which I describe in the introduction. Let me disarm them at once by stating that the thesis was Empson's stubbornly held conviction and there is no question but he intended it to be published. He had been working on the material intermittently for at least ten years before his death and the sheer bulk of typescript drafts and revisions testifies that this was no *jeu d'esprit*.

If he had lived he would doubtless have made final revisions and seen the work through the press himself. In doing this for him I am therefore justified by the knowledge that it was what he wanted, even if the final form falls short of his exacting requirements, however much I have striven to realize his intention. Of necessity this has entailed editing Empson in a manner which others might consider impertinent, since in selecting which variant drafts should be used I have no authority other than my own judgement and the experience of a close working relationship with the author throughout the period of composition (though I must stress that I did not collaborate in the present work other than by providing a translation of the German Faust-book). I have also taken the liberty of omitting a few weak lines of argument which I feel he might have rejected after discussion or which prove to be spurious in the light of information which was not at his disposal. However, I have retained arguments where I know he was unshakeable, even though I do not always agree with them. My own editorial additions to the text (as necessary link passages or to fill a lacuna) do not amount to more than a hundred words. The text used has been referenced throughout to the serial numbers I gave to the surviving typescript pages; this provides an authority for the text and should facilitate the work of scholars wishing to reinvestigate the papers. (The Empson archive is owned and housed by Harvard University.)

I should like to express my deep appreciation of the warm interest of the Empson family in this project, especially of Lady Hetta Empson who has continually urged it forward and provided unfailing assistance in innumerable ways, including the temporary transference of the papers to my custody. In dedicating her husband's work to her I wish to transmit his well-known sentiment and hope I may share in making this offering.

I should also like to thank John Haffenden for his generous advice and ardent support in recommending the venture. His enthusiasm has been greatly sustaining. I am likewise indebted to Barry Carman for friendly criticism of the introductory matter, and to Andrew Best of Curtis Brown for skilfully nursing the enterprise.

Abbreviations

Boas	*Christopher Marlowe*, Frederick S. Boas, Oxford (Clarendon Press) 1940
EFB	The English Faust-book, i.e. *The Historie of the damnable life, and deserved death of Doctor Iohn Faustus* ... translated into English by P. F. Gent ... London (earliest extant edition) 1592; see *The German and English Faust-books: Parallel Texts*, tr. and intro. John Henry Jones (forthcoming)
GFB	The German Faust-book, i.e. *Historia von D. Johañ Fausten* ... (edn princeps), Frankfurt a. M. (Johann Spies) 1587; the translations used in the essay are from Jones, *The German and English Faust-books*
Greg	*Marlowe's 'Doctor Faustus' 1604–1616: Parallel Texts*, ed. W. W. Greg, Oxford (Clarendon Press) 1950
NED	*A New English Dictionary*, 13 vols, Oxford (Clarendon Press) 1933, 1961
Palmer and More	*The Sources of the Faust Tradition*, P. M. Palmer and R. P. More, New York (Oxford University Press) 1936
Sp.	Pagination reference to the GFB Spies first edition, used to indicate sources of material translated

Introduction

The essay

On 27 November 1975, William Empson gave a public lecture at the University of Newcastle-upon-Tyne, entitled 'What the censor took from *Doctor Faustus*'. The text of this lecture has not survived but we are fortunate to possess an advertisement in which he provided the following comment on the subject matter:

A French traveller in 1590 reported: 'Germany is almost entirely occupied with building fires for witches. Switzerland has been compelled to wipe out many of her villages on their account. Travellers in Lorraine may see thousands and thousands of the stakes to which witches are bound.'

The German Faust-book (1587) was one of the first international best sellers, translated into six languages of Western Europe in as many years; and its mass public regarded Faust as a particularly bad kind of witch. But magicians were well received by princes, Queen Elizabeth among the rest; and they claimed to work through Middle Spirits, neither of Heaven nor of Hell. The Church maintained that there were no such spirits, and till 1592 was trying to implement an official right of censorship of plays. The confusion of the surviving texts of *Faust*, and the difficulty of dating them, imply that it ran into trouble with the censor.

How far then can we estimate what Marlowe first wrote? In our surviving evidence he appears boastful about being enlightened, so that he would be ashamed to appear involved in propaganda for witch-burning. Much has been learned about sixteenth-century magicians in recent years, especially from the writings of Frances Yates; they played an important part in the development of the sciences, and Marlowe would hear about them at Cambridge. He

would have to satisfy his mass audience with the drama of the
Faustbook, but would also need to show that he understood the
conflict of opinion. The play inherently tells a sad story, but it need
not gloat so coarsely as the version prepared ten years after Marlowe
was murdered.

   I think that Faust wins at the end what he says he wants at the start,
and is still begging for in the great final speech; that is, having become
legally a Middle Spirit, he is entitled to oblivion, and free from eternal
torture. The parts of the plot that arranged this have been cut out; but
some remaining fragments give evidence for it.

The expansion and substantiation of the thesis outlined in this
summary forms the subject of the present essay which probably
subsumes much of the lecture, modified by the evidence he derived
from the English and German Faust-books in the following decade.
The lecture notice is important since it indicates that Empson's
main thesis was extensively formulated by late 1975, when I first
made his acquaintance, initially as his tenant. Learning that I was a
translator of German, he was anxious that I should help him with
some parts of the German Faust-book which he wanted to compare
with corresponding passages in the English Faust-book, Marlowe's
main source for *Doctor Faustus*. Clearly he was gathering evidence for
his thesis, of which I was ignorant. However, my interest in the
Faust-book had been stimulated and when I discovered that no
accurate English translation had ever been published (the English
Faust-book is very free and imaginative), I decided to undertake the
task with a view to publication, a project much encouraged by the
Empsons. Unfortunately Empson was never to see the complete
work in its finished state, nor was he able to avail himself of much of
the research implicit in my introduction, most of which was written
after his death. However, he was in possession of working drafts of
the translation from mid-1976 onwards and used these as the basis of
his comparison of the two Faust-books. (The quotations he makes
from my translation in the present essay have been revised to accord
with the final draft.)

   Initially Empson had envisaged his Faust essay as a book, or part
of a book, on Marlowe, and possibly he retained this conception as
late as 1979; in an unmailed letter to Ms Roma Gill, dated 8
October of that year and enclosing a short essay 'Kill-devil all the
parish over' (see appendix 2), he says 'I plan to put this in my
eventual book.' Be that as it may, his intention, from late 1976, was

that the Faust essay should form an appendix to the published translation. Presented in this context the reader would have had the material basis for his discussion immediately to hand, together with all the ancillary information I had provided in the form of notes, introduction and bibliography. One consequence of this decision was a need for economy if the appendix were not to be longer than the translation itself; Empson seems to have set himself a target of 60,000 words.

He had prepared a complete reading draft of the appendix by January 1982, and he gave it to me on the very morning of his departure for Miami where he was to teach for the next five months. It was a moment of great flurry and haste and he had been working most of the night to finish the draft. There was barely time for him to indicate to me which parts were which when the taxi arrived and the Empsons were gone. I was soon to discover that the papers he had given me were in considerable confusion and mingled with earlier drafts; he must have got them mixed up during his furious last-minute amendments under the pressure of his imminent departure. The problem lay in the irrationality of his pagination system. The essay was in six parts, each numbered consecutively from 1, but the rewrites were also numbered from 1 or given the same page number as the corresponding page of the previous draft. (I counted seventeen page 1s, fifteen page 2s, etc., besides whole sections without any pagination at all.) Unfortunately I was too busy with other work to devote much time to setting the material in order, but I made what I could of the jumbled essay; in consequence I was apprised of the more *outré* conclusions without the martialled arguments which led to them. It seemed to me then that the thesis was wild beyond belief. I wrote a muted letter expressing my feelings and explaining that the material was in disorder. When he arrived back in Hampstead and inspected his work, he was convinced I had dropped it and we soon ceased to discuss the matter. In any case he had a great deal of other work to attend to: the revision of *Milton's God*, the Marvell essay, and the sundry critical essays for the *London Review of Books*; and he was seriously ill. He planned to retackle the Faust essay next after *Using Biography*, but the preface to that book was the last thing he wrote, the revisions dictated from his sickbed. He died five days later.

As a close friend of the family, familiar with Empson's work, I was entrusted with the task of sorting out the vast accumulation of his surviving manuscripts, notes and correspondence, and this gave me the opportunity to collate all the material of the Faust essay. Reduced to originals and amended copies, this amounted to some 500 foolscap pages of typescript of which perhaps a quarter were paginated in the manner already described. A straightforward listing of page *incipits* and *finits* was not as helpful as I had hoped, since it was Empson's frequent practice to start a page by rewriting the last few lines of the previous one. Also it became clear that not all the pages were present. However, long sequences were soon established and the broad structure of the work became apparent. At this stage there came the problem of deciding which of several drafts of a given section was closest to Empson's final intention and how much in the way of variants might be usefully added. I adopted two guidelines here: the first, that the expanded versions were the more recent; and the second, that variants would only be introduced if they supplied more information or clarification of the argument. To maintain the Empson flow, long sequences from selected drafts are largely uninterrupted and cognate material from other drafts has been submitted as footnotes, although Empson generally avoided using them; however, the rational exposition of Empson's thesis necessitated considerable chopping from one draft to another, and throughout the text superscript letters indicate changes to different manuscripts referring the reader to the textual notes at the back of this edition. Three longer passages which could not be included as footnotes are given in appendix 1. All the Empson material is referenced according to the serial numbers I assigned to the surviving typescript; this reference number is followed by the Empson pagination (E followed by a number 0 indicates no pagination; T indicates an unpaginated title page, corresponding to page 1 of any of the chapters). Footnotes which carry such references (at the beginning) are Empson material; those which do not, represent my editorial comments or references. (Empson only used one footnote in his typescript, the one concerning his usage 'Meph'.)

There was one major problem, however. The material shows that Empson was in doubt about where in the essay to place his denouement. In some drafts he presents his full thesis early on and devotes the remainder of the essay to substantiation; in others he reserves the full exposition till near the end, in the manner of a detective thriller. The second approach is more difficult but I have adopted it, first because it makes a more fascinating book, and secondly because the conclusion is so controversial that the reader needs to be prepared to receive it. I believe this is what Empson would have wished.

The one other liberty I have taken is the insertion of a number of subheadings (the chapter headings are part of Empson's text); this is purely to aid the reader. Some of the chapters are rather long and not immediately digestible as a whole, so a few pointers are agreeable. This is particularly true of chapter 5, where Empson gives a scene-by-scene discussion of Marlowe's play, and here I have used act subheadings as a guide. The reader may find it useful to refer to the concordance of acts and scenes for Empson's proposed reconstruction and for the A- and B-texts of *Doctor Faustus*, provided as appendix 3.

Much of the argument central to Empson's thesis (which I shall not enter upon here) turns upon the vagaries of the English Faust-book as a translation of the original German, which is why he was so keen to have an exact translation for comparison, and, as I have mentioned, envisaged publication as part of a parallel text edition. Although this plan has not been adopted, the essay is nonetheless self-sufficient, since Empson quotes from the translations wherever necessary; however, it still deserves to be presented with some background information for the non-specialist. The remainder of this introduction attempts to supply this information and is based on the fully referenced introduction to my Faust-book translation.

The historical Faust

The legend of Doctor Faustus is based upon a remarkable historical figure of the late fifteenth and early sixteenth centuries, a close contemporary of Luther, Paracelsus and Cornelius Agrippa, though possibly their senior by as much as a decade. There is less uncertainty about the date of his death which was reported in 1541; he was probably still living in 1539. Thus his life spanned an age of great transition. He was born into a Catholic world in the hey-day of humanism, at a time when the recovery and translation of the *Hermetica* had awakened a renewed interest in magic – a magic purified of its medieval dross, its province no longer that of the broth-brewing witch but of the devout, contemplative philosopher. By the time of his death the world was riven by permanent confessional schism, the golden hours of the magus were rapidly passing and the Continent was about to witness one of the most disgusting human delusions the world has ever known – the witch-craze. His life span embraces the discovery and early exploitation of a whole new world, and radical changes in the power structure of the old world. It was also an age of revolutionary scientific advance (the world itself was displaced from the centre of the cosmos), and of discoveries known to the few, which a showman could use to stun his superstitious audiences. Above all, towards the end, because of Luther it became the age of the Devil abroad, going 'like a roaring lion, seeking whom he may devour'.

Faust was one of those famous persons who remain obscure for later generations, largely because they neither left writings for posterity nor occupied positions which would have engendered documentary evidence; so we have to rely on contemporary and post-contemporary reports from a variety of witnesses or gatherers of hearsay, of varying gullibility and persuasion, often with tendentious purposes at which we can only guess. Nonetheless this much can be gleaned of him: he was a man of sufficient education to be styled 'Doctor' without incredulity and it is quite probable that Heidelberg was his *alma mater*, at a time when it was a chief centre of German humanism. He certainly practised as an astrologer, patronized by, *inter alia* the Bishop of Bamberg, and very probably he was also a physician. But beyond these two highly acceptable callings he seems to have been a showman. It is clear that he had humanistic pretensions, but was despised by established humanists such as Trithemius and Mutian, mainly for his wild boasting and for his ability to fascinate the 'ignorant herd'. Plainly he had a vigorous memory, a persuasive bombast and an imposing presence. But his words and deeds were provocative and not agreeable to the civic authorities. There is documentary evidence that he was barred from Ingolstadt and Nuremberg, and according to Philipp Melanchthon he was constantly escaping from one town or another just as he was about to be arrested. There was thus a need for him to travel widely and, indeed, there are reports or traditions of him in a great many cities throughout Germany, besides Vienna, Prague, Venice and Cracow. Melanchthon testifies to his presence at Wittenberg (from which, as usual, he had to flee), though it is clear from Luther's own words that Faust and Luther never met. Both Reformers regarded him sourly (Melanchthon calls him 'a shit-house full of devils'), but the humanist philologist Camerarius, who probably endorsed their opinion of the man, pays grudging respect to his divinatory powers.

However, there was one section of society in which Faust seems to have found a welcome – the Catholic middle classes. We know he had a friend in Daniel Stibar, a town councillor of Würzburg and a member of the von Hutten circle. This was in the mid-1530s, at the height of Faust's fame (in 1536 he is referred to in print as '*Faustus insignis*', 'the famous Faust'). Much earlier (1506), on Trithemius' testimony, he had been patronized by Franz von Sickingen, champion of Ulrich von Hutten. It is also very probable that he had friendly connections at Erfurt with the junker family of von Denstett. Obviously the petty nobility would be the best possible patrons for a man such as Faust; they could afford latitudes of conscience and association which the Great might find impolitic.

From 1536 Faustus seems to have suffered a decline. It may have been precipitated by the posthumous publication of a collection of Trithemius' letters, one of which contained a damning account of Faust, branding him as, amongst other things, a pederast, a vain braggart and a fool. The collection would have been widely read, especially in Würzburg, Trithemius' last domicile, and there was no possible redress. If Faust were staying with Stibar at that time, as seems probable, the revelations would have been especially embarrassing. Faust seems to have gone south. There are two independent accounts of his death, and the soberest and most precise of these says he died miserably as an old man in the town of Staufen im Breisgau, a small town near Freiburg. The other account, by the Protestant clergyman Johannes Gast, who does not locate the death (though Melanchthon, who uses Gast, says it was in a small village in Württemberg), is the first published statement of the essence of the Faust legend: that Faust had sold his soul to the Devil, who had now come to claim his reward. There is no evidence for any such story circulating during Faust's lifetime, although the *Tisch-reden* (Luther's *Table Talk*) mentions that Faust called himself 'the Devil's brother-in-law' and the anti-witch-cult writer Johann Wier (or Weyer) has a story which tends to confirm that Faust was fond of this little joke. If so, he paid the price for it. Whether he died as a result of a chemical explosion, or of inadvertent strychnine poisoning, or was simply murdered (he had enough enemies), it seems his neck was broken or twisted – and this is the classic retribution for those who sell their souls to the Devil. From this point, the historical Faust recedes (or is pushed) into obscurity, and he is replaced by the much larger personage of the legend.

The Faust legend

The man most responsible for the propagation of Faust's diabolical association was none other than Melanchthon, the leader of German Protestantism after the death of Luther. In a series of lectures he gave annually at Wittenberg from 1546 until his death in 1560, he included, by way of anecdotal example, a thumbnail sketch of Faust. This, together with other material, was recorded and published by one of his students, Johannes Manlius, in 1563. It became the definitive account of Faust up to the publication of the Faust-book, for Melanchthon's authority placed his veracity above question:

> I knew a certain man by the name of Faustus from Kundling [i.e. Knittlingen] which is a small town near my birthplace [Bretten]. When he was a student at Cracow he studied magic, for there was formerly much practice of the art in that city and in that place too there were public lectures on this art. He wandered about everywhere and talked of many mysterious things. When he wished to provide a spectacle at Venice he said he would fly to heaven. So the Devil raised him up and then cast him down so that he was dashed to the ground and almost killed. However he did not die.
>
> A few years ago this same Ioannes Faustus, on the day before his end, sat very downcast in a certain village in the Duchy of Württemburg. The host asked him why, contrary to his custom and habit, he was so sad (he was otherwise a most shameful scoundrel who led a very wicked life, so that he was again and again nigh to being killed because of his dissolute habits). Then he said to the host in the village: 'Don't be frightened tonight.' In the middle of the night the house was shaken. When Faustus did not get up in the morning and when it was now almost noon, the host with several others went into the bedroom and found him lying near the bed with his face turned toward his back. Thus the Devil had killed him. (A slightly modified version of the translation in Palmer and More, pp. 101f, where the original text is quoted)

Melanchthon goes on to link him with 'that scoundrel' Cornelius
Agrippa and tells of Faust's escape from Wittenberg and Nuremberg. The passage quoted contains all the main elements of the
death of Faust as it occurs in the Faust-book – Faust's fore-
knowledge that his time was up, the house shaken in the middle of
the night, the discovery of the body in the morning – although the
Faust-book death is more gruesome and is located in the village of
Rimlich, a few miles from Wittenberg. Melanchthon's version is also
the source of 'Ioannes' as Faust's forename (the historical Faust was
George). One would never suspect that Faust had frequented
Melanchthon's company in Wittenberg, yet this seems to have been
the case. This embarrassing association must have motivated the
zeal with which Melanchthon sets out to damn him. The link would
have been astrology, to which Melanchthon was partial, in contrast
to Luther who was strongly opposed to it. But this is beside the
point: Melanchthon had laid a firm basis for the legend.

   That it flourished is the inevitable consequence of Luther's (and
his followers') obsession with the Devil. One may speak of the Faust
legend as the by-product of the changing socioreligious climate of
mid-sixteenth-century Germany; it grew hand in hand with the
increasing momentum of the witch-craze, itself an index to the
insecurity of an age in which the only certainty was the ubiquitous
real presence of the Devil. The Prince of this World had even
assumed a literature of his own: the *Teufelliteratur*, in which each
human failing was associated with a specific devil with special modes
of temptation appropriate to the particular vice. His prize target was
the self-reliant man who did not put his trust in God – the Faust of
the Faust-book. The Devil's enticements were ploys to destroy. This
was proved by the curious finding that the more witches were
burned, the greater their numbers increased, whereas witchcraft
'died out' in those districts where witch-burning was discontinued –
obviously, argues the crypto-Calvinist anti-witch-cult writer Augus-
tin Lercheimer, when the Devil finds his plans are successful he
persists in them but when they fail (that is, his victim the witch is not
destroyed) he turns to other methods. The brave writings of
Lercheimer and, more importantly, Wier, did not go unheeded (as a
direct result of Wier's *De Praestigiis Daemonum* (1563) witch-burning
was discontinued throughout the Palatinate on the orders of the
Calvinist Elector Frederick III), but the devil-cult remained in full
sway until the end of the century, with a spate of publications (such

as the *Theatrum Diabolorum* (1569, etc.) and the *Theatrum de Veneficis* (1586), compendiums of writings on witchcraft and diabolic temptation) emanating from the presses of Frankfurt.

A necessary consequence of this fierce belief in the Devil was the disrobing of the magus. Ficino and Pico della Mirandola had rehabilitated the magus in the late fifteenth century, turning him into a pious seeker of God's secret blessings. This view was extended by Trithemius and Agrippa in early sixteenth-century Germany and taken to its limits by Dee and Bruno at the century's end, but it was not the popular view, nor that of the authorities, at the time of the witch-craze. The enlightened Lercheimer damns the magus more than the innocent women accused of witchcraft. The celestial demons of the Renaissance magus were the Devil in disguise: there was no magic but the magic of the Devil. The popular religious fiction of the *Golden Legend* told of the deeds of Simon Magus, and his exemplary story is expressly put to work to discredit all other magi, as Melanchthon does with Faust in the extract quoted (he is the only source for Faust attempting to fly). Faust was much better material for such debunking propaganda, since his exploits remained in the public consciousness and, although he styled himself 'philosopher', he does not appear to have kept himself on the same high plane as a Bruno or an Agrippa. His picaresque existence, always making hair's-breadth escapes, must have lent itself to the popular imagination. In the years following his death he became the focus for the accretion of anecdotes; the deeds of other magicians, often long dead, were grafted on to this vigorous stock and we see him as author of feats earlier attributed to Albertus Magnus, Trithemius, Zyto and many unnamed magicians mentioned in Luther's 'Table talk'. Many of these anecdotes, now associated with Faust, appear in publications of the 1560s and 1570s, the main period of development of the Faust legend. They are often bucolic, nearly all jovial tricks, with very little wickedness about them, such as Faust eating a load of hay, or punishing a carter for being uncharitable by distributing the wheels of his cart at the four gates of a neighbouring city. They are part of a different genre of folk literature which begins with *Til Eulenspiegel* and is exemplified in the relevant period by Bütner's *Claus Narr* (1572). These elements are strongly represented in the Faust-book but they are ancillary to the legend itself, where the principal theme is the pact with the Devil.

The idea of a pact is implicit in Melanchthon's account and at once Faust is brought into a context very familiar to the sixteenth-century reader. We are back with the ever-popular and widely-read *Golden Legend* and its account of Theophilus of Adana, who gained ecclesiastical promotion by making a written pact with the Devil, sealed with his own ring. The essential clause of his pact is that he denies 'the son of Mary'; this is ironic as it is the Virgin who eventually saves him. When he becomes conscience stricken through fear of Hell, it is she who hears his cries; after testing the genuineness of his contrition she intercedes to obtain divine forgiveness for him, and the pact is miraculously retrieved and burned following Theophilus' full confession before the bishop and congregation. The penitent dies three days later in the place where he had seen the vision of the Virgin, but of course, he is 'saved'. We see here the importance of the written pact and the necessity of its retrieval if there was to be any hope of redemption. The story was also the subject of a miracle play, so it will have been part of the public consciousness.

The more recondite accounts of magicians' pacts with the Devil as they occur in the *Lemegeton* or *Lesser Key of Solomon* were also exposed around this time in Wier's *Pseudomonarchia Daemonum* (1577), and Scot translated some of the rituals from there in his *Discovery of Witchcraft* (1584; Book xv). The Solomonic literature usually assumes that the magician wants to discover buried treasure and his aim is to enslave a spirit (a diabolical minister) to lead him to it. An appropriate spirit to call on is Lucifuge Rofocale, who specializes in such work but of whom one must be wary as he will try to negotiate a bilateral pact in which the magician will have to pay the price. He is subjugated by smiting with a 'blasting rod' and threatening to send him to Hell. Cowed by this technique he will be willing to settle for a small monetary payment and will accept a unilateral pact allowing the magician to escape. Various terms of servitude (twenty or fifty years) are mentioned, but nowhere, so far as I know, the twenty-four years of the Faust-book. (This could be a bit of unnoticed anti-Lutheran propaganda if Faust was known to have died in 1541, for he would then have made his pact in 1517, when Luther nailed *his* to the church door in Wittenberg; we need not hesitate to assume that manuscript copies of 'Faust's pact' were circulating in Germany several years before the publication of the Faust-book, and these need not have been of Protestant tendency.)

As these grimoire elements are a substantial addition to the Theophilus story as inherent components of the Faust legend, we see how important is the timing of Wier's exposure of such material. The other important factor is the nature of the spirit intermediary. The Lucifuge or Fly-the-light is a particular genus of malevolent spirit, recognized by Trithemius in his *Liber Octo Quaestionum*, and he becomes the basic prototype for the Mephostophiles of the Faust-book, a much more developed character who takes on the sophisticated wiliness of the *Teufelliteratur* to ensnare Faustus. Mephostophiles is thus a composite figure, part semi-autonomous and reluctantly obedient but naive Lucifuge, part paid-up member of the Devil, one of the numberless cohort who, according to contemporary belief, were constantly on the watch for a potential victim and were masters in the art of inspiring despair in God – the unforgivable sin.

By the late 1570s, then, the Faust legend was virtually complete in terms of its separate elements: the story of his death, the anecdotes of his magical prowess, his assimilation into the 'pact' drama, the mechanism of the pact and the requisite intermediary. I believe that the stimulating trigger for composition of a coherent story based on these elements was the publication in 1585 of Lercheimer's *Christlich bedencken und Erinnerung von Zauberei* (*Christian Synopsis of Magic*). Lercheimer's book includes many short anecdotes of Faust and also mentions his pact of twenty-four years (the earliest mention of this term I have found), but the earlier chapters, devoted to different kinds of magicians and persons who employ spirits (including card-sharpers), describe the process of diabolical seduction in a manner which translates almost without a leap direct to the Faust-book.

The Faust-book and its story

The first complete presentation of the Faust legend to be published was rushed into print to catch the Frankfurt book fair of September, 1587. It was the anonymous *Historia von D. Johañ Fausten* ('The Life of Doctor Johann Faustus, the renowned sorcerer and black magician; How he sold himself to the Devil in return for a fixed number of years, what strange feats he accomplished during that time, and how he finally reaped his well-merited reward'), generally known as the German Faust-book (GFB). In the preface, its publisher, the Lutheran propagandist Johann Spies of Frankfurt, is careful to stress the devout purpose of the work:

> The multifarious exploits of Doctor Johann Faustus, the famous sorcerer and black magician, have been the talk of all Germany for many a year. Everywhere, at parties and social gatherings, there is great inquiry for a biography of this Faustus. Indeed, a number of modern writers have touched here and there upon the subject of this magician, his diabolic art and frightful end, but I have often wondered that, as yet, no-one has presented this terrible tale in an orderly fashion and published it as a warning to the whole of Christendom. I inquired amongst scholars and learned men as to whether perhaps someone had already written such a work but I was unable to discover anything for certain until recently when I received this Life through the agency of a good friend at Speyer. He requested that I should publish it as a fearful example of the Devil's deception and of his murder of body and soul, so that it might be a warning to all Christians.

There are many pious asides inserted in the body of the work too. We need not doubt the sincerity of these intentions but Spies's haste to capture the market shows he knew he was on to a good thing. Nor was he mistaken: the reception was sensational. No less than five new editions were published before the end of the year, some of them incorporating fresh material such as a number of short incidents taken from Lercheimer in Recension B, and the important Erfurt chapters of Recension C.

The legend of Doctor Faustus is presented in the Faust-book as an authentic account of Faust's life and would have been received as such by the majority of its readers. Some knew better, however. Lercheimer, in the third edition of his *Christian Synopsis* (1597), is among the first to carp and he vehemently attacks the Faust-book:

> I am obliged to give him [Faustus] some considerable attention by reason of a book recently published by some toady, whoever he may be, in which the school and church of Wittenberg are particularly abused and slandered. It says that Faustus was born in the vicinity of Weimar and Jena, that he matriculated at Wittenberg and was there made Master of Arts and Doctor of Divinity . . . This is all badly and childishly told and he lied . . .

Having corrected the Faust-book by regurgitating the Melanchthon version of events, Lercheimer continues:

> Who can believe that a man whom Melanchthon chose to call a shit-house full of devils could have been made Master, let alone Doctor of Divinity, at such a university when he would have besmirched the degree and honourable title with eternal shame and scandal.
>
> I do not touch upon other trivial, false and nasty things in the book. I have pointed out these particular things because it has vexed and grieved me greatly, as it has many other honest people, to see the honourable and famous institution together with Luther, Melanchthon and others of sainted memory so libelled. I myself was a student there, once upon a time ...
>
> ... it is unwarrantable and lamentable that our own [i.e. Protestant] publishers should shamelessly and unhesitantly think to produce such books and make them commonly available ... It is shocking that the noble art of printing, God-given for our benefit, should be misused to such an evil end. (Lercheimer, *Christlich bedencken* ... (3rd edn), Speyer 1597, pp. 41–3; much of the material is translated in Palmer and More, pp. 119–22)

But Lercheimer was too late. By the time he aired his grievance the Faust-book had been translated into French, English, Dutch, and Low German and had inspired a masterpiece of English contemporary drama which was later to reimport Faust to Germany in an entirely new form.

Why was it so popular? Quite apart from its timing at the height of the witch-burnings, when discussion of magic, cosmology and views of the afterlife assumed vital importance, there are characteristics of Faust which allowed him to mirror the aspirations and uncertainties of the age. He presumed to transgress the bounds of licit knowledge, just as contemporary scientists were thought to be doing. He succeeded but paid the price, and in that payment lay the panacea of certainty: that God appointed limits to understanding was a comfort against insecurity. At the same time there was a homeliness about the bucolic japes making up much of the Faust-book which render Faust a folk hero. Orson Welles would think him every bit as 'truly good' as Falstaff. It is this rare combination of the disparate elements, sacred and profane, of the Faust legend which render it timeless. Whoever composed the Faust-book, Spies deserves credit for giving due value to the bathetic elements.

The book is organized in three parts, of which the last is subdivided in two, and the whole of the real drama of the book is in the first part, the seduction of Faust by Mephostophiles and the winning of his soul.

Faust, born of a peasant family, soon shows evidence of a brilliant mind and is adopted by a rich uncle who sends the boy to Wittenberg University to study theology. There he is a star and within a short time has won his Master of Arts and Doctor of Divinity degrees – but 'he was so bent on folly, so unmindful of his vocation and so opinionated that he was nicknamed the Speculator. He fell into bad company ... and began to live a wicked, disreputable life', consorting with

> those who traded in Chaldean, Persian, Arabic and Greek words, in figures, symbols, conjurations, incantations and the whole vocabulary of magic ... Doctor Faustus was set on loving the very thing he ought to have loathed. He meditated upon it day and night and, his fancy taking eagles' wings, he aspired to fathom all the workings of heaven and earth. His vain and insolent curiosity so provoked him that eventually he prepared certain magic words, figures, characters and conjurations, intending to put them to use and try if he might summon the Devil.

So one night Faust repairs to a wood not far from the town and there 'at a place where four roads meet' he draws his magic circles on the ground (the grimoires mention crossroads as among the very best places for conjuring – they were always dangerous, and prime sites for gibbets). The Faust-book does not give the conjurations (Spies says they are expressly omitted lest any rash person should attempt to emulate Faust), nor are any specific spirits named: we are merely told that he 'conjured the Devil'. After sundry tedious manifestations in which 'the Devil appeared none too keen to join the dance', Faust successfully conjures a spirit in the form of a fiery man who transforms, unbidden, into a Franciscan friar. Faust adjures it to appear in his house the following midnight and returns home gloating over his prowess.

When the spirit keeps his appointment (chapter 3) Faust makes three requests: that the spirit should be subservient to him, 'obediently performing whatever he was bid for as long as Faustus should live', that he should not withhold any information required of him, and that he should tell nothing but the truth. We see that at least two of these conditions are concerned with the acquisition of knowledge. To Faust's chagrin, the spirit replies that he hasn't sufficient authority to accede to these requests and the matter must be put before his Master, the 'infernal god'. The spirit explains that 'there is a government and sovereignty amongst us just as there is on earth. We too have our rulers and administrators and servants – of whom I am one.' It is the duty of such servants, he says, to negotiate with human beings and become subservient to them – no man could ever hope to subjugate Lucifer. And he adds an indirect threat: 'we have never revealed the true foundation of our habitation to men, nor that of our government and sovereignty, apart, that is, from the damned who, after their death, will enter and learn about it by direct experience'. It is enough to alarm Faust: 'I won't be damned for that, nor for your sake'. In answer, the spirit recites the following doggerel:

> You won't? But then, you have no plea;
> Having no plea, you'll go with me.
> Our subtle bonds you cannot see,
> From me no plea will set you free;
> Your heart's despair has brought you there.

Faust spits out an oath, 'but as the spirit was about to vanish, Faustus, irresolute from that time on, was of a different mind and adjured it to appear before him again ...' Thus Faust is damned, according to the spirit, right at the outset, because he has despaired in God. Of course, he could easily repent now and save himself (the Faust-book suggests that if he repented God would be merciful right up to the end), but the spirit's task is to prevent Faust from repenting. This is why he tells him he is already damned and names the unforgivable sin. Again and again, Mephostophiles is to tell Faust that it is 'too late', and thus he keeps him on the hook.

When the spirit returns at vesper time, it announces that it has received the diabolic assent. 'I bring you this answer ... and you must give me yours, but first' – and now we have a line which suggests a conflation of two sources – '... but first I would like to hear what it is you want, seeing that you have caused me to appear at this time.' In the context given, this is ludicrous; the spirit already knows what Faust wants and has just been to get the necessary permission. Now, suddenly, he is speaking as if they have never met before; furthermore, Faust's answer is a new set of conditions, nothing at all to do with the quest for knowledge, the foremost being 'that he too might acquire the form, faculties and characteristics of a spirit', the remainder concerning the details of the spirit's servitude, the sort of thing one might expect from a Victorian housekeeper hiring a maid. (Empson has a lot to say about these new conditions and I have no wish to pre-empt him. Of course, his thesis concerns the book as read, not as constructed, and the presence of conflated sources has no bearing on that thesis – it is only important for a consideration of the genesis of the work.)

The spirit is agreeable to the new conditions but makes certain stipulations of his own: Faust is to swear that he will become 'the sole property of the spirit', and he is to put it in writing in his own blood; in addition, he must promise to be an enemy to all professed Christians, he is to renounce the Christian faith and resist any attempts to reform him. 'In return the spirit would grant Faustus a fixed term and when the years had expired he would come to fetch him. Provided he observed the above conditions he should have whatever his heart desired and would immediately perceive that he had the form and characteristics of a spirit.' The bargain is struck but the actual deed of making the pact is deferred to the next day (chapter 5) when we learn the spirit's name: Mephostophiles. Faust cuts his arm, collects the blood and writes his contract (chapter 6) – and once more we are back with the 'knowledge-motivation' material:

> I, Johannes Faustus, Doctor, do hereby make known . . . that, it being my intention to speculate on the elements, finding that despite the gifts . . . bestowed upon me from above, my mental ability proved inadequate, and knowing that such things cannot be learned of men, I have committed myself to the care of . . . Mephostophiles . . . so that he shall inform and instruct me in these matters and whatsoever else I choose . . .
>
> In return . . . I vow . . . that when twenty-four years have passed . . . he shall have full power to direct and govern me as it pleases him according to his way, and all that I have: life, soul, flesh, blood and belongings, shall be his for evermore . . .

There is not a word here about becoming a spirit; the pact is all for knowledge – and we may guess the pact is the oldest part of the book (one might wonder whether the historical Faust himself had not had an edition printed as a ready money-spinner). In this respect the pact harmonizes with Faust's actual demands on Mephostophiles in the remainder of the book; it is not until he finds himself dissatisfied with his spirit informer that he begins to use him for purposes other than a magic key to knowledge. The only evidence in later chapters of him possessing the 'form and characteristics of a spirit' is his ability to render himself invisible and adopt an alien guise (Mahomet), but both aptitudes are recorded of Simon Magus and there was never any suggestion that he had become a spirit.

The vital step of handing over the written contract takes place in chapter 8 after Mephostophiles has provided Faust with a show in earnest of good things to come. The spirit insists that Faust makes a copy of the document, 'and that's just what the godless fellow did'. It is naughty of the author to be hypocritical here for unless his hero made a copy he would have been hard put to answer for his source of the document (no trivial matter, I suspect).

Faust is now securely in the net but he has not been landed and brought to the fire. He has to be reduced to a despair from which repentance is impossible. This is achieved in two ways: he is given a good time so that he may habituate himself to luxury, but he is also shown the reverse side of the coin and brought to despair of salvation by the disputations which Mephostophiles cunningly engineers to this purpose. This forms the plot of the remainder of the first part. We begin (chapter 9) with the good things. Faust has adopted a young rascal, Christopher Wagner, as his houseboy, whom he trains in magic. They are supplied with all their needs – rich clothing, sumptuous food and wines (stolen from the cellars of the gentry), plate and money ('twenty-five crowns a week, making 1300 a year. This was his salary.'). 'Doctor Faustus led an epicurean existence, day and night; he believed neither in God, Hell, nor the Devil and supposed that the soul died with the body' (chapter 10). Curious not to believe in a being one has just made a deal with, but this is the ultimate source for Marlowe's 'Come, I think Hell's a fable'. The author has confused the two meanings of 'epicurean', the hedonistic life with the atheistic doctrine, but the confusion may be intentional.

However, Faust is to discover that the contract sets inherent limits to his pleasures. When he becomes excessively libidinous he decides he will marry (following the precepts of St Paul), only to discover that this will contravene his articles: marriage is a Christian institution and the Devil is wholly against it (except that it provides the possibility for adultery). Although Mephostophiles tells him he will be torn to pieces if he attempts to go ahead, Faust ignores the threat: 'I'm going to get married, come what may!' At once there is a shock, the house fills with flames and Faust is flung down the stairs; the Devil incarnate appears 'in a form so horrid and terrifying that Faustus could not bear to look at him' and Faust bleats a repentance like a beaten child. Having received the stick he is offered the carrot: Mephostophiles promises to supply him with the likeness of any women he wants (they are devils, of course). 'This proposition so appealed to Doctor Faustus that his heart trembled for joy and he regretted the original proposals he had made. He was inflamed with such passion and lust that he spent night and day questing after the shapes of beautiful women. He was so promiscuous that he would fornicate with one devil today and have another in mind on the morrow.' He and 'his devilish mistress' amuse themselves with a magic book presented by Mephostophiles (chapter 11) but Faust's inquisitiveness soon asserts itself and he summons his spirit for a disputation.

There now begins the series of disputations, or lectures by Mephostophiles, which continue until the end of Part I, each new revelation plunging Faust further into a despair from which he is never fully to recover. They begin innocently enough with Faust's query: 'What sort of a spirit are you?'. Mephostophiles tells him that he is a flying spirit, and his realm is beneath the heavens, that is, beneath the sphere of the moon. By a logic which is impenetrable this prompts Faust to ask how Lucifer came to fall. Mephostophiles answers with a brief and garbled summary of the Dionysian hierarchies of the angels, taken from Hartmann Schedel's *Weltchronik*. (There is evidence that the disputations as they are given in the Spies Faust-book have undergone considerable transposition in their transference from an earlier source. This would account for many of the non sequiturs; but such points are not greatly relevant here, where we have to consider the published Faust-book as a seminal work.) We are forced to read this as a fob off, though Faust does not complain; but he is led to think on Hell, and in fact is 'obsessed with thoughts of Hell — it filled his dreams, one might say' (chapter 12): 'Where was it? How and of what materials was it made? How had it been created?' The spirit's answer is brief to the point of obscurity: 'The form and nature of Hell is a secret even to us devils'. This too is a fob off but Mephostophiles has leaked just enough information to keep Faust's curiosity at work, and he reveals a little more in the following chapter (13) when Faust asks 'about the devils' abode, their government and might'. When, in chapter 14, Faust asks the spirit to describe Lucifer and 'his adornments as he was when he had lived in heaven', Mephostophiles begs leave of absence for three days (presumably for top-level briefing) and returns with the story of Lucifer in Heaven 'more treasured than gold or precious stones or any other creation', and how he was banished from his heavenly home when he 'soared up in arrogance and pride and presumed to take command of the East'. The tale evokes a poignant reaction from Faust, the first bitings of remorse: 'without a word he left his spirit and went to his room. There he lay down on his bed and began weeping and sighing most bitterly . . . "Oh, misery, everlasting woe! . . . It will be just the same with me, for am I not also one of God's creatures? . . . Like Lucifer I shall be cast into woe and eternal damnation. . . . Would I had never been born!" So Doctor Faustus lamented but he would not take hope nor have faith that, by doing penance, he might yet attain God's grace.' Faust has finally recognized that he is damned; he must now be taught to accept his damnation. Each further disputation leaves Faust with a heavy heart but he is never again so affecting as he is here.

When he has recovered from this first onslaught of remorse, he wants to know how his fall has come about. He questions the spirit on the Devil's tyranny and his methods of temptation. Although Mephostophiles fears that 'if I answer these questions it will only make you depressed and cause you painful reflection', he none-theless proceeds to do so in no uncertain terms and the result is as he predicted.

> There are countless numbers of us spirits who seek out men to lure them into sin. We range ourselves over the entire world and use every sort of sly trick and subtlety to undermine people's belief and pervert them . . . And you may apply this to your own case too, Faustus. . . . For as soon as we saw your heart and what you had in mind and how none but the Devil could further those plans of yours, why then, we set to work and made your thoughts and fancies still more insolent and daring. We made you so eager that, day and night, you could find no peace but all your thoughts were centred on how you might accomplish sorcery. And since you summoned us we made you bold and reckless so that you would rather be led to the Devil than be

dissuaded from your purpose. Then we encouraged you still further until we had firmly planted the resolve in your heart and you were absolutely determined to procure yourself a spirit. Finally we led you so far that you surrendered body and soul. 'It is true' said Doctor Faustus, 'now there is nothing to be done.'

Already he is beginning to accept his plight and Mephostophiles is able to be brutally frank with him, but he is still not totally downed. 'Doctor Faustus looked earnestly towards Heaven but he could see no place for himself there' – a line echoed in Marlowe: 'When I behold the heavens then I repent.' However, he conceives the notion that by 'prolonged discussion with his Spirit he would bring himself to a state in which he might be counselled to reform through penitence and renunciation of his evil ways'. Accordingly he asks for a disquisition on Hell but Mephostophiles knows at once what he is up to and shatters his hopes: 'If you could climb to the very brink of Heaven I would still dash you back down to Hell, for you are mine and belong in my sty', and he advises Faust not to press for his answer. 'I will know or I will not live', says Faust: he is willing to commit suicide rather than bear the uncertainty, a condition given a more telling representation later in the book. One wonders why Mephostophiles does not then refuse to answer and save himself a great deal of trouble – but this is to ponder on the delay in *Hamlet*; he does answer, and at great length, in a fashion every bit as disturbing as Joyce's 'fire-sermon' in *Portrait of the Artist* which is a close parallel. He surveys the conditions of Hell and the torments of the damned and finally expounds on their hopelessness: 'they will lie in Hell like the bones of the dead, nagged by death and their consciences and their initial confidence and trust in God will be of no avail; he will not even think of them.'

Finally he refuses to answer any further questions on the matter; he does not need to – he has brought Faust to the pitch of despair and Faust himself confirms this condition by begging to ask a supplementary question (chapter 17): 'Suppose you were in my position, a human being created by God, what would you do to please God and mankind?' This causes Mephostophiles to smile (a unique occurrence), but not scornfully, and the touch of apparent compassion humanizes him immensely. He explains how he would 'bow down to God while I still had breath in my body and would take care not to provoke his anger against me . . . then I should know that after my death I should attain eternal happiness', and he contrasts this exemplary conduct with what Faust has done.

> 'That is the sad truth of it' said Doctor Faustus, 'but tell me . . . do you wish you were a human being in my position?' 'Oh, yes' sighed the spirit, 'and small question of it. For even if I had sinned against God I would bring myself back into his grace.' 'Then there would be time enough for me too if I were to reform' answered Doctor Faustus. 'Yes' said the spirit, 'if you could have attained God's grace before you committed your heinous sin, but now it is too late and God is enraged with you.' 'Leave me in peace' said Doctor Faustus.

This last argument by Mephostophiles may appear specious at first sight, but it is a familiar human dilemma to be needing help from someone you have quarrelled with, and it knocks away Faust's last vestige of hope, just as it had been revived by the spirit's earlier answer and compassion. Mephostophiles' one smile is his cruellest weapon and it is used to kill. Thus ends Part 1 and the real drama is over.

The second and third parts of the Faust-book do not need such detailed treatment here, except in so far as the material is relevant to the essay. Having confirmed Faust in his despair, the spirit's brief is to keep him occupied for the next twenty-four years, always guarding against any outside interference or attempts to reform him, at the same time fulfilling the terms of the contract (the Devil is very fair about this). If Faust can be used to provoke mischief and enhance the power of the Devil, so much the better.

It is not surprising then that he begins by becoming an astrologer, supplied with accurate forecasts by Mephostophiles (chapter 18). Luther despised astrology so it is natural that it should appear as the work of the Devil in a book with such a strong Lutheran tendency. The spirit confirms Luther's views: the nature of astrology 'is such that no astronomer or observer of the heavens can make specific predictions with any certainty, for the divine mechanisms are concealed and unfathomable to man' (chapter 19), but the spirits have lived long enough to be experienced in the celestial movements and can interpret the divine plan. This gives Faust the opportunity to camouflage his interest in theology (where further questions have been forbidden him) with queries on cosmology (chapters 20, 21) to which the spirit responds with a conflation of

Schedel and Elucidarius. We learn that 'we spirits and devils' live in the 'gloomy air' of the upper atmosphere where the 'Earth's shine cannot reach' (the spirits shun the light). Faust is not much impressed by these answers and disappointed that his ruse has failed. When he complains (chapter 22) that he has made a poor bargain, the spirit turns on its charm and offers to answer anything he wishes. Won over by this treatment, Faust asks how God had created the world and about the birth of mankind. Mephostophiles, 'true to his type, gives him a totally false answer' ('Devil, you lie', emphasizes Spies, diplomatically, in his margin comment): 'The world, dear Faustus, was never born, neither will it die.' This much is Aristotle but there follows a peculiar creation myth, quoted by Empson, in which the Earth and the Sea divide the natural heritage between them, conceding to God the creation of man and of the heavens. However, the pious Faust prefers the account given in Genesis.

There is now an interlude (chapter 23) in the cosmological section, and it derives from a source in which Faust's 'prince and rightful master' turns out to be Belial. He has observed Faust's thoughts and knows he would like to see some of the principal spirits of Hell, so he has come with his 'main counsellors and servants' to show them to him. This is the scene which Marlowe replaced with the Masque of the Seven Deadly Sins, and Empson gives it plenty of coverage. The hybrid therioforms of the principal devils (Belial, Lucifer, Beelzebub, Astaroth, Satan, Anubis, Dythicanus and Drachus) are given beast-book descriptions, but we are told they are even more hideous in Hell. There is also a multitude of lesser devils, in the forms of ordinary animals, but Mephostophiles does not appear in this chapter. Faust is amused by their transformations and is given a book to enable him to do likewise, but he is not so happy when all the devils transform themselves to insects and drive him out of the house. However, the tone is generally merry and the plaguing is short lived.

In the next chapters Faust makes three journeys, the first to Hell, in a dream (chapter 24), the second to the stars, in a dragon-drawn chariot (chapter 25), and finally a Grand Tour on the back of Mephostophiles, who has changed himself into a horse, 'winged like a dromedary' (chapters 26, 27). E. M. Butler (*The Myth of the Magus*, Cambridge (Cambridge University Press) 1948) shows that 'far-distant wanderings' are one of the ten stock features of the magus myth in its fully developed form, so these journeys are not inconsequential to the legend. Faust courses through the infernal, mundane and celestial worlds, but he does not get beyond the moon, and the supercelestial remains totally out of reach (he is given a tantalizing distant glimpse of Paradise from the top of Mount Caucasus in chapter 27, but this is so that his spirit may comment on its inaccessibility). Hell is very confused, more reminiscent of *Alice in Wonderland* than of Dante's carefully ordered construction, but this is right for a dream. Faust is constantly falling dizzily through populated darkness in a realm of stench and murk; he loses his guide and his dragon-steeds and at one point is stranded hopelessly upon a precipitous crater with a fiery abyss, set in an endless sea. Unable to bear the anxiety of his position he works himself into a rage and 'in a moment of frantic and insane terror' he leaps into the pit shouting 'Accept my sacrifice.' Here, surely, is encapsulated the mad despair of a world unable to bear its own insecurities, somehow much like our own.

The journey to the stars receives sufficient attention in the essay (see also appendix 1, pp. 180–2) to make further comment redundant. The immensely long and tedious Grand Tour (a 'Blue-Guide' nearly a century out of date in 1587) is relieved by the comic episodes at Rome, where Faust blows in the Pope's face and at Constantinople where, having immobilized the Sultan and filled the palace with fog, Faust enters the harem for six days and nights of pleasure, much to the joy of the concubines. When he has finally returned home there is a brief resurgence of cosmology (chapters 28–32) which concludes this part.

The first half of Part 3 is an account of Faust's magic deeds 'and how he used his nigromancy at the courts of noblemen', and it opens (chapter 33) with him raising the spirits of Alexander the Great and his consort before Charles V. (This is a fine example of anecdote-grafting: the original story was told of Trithemius raising Mary of Burgundy before the Emperor Maximilian.) Then, at the same court, Faust plays a trick (chapter 34) on a knight who is sleeping in a window; he sets antlers upon the man's head so that the knight (Marlowe's 'Benvolio') is trapped. This introduces a revenge motif which, with its two appearances (chapters 35, 56), helps to provide a loose framework for this part. Of course, the knight's attempts at revenge only bring him and his company further shame.

From the imperial court we are transported to the world of surly peasants. Faust eats a load of hay to amuse his colleagues at Gotha (chapter 36), but then (chapter 37) he has a more important commission from a group of three 'distinguished counts': he has to fly them to Munich and back to Wittenberg, so that they may see the festivities of the Bavarian Royal Wedding. Mephostophiles is no longer involved (in fact he rarely occurs in this part) and Faust transports them by flying cloak, rendering them all temporarily invisible. But things go wrong, one of the counts is imprisoned and only just escapes being tortured. The story is a warning not to place reliance in magicians.

In these stories, Faust receives princely rewards from his patrons, but in those which follow he has to resort to swindling in order to earn his living: apparently, by a clause not even in the small print, the Devil's promise that he would never lack for money or goods was only valid for four years from the date of the contract. (It sounds like a publisher's invention.) So here Faust deteriorates. He deceives, in turn, a Jew (chapter 38) and a horse dealer (chapter 39), both by means of a supernumary leg, and a swineherd (chapter 43) – both the horse of chapter 39 and the pigs of chapter 43 turn to straw when the animals enter the water and the same motif is used in one of the revenge chapters. These low dealings are interspersed with student brawls and the silencing of drunken peasants (chapters 41, 42), and then Faust returns to the higher plane of court magician, when he performs wonders before the Count of Anhalt (Marlowe's 'Van-holt'). Observing that the Countess is pregnant (chapter 43), Faust satisfies her midwinter craving for fresh fruits by having his spirit fetch them from 'foreign lands where summer is now coming to its end'. Faust's explanation of this mystery to the Count is garbled and shows that an early revisionist has not fully understood the alternation of seasons in the two hemispheres. In the following chapter (44), Faust erects a mock castle (complete with moat, enclosure and a whole catalogue of animals, birds and fishes) in the grounds of the estate and invites the noble couple and their attendants to a picnic; there is another catalogue detailing the menu. But although they glut themselves the guests are famished as soon as they reach their palace. Faust finishes with a pyrotechnic display which razes the mock castle, and he receives a bounteous reward.

There is now a sequence of five chapters (chapters 45–9) set in Wittenberg during the carnival season, and here Faust is at the centre of a company of students and Masters bent on bibulous pleasures and convivial entertainment. Together they raid the cellars of the Bishop of Salzburg (flying there on a ladder), feast on food stolen from noblemen's tables, enjoy magic music and are entertained by Faust's tricks and performing monkeys. They go out masking (Faust has rendered them headless) and then create a dreadful row at night by careering around in a dragon which rumbles over the cobbles. It is difficult, if not impossible, for us to be shocked by their sinfulness as a pious sixteenth-century reader might have been, and the whole tone of these revels invites empathy rather than criticism. The climax to the sequence (chapter 49) takes place on Quasimodo Sunday (the first after Easter) when Faust raises 'Helen of Greece' during a discussion of the most beautiful women. She passes before them speechless but 'with such a shameless and mischievous expression that the students were inflamed with love for her', and later that night they cannot sleep for thinking of her. 'Here we may see that the Devil often inflames a man with desire and blinds him with love so that he falls into loose living and afterwards it is not easy to break him of the habit.'

Following a chapter (50) in which Faust exacts Christian retribution for uncharitableness, he does something really wicked at last. He sees a group of magicians at Frankfurt, performing the trick of magical decapitation; each magician takes it in turn to have his head cut off, shaved and reset upon his neck (chapter 51). Faust is piqued by the presumption of the chief magician and intervenes so that it is impossible to restore his head – so he dies unshriven, having just uttered a blasphemy. Butler regards this incident as a magic duel, another essential ingredient of the magus myth. Other commentators regard it as a further stage in the deterioration of Faust. Both views are probably correct; the author was assembling disparate materials according to a broad plan of gradual deterioration, but he is careless and some of the later chapters show Faust in a better light (for example, chapter 54, where he arranges a happy marriage).

We now return to the serious theme of Faust's plight, and the tick of the unstoppable clock, hitherto barely audible, becomes ever louder. It is the seventeenth year of Faust's term and an old man, shocked by Faust's influence on the young, attempts to reform him (chapter 52). Faust is moved by the old man's sermon and decides to repent, but his decision is no sooner made than his spirit attacks him and threatens to tear him in pieces unless he abandons this idea and renews his pact with more of his blood. Faust complies (chapter 53), introducing a clause expressly promising not to listen to any spiritual teachers, nor to be partial to their teaching. The new pact also contains the peculiar statement that Lucifer 'promises neither to shorten nor extend my life, be it in death or in hell, nor cause me to suffer any pain'. (This induced some reader to add the margin comment: '*Si diabolus non esset mendax et homicida*', 'Is not the Devil a liar and a murderer'. The clause has to mean that Lucifer promises not to curtail Faust's term of years, though it is a very odd way of expressing it.) Confirmed anew in his wicked ways, Faust plans to kill the old man and sends his spirit to plague him, but it is the spirit who receives a drubbing; the old man mocks the spirit and sends it packing, being 'armoured with prayer'. And this is the last we hear of the old man in the Faust-book.

A few domestic displays of thaumaturgy (chapters 54, 55) and the knight's second attempted revenge (chapter 56), fill out the next couple of years, but as his term draws to an end Faust is determined to give himself full rein. 'He summoned seven diabolical succubae and made love to all of them' (chapter 57); they are in the forms of beautiful women he saw on his travels; two Dutch, one Hungarian, one English, the rest German. 'He vented his lewd passions with these seven diabolical whores until his death.' Next, since no account of a magician is complete without the discovery of buried treasure, Faust unearths a hoard with the aid of Mephostophiles (chapter 58). Then, in his twenty-third year of contract, 'so that the wretched Faustus might indulge his carnal desires to the limit' he asks his spirit to bring him Helen of Troy 'so that she might be his concubine'. 'When Doctor Faustus saw her she so captivated his heart that he began to make love to her. He took her as his mistress to live with him and loved her so much that he could scarcely be out of her company for a moment. During the final year she became pregnant by him and bore him a son ... this child revealed many future events ... But afterwards, when Faustus was killed, the mother and child disappeared along with him.'

Helen receives much discussion in the essay and I shall confine myself to observing the (doubtless intentional) parallel between Faust and Simon Magus, who had a female disciple, known as Luna, who was Helen − both Helen of Troy and Helen, the incarnation of Sophia, principle of Wisdom. It is interesting to discover that Giordano Bruno, at the end of a happy stay in Wittenberg from 1586 to 1588 − the university received him with open arms and he speaks nothing but praise of it – gave an *Oratio valedictoria* in which he praises Minerva as 'Sophia, Wisdom herself', and continues 'Her have I loved and sought from my youth, and desired for my spouse, and have become a lover of her form' (Frances Yates, *Giordano Bruno and the Hermetic Tradition*, London (RKP) 1964, p. 312). Of course, this is a year after the Faust-book was published, but it may provide the key to interpreting the marriage of Faust and Helen.

From now on we are in the twenty-fourth year and the grim conclusion occupies the final subsection of Part 3. Faust appoints Wagner as his heir (chapter 60), and at the houseboy's request he procures him a spirit in the form of an ape called Auerhahn ('Heathcock'). Faust exacts a promise that Wagner will write his biography when he is dead; his spirit will recall any details he has forgotten. This Wagner biography of Faust turns out not to be the Faust-book, as we learn in the final chapter that the students and masters who have just buried Faust's remains discover the auto-biography to which they append an end, and this purports to be the source of the Faust-book. However, there is evidence of a 'Wagner biography' in Widman's huge life of Faust (1599), so the introduc-tion of Faust's request to his servant here is logical if such a biography were already known to exist, and gratuitous if not.

When he has only one month left to live (chapter 62), Faust succumbs to depression: '. . . he was filled with anxiety, he wept and talked to himself all the time, gestured with his hands, groaned heavily, sighed and pined, and from that time on he seldom if ever allowed himself to be seen, and he could no longer bear the sight of his spirit.' There follows a sequence of written lamentations (written 'so that he should not forget' them) (chapters 63, 64, 66), interrupted by a chapter (65) in which Mephostophiles uses as many German proverbs as he can remember to mock Faust in his misery. Here the Lutheran tendency is at its strongest. As Butler says: 'The voice was the voice of Mephosto, but the words were the words of Luther . . . with the same boisterous verve, the same inexorable moral judge-ments, and the same blistering wrath, he berated his weak-kneed dupe for his apostasy from God and for his evil life' (*Myth of the Magus*, p. 136). And in his lamentations Faust blames his reason and his wilful self-reliance for condemning his body and soul to torment.

On his last day Faust invites his friends, the students and Masters of his Carnival frolics, to an outing at a neighbouring village, and although he does his best to remain cheerful it is clearly an effort. In the evening, after they have dined at the inn where they intend to pass the night, Faust opens his heart to them and reveals that all the wonders he has performed have been done through the agency of the Devil, that he made a pact with him; this very night the time is up and the Devil will come to fetch him. The students are greatly shocked and upbraid him for having kept his secret from them so long – otherwise they could surely have brought him to repentance and saved him. Even now it may not be too late, they say – but Faust knows better. 'He told them he would gladly pray but he could not bring himself to do it. His misgivings were those of Cain who also said his sins were too great to be forgiven. Faustus was convinced that in signing the contract he had gone too far.' There is a tearful farewell and, at Faust's request, the students retire to bed (they are unable to sleep for anxiety) while Faust remains in the parlour. Between midnight and one o'clock in the morning the house is shaken by a violent wind; the terrified students, not daring to emerge from their room, hear a 'fearful piping and hissing as if the house were full of snakes and vipers and other dangerous serpents. Then Doctor Faustus' door opened and he began to cry out: "Help! Murder!" but with a very weak voice. Soon he was heard no more.' In the morning the students enter the parlour to look for Faust 'but he was no longer to be seen – nothing but blood splattered all over the room and the brains stuck to the wall where the Devil had smashed him from one wall to the other. The eyes and several teeth lay there too – in all, a loathsome, shocking sight.' Finally they discover his corpse 'outside, lying on a dung hill. It was horrible to look at, for the head and all the limbs were hanging loose.'

After burying the remains, the students return to Wittenberg and inform Wagner who is 'grievously upset', and together they discover 'this biography written by Faustus himself, just as it is given here – everything except the end which was composed by these students and Masters, and that which was written by his servant which was made into a new book'. 'That same day the enchanted Helen disappeared, together with her son . . . And from that time on the house became so sinister that no-one could bear to live in it. Also, Doctor Faustus appeared to his servant by night in his own person and revealed many secret things to him. Someone saw him peering out through the window at night to see who was passing by.' The book ends with a pious warning, reinforced by the exhortation from

I Peter 5: 'Be steadfast and keep watch, for your adversary the Devil goes about like a roaring lion seeking whom he may devour. Resist him, strong in your faith.'

The Wolfenbüttel Manuscript and the genesis of the Faust-book

Although the Spies Faust-book is the first published life of Faust, it was predated by at least one other account, of which the manuscript *Historie und Geschicht Doctor Johannis Fausti*, discovered at Wolfen-büttel in the late nineteenth century, is the only extant example. Apart from its orthography and minor variants, the Wolfenbüttel Manuscript (W) is very close to the published Faust-book, except that it contains three extra chapters and a wholly different preface. It is generally accepted as the original (or a copy) of a direct precursor of the Spies Faust-book (there are cogent grounds for regarding the omission of the extra chapters as editorial revision by Spies). On this theory, many of the pious asides of the Spies Faust-book, absent in W, must also be seen as the work of Spies or an earlier editor. (This is more relevant to the present study than might appear since the English translator, P. F., sometimes fails to translate these asides, though it is impossible to determine whether his omissions were stylistic improvements made in ignorance of the manuscript or in the light of its perusal; we may regard it as a hint to such knowledge and P. F.'s most likely source would be Spies himself, in Frankfurt.) Unfortunately, it is not possible to date the manuscript more precisely than 1572–87, and even the latter date is based on the reasoning that any such manuscript would be redundant after publication of the Faust-book. In *The German and English Faust-books: Parallel Texts*, I have argued that the composition of the manuscript W (or its original, if W is a copy) did not long precede the Spies publication, since Spies, in his preface, tells of his search throughout Germany for a life of Faust, and he would have printed it as soon as he found it. As he was a well-known Lutheran propagandist, active in Frankfurt, Speyer and Heidelberg, he could not long have remained ignorant of a sensational manuscript.

The dating is important from the point of view of the genesis of the Faust-book. That difficult subject is only relevant here insofar as it throws light on the incongruities of the Faust-book – the two different motivations of Faust (for knowledge and powers) and his varying characterization. However, a brief consideration may be welcome. The scenario given below is hypothetical but is in accordance with all that is known.

As I see it, some time post 1585, stimulated by reading Lercheimer's *Christian Synopsis of Magic*, an unknown author in a university milieu (the evidence suggests Wittenberg, and Bruno's presence there from 1586 lends cultural support to the idea) composed a Latin life of Faust as a concrete example of the assault of the Devil upon potentially the 'best' of men, whose only weakness was self-reliance. (We may suppose the bulk of this work to correspond to Part 1 of the Spies Faust-book.) The Latin manuscript was circulated amongst a select university readership, but one member of this group mentioned it to a colleague at Speyer who was in touch with Spies and knew that the latter was anxious to acquire a life of Faust. The man at Speyer wrote to his informant begging him for a translation but without mentioning his purpose, and after repeated requests (attested by the Preface to W) his correspondent (whom we may call T, for translator) obliged. T, like the author of the Latin MS, is an academic (resident, perhaps, at the neighbouring university of Erfurt) with a considerable library at his disposal, and he pads his translation as he goes, with extracts from Schedel, Elucidarius, Dasypodius and, probably, verbal tradition (supplying many of the short 'jest' chapters which have plainly never been in Latin). He is slovenly and works at terrific speed, never bothering to correct completed parts on the basis of second thoughts, as is apparent from the chapter on the Grand Tour. The result is basically W and the preface to W is his work, beginning:

> My very dear friend and brother, this translation of Doctor Faustus and his wicked design is the result of your repeated request that I should put the Latin into German, which, so far as I am aware, has not been done. The reason it has not been printed or written in German is clear: so that no wicked and uneducated persons will use it as a model on which to build their fantasies and attempt to do as he did.

He ends:

> I could not forbear from adding this preamble and the anecdotes within the work itself, both as an apology and a caution. I am quite confident that you will find the deeds of Doctor Faustus a pleasant

diversion, especially since these events are true and consequently you
will enjoy them more than other, fictitious stories. Dear friend and
brother, take it and read it to enliven your garden walk.

He might have been horrified to learn that he had sent his
translation to one who was to pass it directly to a publisher, with the
express purpose of making it public as a pious and terrifying
warning. The surviving manuscript, W, is then a copy of the
translation as sent. I propose that the man at Speyer removed the
preface (to hide T's identity from Spies) and then sent the truncated
MS on to Spies at Frankfurt who, after making his own editorial
amendments, rushed it into print.

Even if this hypothesis is rejected (none of the several other
possibilities which have been mooted is simpler), it is impossible to
deny that the Spies Faust-book shows much evidence for a
conflation of Faustian source material, indicating multiple revisions
and precursors. Setting aside the topographical and cosmological
padding of the Faust-book, the theme as provided by Lercheimer
and its realization in the disputations, we may recognize five strains
of material which contribute to the work:

1 traditions of the historical Faust. Older members (age 60+) of the
population, of Wittenberg or Erfurt, for example, would have
witnessed the historical Faust or have been youngsters when his
actual deeds were hearsay. Some of their memories, much em-
broidered no doubt, would have provided a verbal source.

2 pseudo-Faustian anecdotes, in which Faust appropriates the
central role in a well-known tale of magic. Many of these had
emerged during the mythopoeic period of the 1560s and 1570s and
are taken directly into the Faust-book.

3 pseudo-Faust 'autographic' material. This would include the two
pacts, as they occur in the Faust-book, several of the 'written'
lamentations (the Faust-book author's apology that Faust wrote
them down lest he should forget them, when he knows he only has a
month to live, is rather weak), Faust's will, and probably the letter to
Jonas Victor describing his trip to the stars. All this material would
have been circulated as manuscripts or pamphlet publications.

4 pseudo-Wagner material. The Faust-book refers to a life of Faust
by his servant Wagner, and it is made clear in the final chapter of the

Faust-book that this is not the Faust-book itself, but another work. There are also one or two places in the Faust-book where Wagner is invoked to supply additional detail, so such material must have been available when the work was composed. There is much more evidence for a 'Wagner' Faust-book in Widman's *Warhafftige Historie*, a greatly augmented version of Faust's life, complete with exhaustive commentary, published posthumously in 1599. (Because of the late date of publication this work is unduly neglected as a contemporary treatment of the Faust story; its date of composition is uncertain but it need not be much later than 1587, when the pool of source material was still available.) Widman draws upon the material of the Faust-book but he employs other sources, a main one being Wagner or Wäiger, as he calls him. (This material is quite independent of the so-called 'Wagner-books' which concern the deeds of Wagner after the death of Faust.) The possibility of invention of sources by Widman can probably be ignored: he was not an inventive writer. It is thus quite likely that Widman incorporated some material which was older than much of the material in the Spies Faust-book. One aspect of Widman's treatment important for Empson's discussion is that in it Mephostophiles claims not to be a devil but a *spiritus familiaris*.

5 material from civic carnival plays. There is evidence for a carnival play of Faust (in which he seduces 'Grethle' with the aid of his devil 'Rabuntikus') given at Nuremberg in the year of the Faust-book (and so predating it). A principal float in the carnival procession was a huge dragon: manned by the young citizens who were to perform the carnival plays later in the day. One sat on the head, others in the belly and on the tail, all dressed in masquerade or character costume. But surely this is the dragon of the Faust-book (chapter 48) in which Faustus and his student companions 'career around till midnight' on the fourth day of carnival: '[Faustus] equipped himself with a sleigh in the form of a dragon. Dr Faustus sat on the head and the students in the belly. On the tail four enchanted monkeys tumbled merrily with one another.' The descriptions of the manifestations accompanying Faust's conjuration of the Devil also read like an eye-witness account of a dramatic representation.

Considering the diversity of the material and treatments, it is remarkable that the Faust-book displays any sense of unity. That it does so is largely due to the encompassing framework of the main theme which I suspect was the essence of the Latin original.

Any further discussion of the genesis or assignment of strata would be out of place here, but there is one final Faust-book related topic which should be mentioned, namely the Erfurt material of Recension C. This recension appeared in the same year as the Spies first edition and contains an additional six chapters, one describing the famous Leipzig barrel ride, the other five set in an academic milieu in Erfurt. Faust is represented as lecturing in Greek literature at the university, and at the request of his students he 'raises' the Greek heroes (including the terrifying giant Polyphemus) for their entertainment. In the other chapters he is the genial companion of local junkers by whom he is much regaled. These chapters differ from the rest of the Faust-book in the degree of (correct) topographical and sociological detail and it is quite probable that they have a historical basis. In the last of the 'Erfurt chapters', a famous barefoot friar, Dr Klinge (a well-known historical character and vigorous opponent of the Reformation in Erfurt) attempts to persuade Faust to reform, just as the anonymous old man does in the Faust-book. Faust listens patiently to Dr Klinge, and agrees that what he says is true, 'but I have gone too far and have made a compact with the Devil himself in my own blood delivering myself up to him, body and soul, for all eternity. How can I go back? How can anyone help me?' The monk explains that all that is required is true remorse and penance, followed by rigorous abstention from magic: 'Then we shall hold a mass for you . . . and that will surely free you from the Devil.' Faust's reply is superb and heroic and can only stem from memory of the historical Faust: 'Mass here, mass there' said Doctor Faustus, 'my promise binds me too fast. . . . Besides, it would not be honourable, nor redound to my credit if I were to revoke my letter and seal compacted with my own blood. The Devil has kept his word in his promises to me and I will keep my word in what I have promised and contracted to him.' Faust's code of honour, sincere or assumed, was too much for Dr Klinge, who went off in a rage and had the magician banished from Erfurt. But what a contrast here with the would-be repentant but degenerate Faust of the original Faust-book treatment. The Faust of the Erfurt chapters is a grand figure, a Falstaff, much the same as the Faust of the 'carnival' chapters, wining and dining with the students; I cannot but believe that this presentation of Faust retains some historical accuracy, and was in no small measure responsible for his popularity and the official condemnation of him as a corrupter of youth. Indeed, one could go further: the widespread public popularity of Faust before the appearance of the Faust-book was probably a key to its success.

The English Faust-book

The continental rage for the Faust-book was a near guarantee that the book would be translated, especially for Protestant readership. Thus the early advent of Dutch (1592) and English translations is not surprising. A detailed review of the English Faust-book (EFB), as the English translation is generally known, is scarcely necessary here since it is given very ample consideration in the essay (see chapters 2 and 3). All attempts to identify the translator, known only as 'P. F., Gent.', have proved fruitless; this is one tantalizing aspect of the book. The other is the difficulty of dating either the translation or the first edition, no longer extant. The earliest surviving edition is from late 1592, 'newly imprinted, and in convenient places imperfect matter amended'; it is this information on the title page which attests to the existence of the earlier edition. But 'Faust' was by no means new in England in 1592. On 28 February 1589, there was entered in the Register of the Stationers' Company 'A ballad of the life and death of Doctor Faustus the great cunngerer'. But it is not known for certain whether this is the same as 'The Judgement of God shewed upon one John Faustus' in the late-seventeenth century Roxburghe collection of ballads, which does show a knowledge of the EFB; so although the appearance of the ballad is suggestive of an English Faust-book prior to the end of February 1589, it cannot be taken as proof. However, it does harmonize with one equivocal piece of internal evidence from the EFB: P. F. adds to Faust's Grand Tour a description of the obelisk at Rome, saying 'it stood in Faustus his time leaning against the Church wall of Saint Peters, but now Papa Sixtus hath erected it in the middle of S.Peters Church yard.' P. F. writes as if Pope Sixtus were still living (he died 27 August 1590), thus suggesting a relatively early date for the translation. But P. F. might have used uncorrected material from an earlier source, and in any case, the evidence could hardly be considered conclusive.

The gross tolerance in the date of the EFB is most unfortunate, since it is indubitably the prime source for Marlowe's *Doctor Faustus*, and a firm limiting date for the composition of the latter would have been most welcome. As it is, *Doctor Faustus* might have been written at any time between 1588 and Marlowe's death (30 May 1593), allowing much ground for controversy, as the Empson essay indicates. As I cannot profitably add more detail here without duplicating the material of the essay, I will leave the rest to Empson. What comments I can offer regarding his theories, and some consideration of the more recent Faust/Marlowe literature are best left to the postscript.

The English Faust-book
and Marlowe's *Doctor Faustus*

a1

The Problem

In a report on the English reaction to the Faust-book soon after its appearance, the play by Marlowe needs to take the first place, because much of it is very good and also because its bad parts are a mystery. But the translation used by Marlowe, which had made some very bold changes, is of more immediate interest to the reader of this book,[1] and in itself calls for explanation. Besides, the play is a ruin, as all agree, and we need advice about how to reconstruct it. The cuts which were made from it are lost for ever, but the changes in a translation, when the original survives, are plain to see. Here they should at least tell us what was the main disturbing factor.

Our sources for it are uniquely bad, among the plays of that era which got printed at all. The earliest surviving text, usually called the A-text, is dated 1604,[2] but the book was registered in 1601[3] and probably first appeared then (these flimsy quartos giving only one play soon fell apart); even so, it would be about ten years later than the first performance. The controversy about the play has centred round whether it was written in late 1589 or 1592, and Marlowe's life was so tragically brief that this means a great deal;[4] but either view

Throughout, superscript letters refer to the textual notes (see pp. 209–12).

[1] Empson is referring here to *The German and English Faust-books: Parallel Texts*, tr. and intro. John Henry Jones (forthcoming), for which this essay was to have formed an appendix.

[2] For a listing of known editions to the end of the seventeenth century, see Greg, pp. 12–14.

[3] Greg (p.12) quotes from the Stationers' Company Register. See *A Transcript of the Register of the Company of Stationers of London 1554–1640 AD*, ed. Edward Arber (London 1875). The relevant entry is dated 7 January 1601 and the publisher is Thos. Busshell.

[4] February 1564–30 May 1593. See Boas.

leaves the first text very belated. It is about 1,500 lines, too short by 500 for the public London theatres, and it has obviously been truncated with harsh indifference to the dramatic effect. ᵇThe B-text (1616) is merely an expanded version brought out by the same publisher, which completely replaced the old one; it gives almost all the A-text, sometimes perhaps from a slightly different version, and is a little over 2,100 lines, quite long enough for a play with so much business.⁵ Most of the added text is generally agreed to be padding, not by Marlowe, written in undistinguished verse and often irrelevant to the story; especially the anti-papal bits about Pope Bruno, which have practically nothing to do with Faust. ᶜHowever, it gives us one comic scene by Marlowe urgently needed for the structure of the play; somehow that had been recovered. ᵈSir Walter Greg,⁶ my chief opponent here, recognized this; and it is much to his credit, as he hated the comic scenes, feeling no doubt that so terrible a story ought to be tragic all along.

The A-text has worse incongruity than that. There are long sequences in very good poetry, ringing, sensitive and profound, and then one is dropped abruptly into bilge, as through a trap door. Scenes II.i and II.ii are run together, though events between them have made a radical change. Not only critics who dislike the play, but editors giving it devoted labour, let drop at certain points that here Marlowe 'parodies' himself – of course, they may assume that he does it like Ancient Pistol, who was a sincere admirer of the style. Most of them posit a collaborator, an incompetent hack who took over when Marlowe was too bored to go on; though surely this does nothing to excuse Marlowe, as it makes him refuse to correct work which he knew to be bad. Also, scenes that would be welcome to the first audiences are half-promised but do not occur – perhaps there are only two cases, the second visit to Faust by the magicians and Faust's visit to the Sultan. More important, there is a violent indifference to the feelings of the audience; all through the middle of the play Faust is assumed to be a popular character, a great source of fun, and yet his enormous punishment at the end is accepted as a matter of routine. Not by himself, however; he remarks in act IV that he expects to be saved ('Tush, Christ did call the thief upon the

---

⁵ [257; ET]Shakespeare often runs to 3,000 lines, but plays with conjuring and such like were commonly short; the B-text is about 2,100 lines, and so is *Macbeth*.
⁶ See p. 41.

Cross'[7]), and pleads at the end with astonishment, perhaps also indignation; and yet he has devised no plan to escape the doom of which everyone has warned him. The B-text, at the end, gives Faust a vision of the tortures soon to come and makes the audience share in it, with an orgy of spiteful gloating from the devils in which the Good Angel takes part. The audience feels it would be unsafe not to join them in their evil pleasure. No new fault in Faust has been offered as a reason for this vehement change in attitude; it merely rounds off the play.

'Between thirty and forty years ago, there was a literary-critical revolution about such matters, making Renaissance authors more medieval, and less abreast of modern thought, than had been believed before.[8] For this play the bulwark of the movement is a grand parallel text edition by Sir Walter Greg, *Marlowe's 'Doctor Faustus' 1604–1616*, published in 1950; its notes are powerful and tireless, and it is still dominant though in detail it has been much whittled away.

Greg's scheme for A- and B-texts

'Greg has a scheme[9] for the sources of A and B, which in the main I gladly accept. Marlowe wrote the play for Pembroke's Company, which became bankrupt and had to sell it to Henslowe, for the Admiral's Company. Pembroke's men went on tour, and found they

---

[7] A: 1173, B: 1550. This and all further references to the text of *Doctor Faustus* are based on Greg. Both A- and B-text line references are given unless the quotation is specific to a particular text.

[8] [16; E3] . . . saying [of Marlowe's *Faust*: ed.] that wrong meanings had been read into the play by sentimental liberals: it was entirely Christian, more so than any other Elizabethan play. The trouble with these enthusiasts, I dumbly felt, was that they would swallow anything; they thought witch-burning entirely Christian, whereas many Christians at the time knew better. Marlowe was in an uneasy condition after leaving Cambridge, with no source of income except his spy contacts which would bring in little; but he considered himself a progressive man, in touch with the Ralegh group. He was not a tactful boy; he made rude jokes about the Virgin Mary in pubs; he pretended to be more friendly with Hariot than he really was. Not a perfect character; but he really would feel bitterly ashamed, on high moral grounds, if he knew that just after his death his play was being twisted into recommending eternal torture.

[9] Greg, p. 50

could recreate the play of *Faust*, or some shortened performance of it which they had given at a grand house, by 'memorial reconstruction'; when cut further for easy production, this became the A-text. ᵍGreg, in arguing that Marlowe wrote all the B-text, puts forward an argument which is usually ignored by his supporters. He thinks that the sadistic parts are purely abstract or allegorical, written by Marlowe when he was merely trying to versify the theology, but when he wrote the final soliloquy he 'moved onto the human plane', so he cut out these earlier drafts (Greg, p. 131, etc.). But Henslowe, says Greg, had kept the 'foul papers' (the first draft) for half a lifetime, and at last they were released – a thing to make Marlowe turn in his grave.[10] Thus the B-text did not give what was currently being acted, only a remote historical curiosity. ʰThe innocence of the pure aesthete makes Greg an attractive figure here, though it makes his theory quite incredible. And at any rate he agrees that Marlowe would not have intended to put on the last act of the B-text, as it would feel a bit out of key, somehow.

Two other aspects of the complicated and exhausting controversy over this play need to be mentioned. Like the English Faust-book, it cannot be dated. Some information comes from Henslowe's *Diary*,[11] which lists his daily takings from named plays at the Rose Theatre from early 1591 till 1597. He has all of Marlowe's plays known to be then available, but never acquired *Edward II*. He records his first performance of *Faust* in September 1594, and does not mark it as new; but the takings have the usual form for a new play: over £3 on the first night, and then a rapid falling off. This does not look as if he had simply bought it from a rival. If Marlowe had sold it to Henslowe shortly before he was murdered (30 May 1593) a bit of

---

[10] [18; E0]Nobody ever kept 'foul papers', and the only man in the business who might have done it was Alleyn the founder of Dulwich College, who was Henslowe's heir. [402; E7]Henslowe died in 1616, and probably Alleyn saw no advantage in hiding the acted version any longer. [18; E0]It makes Marlowe begin writing with a number of absurdly mistaken false starts. [20; E5]No supporter of Greg now recalls this theory. Besides, Marlowe would not have thought up Pope Bruno, because he was a concentrated dramatist who never used double plots; this padding was needed (and paid for by Henslowe in 1602) because so much had been cut by the original censor. Greg's scheme for the A-text does lead one to the truth, but it is impossible to explain the cuts as made by a working producer; they are against his interests repeatedly.

[11] *Henslowe's Diary*, ed. Walter W. Greg, London (A. H. Bullen) 1904, or for a more recent edition, that of R. A. Foakes and R. S. Rickert, Cambridge 1961.

time might well be needed before it was cleared with the censor, and an elaborate production had to be got ready; this date is not impossible. It does need some explanation, but the disciples of Greg regularly find another use for this dating, and talk as though Marlowe saw the light before the end. On the other hand, Greg is an aesthete, and appears surprised at the idea that Marlowe would care about the beliefs expressed in his plays. Well, the author may have agreed with Oscar Wilde,[12] but his audience didn't; he would be jeered at heartily if he ratted on his beliefs, after making so much noise about them. Not, indeed, if he had announced a conversion, but that we would hear about; the delations make clear that he announced his opinions recklessly, and there could be no advantage in a secret conversion, whether sincere or a last bid for safety.[13] It is generally agreed that he 'died swearing'; maybe his friends dared not speak up at the time, but consider Michael Drayton, a friend of about the same age who lived after him for a generation longer, and then said he had been 'all air and fire'. Surely he would have mentioned this conversion.[14] The explanation has to be something different.

Secondly, *Faust* was designed as a five-act play with choruses

---

[12] That any lie is permissible for the sake of art.

[13] [15; E2]He died leaving unfinished his *Hero and Leander*, which is not penitential.

[14] [187; E0]Also, supposing that he did, and that his play was as pietistic as our B-text, described by Kirschbaum ['Marlowe's Faustus: A Reconsideration' in *Review of English Studies*, xix (1943), p. 229] as the most Christian play in the Elizabethan canon, why did no one mention it? Surely his atheism was notorious ... and the accusation in the death-bed repentance of Greene in *A Groatsworth of Wit* was published in the year before the murder. It is theatrical, but as Greene says he was practically an atheist too it is not spiteful, merely urging his friend to repent. There is an impressive amount of agreement between these sources and what was extracted from Kyd. After the murder various people say he deserved it for his wickedness, and though friends speak up for him later it is with caution; one says 'he was all made of air and fire', another pretended he had died of plague. Nobody says he repented at the last and wrote a glorious Christian play, though plenty of Elizabethans were quite as silly as Kirschbaum. Nor does anyone even hint that he [190; E0]became a hypocrite out of cowardice, giving slavish reverence to the evil beliefs he had denounced. ... He might repent sincerely, or from mixed motives, but surely somebody would accuse him of bad ones. The Henslowe version of the play was produced a year after the murder, when his career was still widely discussed; and either of these views of him would be a good gossip-point. There is an explanation; the play by Marlowe had made a brief appearance four years earlier, and had implied no change in his opinions, and discussion of it was totally forbidden.

between the acts, as was believed to be the classical manner. Horace had remarked, in one possibly ironical line, that a play has to have five acts, and the university wits were prone to obey him when they first hit London. The *Spanish Tragedy* seems to break the rule, having only four acts with the last one twice the usual length; but it lost a Chorus for an obvious reason during the same outbreak of censorship as ruined the play of *Faust*. The latter was crippled much more severely, but at least parts survive of all the Choruses except the first one (that is, the harangue between acts I and II; they were all like the initial prologue). And acts I and II of *Faust* make nearly half of the play,[i] even in the B-text; there is an obvious gap, as even the A-text says 'Enter Chorus' for the one between acts III and IV. So there we may be sure that something was cut, and not cut for convenience in staging.

Censorship of *Doctor Faustus*

All these complaints, though they seem scattered, are met by one explanation:[15] the play was disrupted by an explosion of censorship. There is a real likeness to [j]the ruin left by volcanic action, where a specially hard pillar of rock often marks the place where the hole used to be, through which the molten lava forced its way.[16] The insistence in the B-text upon sending Faust to a real Hell marks the source of the trouble; in Marlowe's play he had escaped. There is a trace of this in the nasty gloating of the transformed Mephosto of the B-text, when he tells Lucifer that Faust is already being tormented:

> his labouring brain
> Begets a world of idle fantasies
> To over-reach the Devil; but all in vain . . .
> (B:1908–10)

[15] [258; E2]It should have been plain, but our political innocence kept us from seeing it.

[16] [218; E4]In the same way, the eighty lines of sniggering sadism near the end of the B-text correspond to the growing realization of the first audiences that no devils would appear at all; of course, the brief direction 'Enter devils' near the end of the A-text would be added by the editor, ten years later, if he found it lacking.

Marlowe the Overreacher[17] was made the title of a perceptive and useful book, but Faust himself has no idea of planning any escape; that, in fact, is what is the matter with the play. He is too much of an ass, and surely the real play by Marlowe was likely to have avoided that weakness.[18] The author of this nasty talk, an actual cleric perhaps, feels sure that the new audiences will remember the old play, and his chief business is to refute it. There is another reference in the disillusion of Old Man, when Faust walks off with Helen:

> Accursed Faustus, miserable man,
> That from thy soul exclud'st the grace of heaven,
> And fliest the throne of his tribunal seat.
>
> (A:1377–9)

This comes in the A-text, and is probably by Marlowe himself; why the whole speech was cut from the B-text one can only conjecture. In the play as we have it Faust makes no attempt to escape from Judgement Day, and the thought is an intriguing one; but how would he do it?

It will be answered that these are mere careless expressions; Faust could not be made to escape Hell, or even to imagine a method, because Marlowe was expected to dramatize the Faust-book. Probably he was commissioned to do simply that, as the ᵏA-text follows the English translation closely; and anyway, most of the spectators would have read the book, accepting it as historical truth. Marlowe would have to claim, one must agree, that his version was even truer; he was telling the real story, which the Lutheran censors had hushed up.[19] He could be plausible: the Faust-book itself hints that there is some mystery about Meph.[20] Anglican doctrine had not

---

[17] Harry Levin: *Christopher Marlowe: The Overreacher*, London (Faber & Faber) 1954.

[18] [406; E10]In a legend he does not need a plan; the sentiment of the Faust-book is that of course he is a fool, as all young men are, because they do not realize their true interests. It is a difference in the media, though no doubt also in nationality and historical periods.

[19] [5; E0]Very likely he convinced himself of this, after a number of brief sessions with a friend who could do running translations from the German, at the points where Marlowe felt suspicious of the English version; but in his sceptical heart he would recognize that this was not legally a scholarly procedure, even though it fetched up nuggets so often.

[20] [337; E0]It seems as well to put 'Meph' for the familiar spirit of Faust, not to raise a laugh but to solve a difficulty. The best form of the name is 'Mephistopheles', with

sided with the Lutherans on the point at issue, so Marlowe was safe
there; and popular opinion was with him. Luther and Calvin had
denied that there are any other spirits beside angels and devils,
excluding even ghosts, but the ordinary practice of a magician had
long been to deal with Middle Spirits, and deny energetically that
they are devils. The first half of the sixteenth century, when Faust
was alive and busy, had seen this Renaissance cult in full flower; by
Shakespeare's time it had lost credit and become playful, among
some people at least, but the group is hard to define. Simon Forman,
a successful London medical practitioner who treated many of
Shakespeare's acquaintances, accepted changelings as a matter of
course, and describes his attempts to get into contact with spirits
merely as part of his professional study, with no sign of fear that he
might end up in Hell.[21] And come now, it is all very well telling us we
must not believe what devils say, because we know they are liars, but
perhaps Meph is telling a lie when he says he is a devil. The Faust-
book makes the claim look extremely flimsy.[22] The playwright had a
bit of room to manoeuvre here.

Spies[23] or whoever edited the Faust-book material realized that
there were in effect two Faust legends, and wanted to retain both. No
doubt some bits had to be cut out because they would have caused
trouble, but there seems to have been no rewriting to soften the
contrasts. One Faust has committed the unforgivable sin and is the
enemy of mankind, knowing himself doomed to eternal torture; the
other is an avatar of the demigod rogue, found in practically all

---

an i, well known from Goethe but invented earlier in the eighteenth century. It
makes the spirit a cool civil servant, a tax collector perhaps, or an inquisitor. The
Faust-book calls him 'Mephostophiles' with an o, so that he is a rather clumsy but
forceful, even a jovial character. The A-text of Marlowe, which we have no adequate
reason to doubt, calls him 'Mephastophilis', so that he is a bleating sheep-like
figure, who demands love but could bite. It would be tiresome to insist upon the
correct spelling. [See Postscript, p. 203. This is the only footnote in Empson's MS:
ed.]

[21] See *A Selection from the Papers of Dr Simon Forman*, London (Camden Society)
1843, p. 19 (from the Diary entry for 1588, almost as an aside: 'This yeare I began to
practise negromancy and to call aungells and spirits.' Had he been stimulated by
the Faust-book?)

[22] See chapter 4 for a full consideration of Meph's status in the GFB.

[23] I have italicized the name of Johann Spies, the publisher of the GFB, wherever
there is a possibility (especially in a piece on Marlowe) of confusion with espionage
agents.

ancient literatures and surviving oral cultures – the ideal drinking companion, the great fixer, who can break taboos for you and get away with it. Falstaff and Samson are merely parts of him. 'This half of Faust was of course unwelcome to the authorities; just around the time when Spies published his version at Frankfurt, another one came out in Tübingen,[24] and the two authors and the printer went to jail. *Spies* in his introduction and marginal notes makes a fuss about his piety and orthodoxy, but he was merely being cautious. English critics have been prone to say that the coarse German original is too crude for their attention, but at least the editing of it was delicate.

This is made clear in Jones's edition,[25] where the two groups of material added during the very year of publication are separated out. Evidently the book was a roaring success, and for the third edition,[26] the second demand for more, Spies felt safe enough to print the Erfurt material.[27] There could be no theological objection to the anecdotes from Erfurt, and surely Spies would already have known about so obvious a source; but they would be annoying to a Lutheran official because they present Faust as a great social success. No smart party for young men is complete without him, even if he has to arrive on a flying horse. He is helpful too, but this was already clear in the first edition. Modern Eng. Lit. critics, determined to make the story Christian, always say that Faust steadily degenerates.[28] The last action recorded of him before he is caught up into disaster is his best one, so far as we know; he brings together for marriage a loving couple of the upper-middle class – no wonder the dons avoid any mention of it, finding no opportunity to express their contempt for peasants and duchesses. The book has great merit as a factual report of the various legends about Faust which had grown up during the thirty or forty years since his death.

It went across northern Europe like a prairie fire. Greg says that six translations appeared within six years,[29] which has been

---

[24] *Ein warhaffte und erschröckliche Gesicht; von D. Johann Fausten ... in reymen verfasset*, Tübingen (Alexander Hock) 1587/8, available as a facsimile edition: *Der Tübinger Reim-Faust von 1587/8*, ed. Günther Mahal, Tübingen (Schweier) 1977.

[25] *The German and English Faust-books*.

[26] [274; E5]Not used by the English translator.

[27] See introduction, p. 34.

[28] This view is not confined to the English, but prevails amongst most German commentators.

[29] Greg, p. 1n. The five early translations are: Low German (1588), Dutch (1592), English (2nd edn,1592), French (1598) and Czech (1611).

questioned but gives the right impression. Most international best sellers were in Latin; to have one aimed at a public which did not know Latin, so that this massive work of translation was required, was in itself rather alarming. The voice of the people ᵐhas so often meant trouble.

The theological left wing in England was being particularly tiresome just then; ⁿone might expect that the destruction of the Armada in 1588, confidently assumed in England as elsewhere to be an act of God and not of the Queen's Fleet, would be to create a confident national unity. Just the opposite; they had got that before, and the effect of feeling safer was to make quarrelling permissible. The Marprelate Pamphlets,[30] for example, appeared, demanding to abolish bishops; and the position of Archbishop Whitgift is rather hard to grasp, since he like most of the higher Anglican clergy at the time was a Calvinist except upon this point of Church government. But none of them were Lutherans, and the Faust-book would seem to them much more plainly Lutheran than it does to the average reader nowadays. Luther, though he had ratted on the peasants in the Peasants' War, was considered a rabble-rouser, and like all demagogues very tricky.[31] Scrutinized in this light, the Faust-book

---

[30] See, e.g., *The Marprelate Tracts, 1588–1589*, A Scolar Press facsimile. 7 parts. Leeds (Scolar Press) 1967.

[31] [420; E12]Luther had cheeked Henry VIII, and Shakespeare in his *Henry VIII* makes Wolsey call Anne Boleyn a 'spleeny Lutheran'. Apparently he means 'liable to produce out of the blue an inconvenient religious scruple'. [45; E4]Intense curiosity would however be excited in the Anglican censor at the time, as it has been in many subsequent commentators. Can this be a secret attack upon Luther? He had sometimes advised men, since they cannot avoid sin, to sin vehemently and repent vehemently, and had sometimes maintained that total despair of the divine gift of grace was the most probable condition for receiving it. Faust seems to have followed this advice, and is commonly supposed to have met doom. But no Reformer denied that the judgements of God are inscrutable, and the book makes no attempt to imply that Faust had been misled by the theories of Luther; when he signs the pact he is just a careless sceptic, aiming chiefly at knowledge, but also pleasure and power. At the end he tells the students: 'I am sincerely remorseful and pray continually in my heart for the grace that would save my soul . . . I know the Devil will have my body and I will gladly let him have it if only he will leave my soul in peace.' [Sp. 221]. Repentance here is become a highly technical conception. In both his pacts (GFB, chs 6, 53) Faust promised to give both body and soul to the Devil, but neither of them, as the story ends, has gone to Hell. His body is left, ripped to pieces, around the neighbouring inn, and his ghost can be glimpsed in his own house, presumably dictating his memoirs to Wagner. No doubt this is merely a result of the editorial policy, of reporting all tolerable legends about Faust, but it

excites immediate suspicion; why is it exciting so much enthusiasm among the masses? Which side is it on, anyway? There is no need to argue that the censor behaved at all cleverly, but it is reasonable to suppose that he had been alerted from above to take special care.

However, compared to the mainland we were a haven of peace; this period was the height of the witch-burnings. A French traveller reported in 1590: 'Germany is almost entirely occupied in building fires for [witches]. Switzerland has been compelled to wipe out many of her villages on their account. Travellers in Lorraine may see thousands and thousands of the stakes to which witches are bound.'[32]

It sounds like the Black Death, and of course the sects were still persecuting one another as usual. But the special witch courts, with any accusation accepted and the torturers waiting to extract confessions in the next room, had not been established in England. °The high officials of the Church, in England as elsewhere (Professor Trevor-Roper has remarked),[33] tried to keep the lunacy out of their countries or districts, but some of the clergy were keen for it and could raise some of the mob, Pand presumably there was pressure to bring the witch-courts in. Was that what the Faust-book was concerned to recommend?

qMagicians were not as a rule treated so badly as witches, as it was granted that they usually did not make a pact with the Devil but merely found means of forcing him to work for them; but Faust, even more in words than in deeds, does enlist under the Devil completely, and the play as we have it agrees with both Faust-books in assuming that other magicians do the same. rIf the persecution came to England Dr Dee, a learned adviser of the Queen, and her cousin, would certainly have to be burned on his return from his long visit to the Emperor,[34] and so would helpful Dr Forman,

---

gives no assurance that he went to Hell. And what is one to make of all that facetiousness in the middle of the book, evidently rejoicing at the horseplay of Faust; surely that takes an 'antinomian' position? (It is still completely unforgivable to the modern critics of the play.)

[32] Henry Boguet: *An Examen of Witches* (translation of *Discours des Sourciers*, 1590), tr. and ed. Montague Summers, London (John Rodker) 1929, p. xxxiii.

[33] H. R. Trevor-Roper: *The European Witch-Craze of the Sixteenth and Seventeenth Centuries*, Harmondsworth (Penguin Books) 1969, p. 69 and n.75 (pp. 129f).

[34] [196; E8]Dr Dee's house was sacked soon after he went abroad (September 1583), but as he recovered most of his books after he got back (December 1589) the mob was probably actuated by greed rather than piety.

though ⁵he did not claim to have got at all far with necromancy, and who knew what other plainly innocent people?³⁵ 'All three accusers of Marlowe say he was a friend of Hariot,³⁶ a single-minded scientist who was under grave suspicion of being a conjurer as well as an atheist, so he would be burned alive if the Faust-book prevailed. However, this need not have worried Marlowe, who deals with the point firmly at the start of his play. The two advisory magicians are not presented favourably, since they want Faust to take the risk while they get the advantage ('Faust may try his cunning by himself'), but they are too timid to have sold their souls. And Marlowe's Faust intends to do good with his powers, though he ᵘseems to get distracted from it. This need not distress Marlowe, but surely he could not send Faust to eternal torture for his good intentions. The Baines delation says: 'almost into every Company he cometh he persuades men to atheism willing them not to be afeard of bugbears and hobgoblins' (see Boas, p. 250). Of course the chief hobgoblin would be Hell itself. ᵛA great fuss about atheism in high places was brewing up, settling upon Ralegh and his asssociates in later 1592, but by 1594 it had become a campaign against a Jewish doctor of the Queen.³⁷ These shifting fads in Court circles cannot be argued about as if they were sensible; but the year or two after the great victory were a time when the censors would be especially sensitive about a Lutheran best seller. ʷIt seems plain that they had doctored the translation before they captured the play.

ˣBut, I may be told, no such argument can be set up, because the censorship of plays rested only with Sir Edmund Tilney, appointed by the Queen. There is a decisive answer. In 1589 a committee was set up, including representatives of the Archbishop of Canterbury and the Lord Mayor of London, and of course Tilney, whom it was to supersede.³⁸ He demanded a pension in lieu of the comfortable

---

³⁵ [196; E8]One should remember that Reginald Scot's *Discovery of Witchcraft* had come out in 1584, deriding and refuting the whole cult, only three years before the Faust-book. So it would be wrong to present the first readers of the English Faust-book as personally agitated over the witch-problem; but still, that was a major part of its thrilling background. Even so, one might be an earnest Christian without believing that to burn witches alive was a basic duty; this aspect of the book was a distinctly foreign one.

³⁶ Thomas Hariot (BL cat.: Harriot) (1560–1621). See Henry Stevens: *Thomas Hariot: The Mathematician, the Philosopher and the Scholar*, London 1900.

³⁷ Dr Lopez, executed in 1594 for 'attempting to poison the Queen'.

³⁸ [194; E5]It shows that the censorship was pressing forward just then, and also the

income he had been making, and the Archbishop wrote to the Lord Mayor, and the Lord Mayor wrote to two of the rich city companies, who replied that they ʸrefused to pay. It may be presumed that they said they fully appreciated the importance of the matter, but considered that Tilney was trustworthy. By 1592 he was 'fully in command' again, and remained so till he retired with honour after several years under James (Glynne Wickham: *Early English Stages 1300–1600*, London 1959–72, vol. II, part I, p. 88). It is a mysterious triumph, and a most fortunate one, because *King Lear* could hardly have been produced otherwise (not that it is really heretical, but that a conscientious clerical censor would have become intolerable to the author). Tilney must have done something decisive to save himself, for example throwing Marlowe to the wolves. ᶻHe was extremely fortunate to have a play available which expressed a heretical opinion; that was probably unique. He had only to hand it over to the Archbishop, expressing entire readiness and submission. He may have been rather relieved at having his authority strengthened by this affair.

The date of Marlowe's *Doctor Faustus*

In assuming that *Faust* was sacrificed, I am adopting the earlier date for it. ᵃᵃSeveral plays of 1590 and 1591, such as *Friar Bacon and Friar Bungay*, *The Looking-Glass for London*, and *John a Kent and John a Cumber*, appear to be 'influenced' by *Faust*, or rather, to be cashing in on its notoriety. They introduce devils, or characters disguised as devils, and other spirits called up by magicians, but they are mild and playful about the subject, orthodox too. Greg of course has to argue that, wherever 'borrowing' is obvious, Marlowe has taken a tip from one of these humble catchpennies.[39] In recent years the argument or the state of opinion has been moving against him; it is a

Archbishop begins giving his personal licence to selected literary works. I suspect he came a cropper in early 1593, when he gave it to *Venus and Adonis*, assured no doubt that it described how love led only to suffering; but when it came out it was considered so libidinous that every lustful student slept with it under his pillow. No book was licensed under the Archbishop's own name during the next year; as he was very impervious to ridicule, the Queen herself must have told him to stop making a fool of himself.

[39] See appendix 2: 'Kill-Devil All the Parish Over'.

lengthy business, and only the result can be reported here.[40] Well then, Marlowe's original *Faust* must have been acted fairly often in 1589 or 1590, say ten times;[41] the audience of a catchpenny must be expected to enjoy an echo from that *Faust* — it is not merely that the author got a good idea from reading it in manuscript.

Hence the text must have passed the censor, presumably the Queen's censor Tilney, but even he would be quick enough to spot a cause of theological trouble. After ten performances, the censors realized that the audiences were enjoying a heretical conclusion — that Faust died in an ecstasy of relief and gratitude, having somehow learned, immediately after the soliloquy, that he had escaped Hell. There was an immense shutdown; all mention of the play was stopped, and all sale of the translation of the German original; but there could be no legal penalties, as they could not be imposed in secret.

[bb]Here there are two major improbabilities; first that the trick could succeed for a time (Marlowe would know that it must soon be discovered if successful), second that it could be hushed up after discovery. As to the second, historians have been coming to give more recognition to the energy and powers of the Elizabethan censorship, Christopher Hill especially,[42] but here an example may be enough. In 1597 a play called *The Isle of Dogs* was suppressed,

---

[40] [189; E0]On Greg's theory, Marlowe could not even have started considering a Faust-play before May 1592, and in July all theatres were closed because of riots until September, and before that date had been reached they were closed because of plague for the rest of Marlowe's life-time — he was murdered in May 1593. Or rather, the theatres had occasional remissions for a month or two, but they then put on old favourites; they were too poor and depressed to plan a major new production. Like Shakespeare, Marlowe was writing a long allegorical poem for some patron; it would not be a sensible time for him to write *Faust*.

[41] [15; E2]I agree that he would not write *Faust* next after the two *Tamburlanes*, but he might well write it after the uproarious *Jew of Malta*, which has many dangerous thoughts from Jews and Turks but was encouragingly successful. So it can be dated 1589–90, when the approaching roar of the Faust-book was first heard in England, and recognized by a licensed ballad (February 1589). ['A ballad of the life and deathe of Doctor Faustus the great cunngerer' was 'allowed' to Richard Jones 'under the hand of the Bishop of London', according to an entry, dated 28 February 1589, in the Stationers' Register. It is still uncertain whether this ballad is 'The Judgement of God shewed upon one John Faustus' in the Roxburghe collection (ii, 235): ed.]

[42] See *Society and Puritanism in Pre-Revolutionary England*, London (Secker & Warburg) 1964, and *The World Turned Upside Down*, London (Temple Smith) 1972.

apparently after at least one performance.[43] There was a threat to close all the theatres for ever. It seems to have been a kind of 'revue', a collection of skits on current topics and personalities, by various hands, and all the authors were to be thrown into prison. This is why we hear about the play; probably the Queen herself had demanded imprisonment, not realizing that it would give a loophole for gossip. We know that Ben Jonson demanded to join them in prison, while denying that he had written any of it. But we do not know anything about this play, not even why it was considered wicked; not a sentence, not a phrase from it has survived. A censorship which can do that much, in a case where there is keen gossip-interest and nothing (apparently) to feel solemn about, has considerable power to impose silence. ^{cc}A more moderate attitude was taken about *Faust*, and only parts of the play were forbidden by the censor – but these parts, when added up, were enough to prevent any further London performance. It is not surprising that no mention of ^{dd}the suppression of the 1590 *Faust* survives, because anything written, such as might survive for a modern historian, might also be used in a law court; on the other hand, people seem to have talked pretty freely. The disastrous changes in the modern world, often returning to earlier conditions, should at least have one good effect; historians may now understand better what happened under a Thought Police. ^{ee}People living under such a regime are usually aware of it, and the play of *Faust* might naturally suggest a parallel here. It was usual to believe that devils could hear anything you said, and otherwise observe your movements, but not your thoughts. If Faust enters into a plot with Meph, which the Devil would prevent and punish them for, they must never tell one another, though probably they drop hints the Devil will not understand. Marlowe would realize quite early that his rash talk was being followed by official spies, and would enjoy hinting to the audience: 'You are all like Faust; all being heard by official spies'. It would help to alert them for the main trick.

^{ff}The immediate question is how such a plan by Marlowe could have got through the censor. But ^{gg}all propaganda has to admit that some opponents hold other views. ^{hh}Many a pious tract describes how a young man was misled into forming a very wrong belief, and then repented of it, preferably on his deathbed, after finding that it

---

[43] [417; E8]therefore past the censor . . .

did great harm. Maybe some foolish reader might learn of the wrong belief in this way, by reading this tract, and reject the recantation, but the author could not be blamed. A play has more powerful means of insinuating a surprise at the end, not visible to a censor who only read the words; and this play does all it can to make Faust popular with the audience, so that they want him to be let off at the end. Censors were not theatregoers, and might well take time to realize what was happening. The traces of influence by *Faust* upon catchpenny plays of 1590–1 support the belief that it had already been acted, and this is a help in considering the texts of *Faust* – a fully prepared prompt copy was what had the final censor's cuts marked on it.

Origin of the A-text

[ii]The origin of the A-text, at any rate, is now clear. On the day in the summer of 1590 when the dread summons arrived, demanding the prompt copy of *Faust* and forbidding performance till further notice, Marlowe had taken out the brief comic interludes for further work on them; they were a new kind of assignment, for him; he was anxious to manage it right. [jj]He had first written them in the style of his college friend Nashe, making them all talk as if they are drunk, which is tiresome enough in print but worse for an audience who want to follow the story. (Hence the argument that the A-text must be later than the B-text, because the sinful comics had become more hopelessly confused there, is completely upside down.) This feature of course was quite out of sight at the time of the disaster.[kk]In answer to the summons all the drafts were huddled up at the end of the play, and they have never since been put in the right order.

When the text returned it was marked with savage cuts, amounting to a quarter of its length, including two of the most uproarious scenes, and making it quite unfit for production in London, [ll]and all the manager could think of was to tell the scrivener to make a copy of the parts not rejected, so that the committee could look them over and decide what yet might be done. [mm]Thinking this a fairly pointless sudden demand, he did it rather casually, and got another man to dictate to him what he was to copy – such is the quickest way to do it, and all the supposed evidence for 'memorial reconstruction' (such as 'a dog so bade' for 'a dog's obeyed')[44] can arise from this one process;[45] [nn]but he was careful enough to ask one of the actors where the comic interludes should be placed. The distracted man gave the wrong answers, irretrievably.

Then matters became slightly less bad; the friendly Edmund Tilney, representing the Queen, was prepared to write on all pages of this text that they had been passed for public performance,[46] so it could be acted on tour, where it would excite great interest, all the more because of the London suppression. Being in regular use, though chiefly to lay before the officials of each city, it was sometimes scribbled upon, as in the case where a comic might drag in a mention of the trial of Dr Lopez (1594); and the copy of it used for the A-text had been badly mangled once, where Faust comes to Rome, to suit performance without a balcony (so Greg is correct in his account of the main story).

[oo]It is clear that Henslowe became master of this situation, whether or not he had owned the play beforehand.[47] Holding a complete text with the censor's marks on it, he negotiated at leisure, but only succeeded in winning [pp]back the comic scenes at the end of act IV, usually despised by modern critics, but this part, rounding off the sub-plot, [qq]he would think a necessary part of the structure. The reason for being sure it is by Marlowe, apart from its firm grasp of the assembled characters, is the smooth grandeur of the transition at its close. [rr]All the victims of horseplay by Faust are complaining in a pub, and they are somehow transferred to a grand room in the

---

[44] *King Lear* IV, vi, l. 159 (Riverside edn).

[45] [40; E5]This question is important because the A-text is very much more lively and natural than the B-text; both have careless errors, but when they differ I estimate that the A-text is right, up to the end of the second act, which is the crucial part, four times out of five.

[46] [406; E10]His help would be needed; plays on tour were left to the local officials, but in a notorious case they would have to be shown a text with a licence on it, [211; E14]and without that the performance at Exeter, for example (when the actors found they had one devil too many), could not have occurred.

[47] [263; E6]It is not important whether Henslowe bought for the Admiral's Men an apparently worthless script with the censor's marks on it, intending to negotiate later, or merely sold the permitted A-text for use on tour. His business procedure should be accepted as impenetrable. However, it is slightly more likely that he had refused the text for the Admiral's Men, as likely to cause trouble, and then bought the manuscript for a song after the collapse; because if he had owned it all the time he would probably not have allowed the A-text to escape.

castle of the Duke of Anhalt, which they continue to treat as a pub. After they have gone far enough, Faust strikes them dumb each in turn. The Duchess says she is pleased, and the Duke has a tremendous final thought:

> ^{ss}His artful sport drives all sad thoughts away.
> (*Enter Wagner dressed as Chorus*)
> Wagner   I think my master means to die shortly.
>
> (B:1773–8)

As Greg very sensibly remarked, this bang must have been intended by the author, and also the whole idea of a scene collecting the comics before the end. ^{tt}Then Faust is giving feasts as he approaches the agreed time, to please very high-minded students as we soon find, who bring him to the love of the divine Helen. The absolute conflict between two judgements or world-views gets presented with fierce brevity, and Faust implies in his great soliloquy that he does not deserve the eternal punishment he has incurred. A surprise ending could not feel out of place after so much preparation for it.

Greg did well to recognize that the speech of Wagner was the Chorus before the last act (delivered as usual from the balcony), and deduce that the scene leading up to it in the B-text was part of Marlowe's original design. But this gave him no reason to deduce that the whole of the B-text, however flabby or disgusting, was Marlowe's too,[48] so that the A-text was merely a vulgarized cut version easy to produce on tour. Consider, the grandeur of a papal feast was notorious, and much was known about the uniforms employed there. An attempt at this was kept in, but a simple pub scene with fewer actors in ordinary clothes had to go out. It may be answered that boxing the Pope's ears was so popular that even an ^{uu}absurd presentation would be welcome. But there would be no difficulty in presenting some at least of the attempts at revenge by Benvolio, who had been ridiculed by Faust in the presence of the Emperor, and tries hard both in the B-text and the Faust-book.

---

[48] [229; E9]As Henslowe's *Diary* for 1602 records his payments for these 'additions to Faustus', it had always been wild of Greg to argue that Marlowe had written the whole of the B-text; he had also argued that Ben Jonson had not written the additions to the *Spanish Tragedy*, though the *Diary* records his payment for them. (Henslowe liked to keep useful men attached to him, by payments due in either direction, and Greg found this procedure unbelievable.)

They make lively fun, and are at least a token filling of the great gap in time. They make no special demands on the producer. Also, Greg does not appreciate that any peculiar dress had to be dragged along in the wagon, so that a thrifty wardrobe master would expect it to be used more than once. A peculiar dress for devils would have to be invented, and in the B-text is used often from start to finish, implying that Faust is damned by Calvinist predestination; but in the A-text they are only wanted for the absurd scene of the Masque. (They are allowed a mention as carrying off the corpse.) The two magicians also have special clothes, and they promise to return but never do; ^{vv}and what reason for it could Greg propose? The first Chorus (between acts I and II) is also missing, and again offers no difficulty to a producer or a wardrobe manager; but these last two items would have to include explanations to the audience about the plot of Faust – he can only have learned the name and the dubious character of Meph from the magicians, before the play begins, but the audience need not be told this till the end of act II scene i, when he is triumphant, and defies them. Neither cut is explained by the Greg theory at all.

The cuts

^{ww}Literary critics are equipped to deal with documents, and feel uneasy outside their field; I do not see any other reason why they have refused to recognize the obvious fact that *Faust* has been censored. As it happens, by good luck, we are not left to gasp in the void; the important cuts are quite plain and make up the required length. The first is the Chorus before act II,[49] which all agree to be 'lost'. This play, like the two *Tamburlanes* and the *Jew*, but unlike the later ones, had a five-act structure (thought decent by young graduates, but despised by London producers); and in this case, as a well-known book was to be followed closely, and not much shaping could be done, but it happened to suit five acts, the shape was emphasized by a chorus before each act. In the first two of them Faust is usually telling lies to others or expressing in soliloquy what is only a passing mood, and so the audience needed very much to have a firm assurance about his intentions. The Chorus explained

[49] See appendix 3: 'Concordance of Acts and Scenes'.

his plan to escape Hell, admitting that the procedure was very tricky and ˣˣmight reasonably excite extreme anxiety; also that he was well aware, having attracted the attention of spirits, that he might be overheard by a multitude even when he seemed to be alone. ʸʸAnd now it is clear why there had to be a Chorus between the acts, and why the first Chorus has disappeared; the Chorus talks directly to the audience, so he does not live in the world of the play, so its devils cannot hear him. The prologue, spoken of course by the same actor, had already taken a slightly clinical attitude to Faust, explaining him with the minimum of comment; and he explains him further after act I when the audience ought to be feeling that there is much to explain. ᶻᶻThe next item is a soliloquy ending with a promise to Beelzebub:

> To him I'll build an altar and a church
> And offer luke-warm blood of new-born babes.
> (A:450f; B:400f)

The actor should say this leering at the invisible multitude who overhear him. Faust in the play is never made to promise that he will work against Christians, or against all mankind, though he blurts out the offer again when confronted by Lucifer; but it is one of the conditions in both Faust-books (GFB, EFB, chapter 4), though no devil ever asks him to carry out the required promise, and he ends up enjoying his popularity in his own district. This soliloquy has also been cut; when blank verse was a new technique, Marlowe would not offer 'To God? He loves thee not' as a blank verse line, and anyhow Faust would have more to say about his views on God (maybe the censor here taught Shakespeare something about short lines in soliloquies). This initial cut is the radical one, altering the whole attitude of the audience, but it would not add up to more than fifty lines.

The next cut is at a point where everyone agrees that a scene is 'lost': what most editions call the start of act II scene ii, when Faust looks out at night from his study window and says 'When I behold the heavens, then I repent'. The A-text allows no break at all, which only one textual expert thinks possible, and the B-text tries to make do by inserting part of a later chorus. We soon learn that Faust has had at least a week or two of experience in his new life, and has found that Meph as a musician fits in splendidly with the ancient Greeks;

unless he had had this solid satisfaction, he says, he would have obeyed the voices urging him to suicide. A new scene really must begin when Faust is presented in this entirely different mood, and Faust must not appear in the interpolated scene because the chief purpose of it is to mark the lapse of time. However, as a problem this is ridiculous; all you need do is put back the short comic scene (B: act II.iii; A: scene viii) between Robin and Dick where it belongs. Greg thinks there needs to be an extra scene, showing Robin escaping from Wagner with a magic book; but he need only leer at the audience at the end of his first scene, saying 'I'll follow him, I'll *serve* him, that's flat', and his [aaa]next appearance, free and boasting of his theft of a magic book, will be what the audience expected. Wagner had tried to enslave him by magic but failed; what now will he do when he learns how to read the stolen book? The audience feels only a mild interest but enough to make it remember; the later summoning of Meph from Constantinople (B: act III.iii; A: scene ix) comes as a surprise, but 'fits in', whereas a long gap between the first two comic scenes only confesses they are both a needed interruption. And really the presence of these sinful comics, though no more than a habitual requirement of the Elizabethan stage, is enough to make nonsense of the whole story; what Robin does is precisely what Faust does, and yet nobody could feel, as his case is treated, that he is to serve eternal torment.

However, there was another scene at this point, which the censor cut; at least, it must have come somewhere, and perhaps before the Chorus for act II, but Faust would not then have felt ready for it. The break not visible in the A-text is his brief time of triumph; he has been allowed all he asked, even human women, and then a magic book; he is exultant. Then the visiting magicians are announced by Wagner and admitted, and he boasts to them of his success, exulting over them, and they walk out at once, indignant at his wickedness. No dramatist would promise the audience a future scene and then leave it out, and no producer, having already provided clothes and make-up for two magicians, would think it a saving to cut the scene they have prepared for. The same argument runs through nearly all Greg's details about the A-text; the cuts could not have been made for any purpose except that of a censor. Marlowe would think it only decent to protest (in effect) that some respectable magicians existed, even while allowing them to look silly; this is what he is preparing to do in their first brief scene. Their second visit should interrupt the bookworm while he is absorbed in his newly presented book, and he is no longer their disciple; the scene should be witty and brief, hardly more than thirty lines. Then the interesting comic scene, then we see Faust in an entirely different mood, gazing at the stars. From then on he runs straight into disaster, but we are free to regard the failure as one of his own nerve, not of his original plan.

[bbb]After the second act there were two major cuts, but both were malignant rather than doctrinal, that is, they were intended to make the play unactable in London; but reasons of state would not be hard to find. I need first to consider the beginning of act III, the most evidently corrupt part of the text. Faust has a guide book speech, describing his tour of Europe, and Marlowe does the job with perfunctory haste, irritated perhaps because this is not the important thing for Faust to be saying. Greg imagines that he had a small platoon of hacks, whom he would order to write any link-passages he found boring, but this is enormously improbable, because he could not afford it. [ccc]Marlowe was a great success as a playwright, but he had to sell each play outright for £5 or so. [ddd]Probably he went on earning money as a spy (a document to secure his MA testifies that he was working abroad for the Queen) because otherwise he would have starved, and he was finally murdered in a huddle of spies; but such work was very ill-paid. [eee]Each play would be a sum of money to him, and of course he would not share it out. [fff]He would certainly believe he could make better jokes than the next man, however wrong he was; I cannot see him wanting these hacks, even if he had been rich. The belief results from the mandarin superstition that one can always 'spot' an author, as if he were a glass of port, whereas young men caught up in a literary movement, as Marlowe was, spend half their time imitating one another. Besides, the bad parts have flashes in them which I too would 'spot' as Marlowe.

What does seem clear is that he had not yet found how to start act III effectively when the text was sent to the censor. Faust, as Marlowe interprets the story, has lost his flippant assurance just at this point; he has become certain of Hell, and the devils are entertaining him only to keep him from repentance, which he does not realize to be still possible. He is very glum, but he becomes determined even now to appreciate the world. The surviving words say it clearly enough, but they are in confusion; and a real bit of reconstruction needs to be done, of the second thoughts of Marlowe here.

A well-known entry in Henslowe's *Diary*[50] lists the properties of his theatre, and among them come: 'One city of Rome ... one dragon for Faustus'. Many people must have realized that these would be best used by putting the 'city', a large backcloth, fairly high behind the upper stage, and dragging the dragon across the upper stage with ᵍᵍᵍFaust and Meph sitting on it, Meph pointing out the seven hills and other educative details. This could certainly be done on the stage *The Jew of Malta* was written for. Henslowe has taken over Rome only, because he had been forbidden Istanbul; but the real impudence of the thing only came over, towards the end of the early performances, in 1590, when you had hardly recovered from the pleasure of seeing Faust box the Pope's ears before the dragon appeared again in the heavens, hovering now over the less well-known city of Istanbul, as it led Faust to the harem of the Sultan. This time Faust would ask questions, but earlier while over Rome, he would have been silent and glum, leaving Meph to give the lecture of a guide. It is therefore not so ludicrous when he breaks out, probably in the next scene, after arrival, saying:

> Now, by the kingdoms of infernal rule,
> Of Styx, of Acheron, and the fiery lake
> Of ever-burning Phlegethon, I swear
> That I do long to see the monuments
> And situation of bright splendent Rome.
> (A: 862–6; B: 848–52)

Greg is witty about this, saying that the tourist has only come to do the sights;[51] and therefore that the lines agreeing to look are only a parody of Marlowe written by a hack. I agree that Faust needs to say this when breaking a long silence, and that the remarks of Meph just before are inadequate to cause it. And the actor needs to emphasize with an air of astonishment the small word *do*, having treated the three earlier lines quietly and reflectively. It is anyhow a big decision, affecting the whole of the later life of Faust, and the cause of the affection and respect with which at the end he is so widely regarded. James Smith would have said, I must not forget, that Faust is none

---

[50] In the papers supplementary to the *Diary*; see *The Henslowe Papers*, ed. W. W. Greg, London (A. H. Bullen), 1907.
[51] Greg, p. 113.

the less fatuously wrong;[52] but a poem by Roy Campbell called 'The Skull in the Desert' (of a horse) assures us that 'the brainless laughter of the ranker' has again and again saved mankind.[53] I would translate this, in our example, into saying that the basic parts of the mind of Faust were not so easily deluded as his educated parts. [hhh]The opinions of the author do not much matter here (anyway he was probably a Socinian, expecting no afterlife for Faust); his mind would be concentrated upon the reactions of his audience. He expected that they would enjoy a rogue demigod, while not denying that he must expect some punishment, but that (when confronted with the end of the play) they would feel quite positively that he did not deserve eternal torture. And to have the Pope damn him to Hell in full form would strike them as a very hopeful indication.

The Chorus to act IV says he has been to 'courts', in the plural, but we have only seen him visit the Pope, and act II is only about 100 lines long, or 160 including the comic scene with the stolen goblet; whereas the average length should be about 400. Also, the comics when almost caught by the vintner summon Meph to help them, and he arrives furious because he has had to travel from Constantinople (so he says even in A, and in B that he was at the great Turk's court). It would merely annoy the audience, many of whom had read the book, to remind them of Faust's exploits there while refusing any presentation; hence, I submit, it is quite certain that both our texts bear witness to an earlier version which gave the harem scenes. Consider, it is planned as a climax, funnier even than boxing the Pope's ears; and two state banquets, close together, are no harder to present than one. At this point Greg's explanation of the A-text, often absurd, becomes impossible; the more coarse and vulgar the country audiences were, the more they would want the scene with the Sultan, and it cannot have been too hard to stage because this text retains the scene with the Pope. Nor would it be indecent; after breaking up the banquet, dressed as a pope (say both Faust-books) but easily mistaken for Mahomet, Faust retires behind the white resinous smoke used in plays, and the next scene shows the ladies of the harem explaining to the Sultan that Mahomet is much better in bed than he is. They call Mahomet a god but the Sultan knows better; probably Marlowe gave him a crack against Jesus

---

[52] James Smith: 'Marlowe's *Doctor Faustus*', *Scrutiny*, VIII, i (1939), pp. 36–55.
[53] In *Talking Bronco*, London (Faber & Faber) 1946.

here, and probably it was taken out early. Only censorship can explain why the whole visit was suppressed; I can hardly believe that I am the first to say so. Nor was it hard to find an excuse; when Philip II had taken over Portugal in 1580, he announced that nobody in Europe ⁱⁱⁱmight trade outside Europe except himself. Nothing less would have induced Elizabeth to initiate the British Empire, but this drove her into several actions, of which the first and simplest was to open trade relations with the Sultan, forming the Levant Company. Plainly then, he must not be insulted; and the official protection of him would be talked about in London because it would seem almost as funny as the similar protection of the Devil. The scene remained forbidden till the Restoration, when the boxing of the Pope's ears was forbidden instead.

The last cut is at the end of act IV, usually called scenes vi and vii. Greg writes well about the merits of this sequence, which is the more to his credit as he hates the vulgar scenes otherwise. It is his chief evidence that the B-text contains material written by Marlowe, and hence that the A-text is a later corruption. But the deduction is unnecessary; I maintain that these scenes are the only parts written by Marlowe which survive in the B-text but not the A-text, and the reason is that Henslowe was able to win them back from the censor, in 1594, when the excitement had died down, pointing out how harmless they were, and how absolutely necessary if the play were to have a tolerable shape, as the London theatregoer saw it. The current ruler of Anhalt, now a Prince, was a quite prominent ally of the Queen, and of course ought not to be insulted; but Henslowe could get a contact with his representative in London, and at last a written assurance that the great man did not object to this entirely favourable treatment of his grandfather. Such a rebuttal of the official excuse would make his request hard to refuse, ⁱⁱⁱand perhaps by that time the rebuttal was accepted readily. Archbishop Whitgift was a ruthless but adroit man, and had literary interests; he is unlikely not to have taken an interest in the negotiations. ^{kkk}Henslowe was probably quite willing, as a pious man himself, and needing to lengthen what was left of the play, to add some impressive stuff about Hell at the end; enough to make the audience sure that Faust went to Hell. The censors allowed the translation to reappear in 1592, and the doctored play in 1594, after the author had been safely murdered. There was nothing else so fiercely pious in the public theatres, and the clerical censors were lucky to be able to impose it.

IIIWell, then, the heresy which the censor was determined to stamp out was some belief first expressed by Faust and the Chorus quite plainly, as a plan for him to escape Hell, then (after act II) renounced by Faust as quite useless, merely a mistake he had made, fatally; so far no censor could object, and Tilney could not be blamed for passing the script; but then the authorities discovered that the audiences were believing at the end that Faust had succeeded in escaping Hell, because his first plan, unknown to himself, had been correct. The play is in any case tremendous, and softening it would be no good; but in its present mangled form it is, rightly I think, found intolerable. The question raised by Faust in his last speech needs to be admitted as a real one, and so it was at the time, by the Socinians and the Anabaptists and the Family of Love, who were the nearest home. A prying censorship backed by immediate money penalties and a not remote threat of torture immediately excites a fellowship for people with offbeat opinions, especially after the government has altered its persecuting opinion within living memory, even though most of these sympathizers would feel determined not to be led into trouble. The first audiences would be quite ready to accept the kind of play I am proposing. But there is still a great gap to be filled; what plan could Faust possibly put forward, which would feel solid and practical, so far from being a modern theory, which somehow joined on to what you had learned at mother's knee? The trivial horseplay of Faust joins on there, and so must his method of nipping out from eternal torture.

ª2

The Translator

Evidence that the translation was censored is what needs presenting first, as the basis for the argument. But an obstacle comes up at once, because this translator is jovial and easy and makes alterations of his own ᵇ(Elizabethan translators are often wilful, and this one especially so). ᶜSome of his amendments are flippant or whimsical, but by no means all; and they need to be considered beforehand, so that they can be distinguished from the grimly consistent changes demanded by the censor. Even that does not end it; the translator is sometimes willing to collaborate with the censor. Tiresome as it may appear, this is the standard situation; a censor docs not write the new text, he merely states the conditions which the author must satisfy if he is to get his licence.[1] Still, the extra obstacle is not so bad as it may appear; the grudgingness or awkwardness of an author, as he tries to collaborate, sometimes gives us the chief indication that he has been forced.

ᵈMany commentators have taken an interest in the character and preferences of the unknown 'P. F. Gent', without arriving at noticeable disagreement. He is more Renaissance or enlightened than his original, though he does not deny that Faust is damned. In both Faust-books (chapter 1) the students at the recent Protestant University of Wittenberg call him 'the Speculator', but P. F. makes Faust use that title himself in the guest book of the freethinking University of Padua.[2] ᵉHe has his serious side; he pulls the details

---

[1] [431; ET]Tilney, on the margin of the abortive play *Sir Thomas More*, wrote a short sequence of the scenes which might begin it without political embarrassment, but even that was going far (perhaps he knew that the Queen would never permit such a play anyhow).

[2] EFB, chapter 22, p. 35.

together, making the story more coherent, and he does as much as the story allows to recognize the claims of a magician. It cannot be said, as some have done, that he introduces the scientific craving for knowledge; ᶠalready in the GFB Faust has an obsessive desire for knowledge, at least in his initial demands,[3] but there it is the sin of 'curiosity',[4] whereas P. F. seems to expect that there are some useful laws of nature as yet undiscovered. For example, he adds at the start of Part II,[5] when Faust has become sure he is damned, that he 'forgot all good works'. These must have been speculations, because neither the GFB nor the EFB suppose him to have charitable or patriotic plans, helping mankind or his fellow Germans, as Marlowe does in the play. GFB, chapter 21, tells us that Faust had only pretended to be interested in astronomy, hoping that some gossip about Heaven might be let drop; P. F. cuts this out. Both are jovial about the recurrent horseplay, but P. F. seems to find it rather an effort. ᵍThere is no direct palliation of Faust's crime, which even P. F. might think too like quarrelling with his original, but he cuts the whole of the triumphant chapter of oafish jeering by Meph near the end (GFB, chapter 65), ʰand he reduces the final moaning of Faust, perhaps not wishing him to appear unmanly. He also omits his absurd assurance, in the second pact, that he will not suffer any pain in Hell (GFB, chapter 53).

This seems a definite enough picture. Two rules can also be found, requiring changes at a number of places, which P. F. is unlikely to have invented for himself. But this need not imply that he was acting against his conscience; on one occasion he speaks up boldly. Some of the changes that were demanded, he may well have felt, made his version more lively and coherent. It is as well to begin with one of the delusive cases, where he is jovial about ⁱhis additions, so that he might be making them to please himself, except that they agree with what the censor is known to want elsewhere. In these other places it is known because the changes are made with sullen patience, as by routine. The logic feels rather remote, and perhaps this is a reason why the difference has not been pointed out long ago; but the literary recognition, once a reader is alerted to it, feels very direct.

[3] GFB, chapter 3 (Sp. 11, 12).

[4] GFB, chapter 2 (Sp. 6): 'His vain and insolent curiosity so provoked him . . .'

[5] EFB, chapter 17.

Visit of the seven principal devils: GFB version

P. F. makes the visit to Faust by the Devil and his court (GFB, chapter 23; EFB, chapter 19) much grimmer. The original story is consistent here. Meph has gradually undermined the unreasonable confidence of Faust, working up to the terrible sermon on Hell, so that he recognizes he is doomed. Then in Part II the devils try to make him feel tolerably at home in his new situation, presumably so that he will do useful work for the devils, though this work is left obscure. He is made to publish an almanac, containing true prophecies supplied by Meph, which wins him fame,[6] and he is allowed to gratify his curiosity by surveys of the earth[7] and the stars.[8] A personal visit by the Devil, introducing the chief devils who form his cabinet, is in line with the policy. [j]It is a grand show, with seven major devils (corresponding to the Masque of Seven Sins in the play) which, as in the play, is offered merely as an entertainment.[9] [k]What is queer is that the devils are so convincingly playful, [l]so very unlike the description of them in Meph's grand sermon about Hell (GFB, chapter 16; EFB, chapter 15) where he speaks of 'the remorseless lash and the hideous faces of the devils';[10] [m]it is hard to believe that they are hiding their real evil. The Devil brings with him his usual train of servants, as well as his cabinet of seven; but there is no room for the servants in the study of Faust, so he kindly begs a holiday for them, and they are dismissed. They appear as animals, in great variety but each as a genuine copy, whereas the top devils are fantastic hybrids. When the servants have gone, Faust asks the leaders to show some of their skill, 'and, each taking his turn as before, they transformed themselves into all kinds of animal, including great birds . . . Faust was delighted and asked whether he could do it too. "Yes", they said, and tossed him a booklet of magic so that he might try it,[11] which he did' [Sp. 81]. We would

---

[6] GFB, chapter 18; EFB, chapter 17.

[7] GFB, chapter 26; EFB, chapter 22.

[8] GFB, chapter 25; EFB, chapter 21.

[9] [171; E0]This is the chief point where Marlowe follows the original German rather than the English translation, but he might have re-invented it.

[10] Sp. 57.

[11] [171; E0]English critics are rather fond of saying how crude the German text is, and one has to reply here that Faust, once he had been made a spirit, could not

presumably be told if he had failed, but as he never does magic for
[n]himself elsewhere one may suspect that they helped him out. At the
end Faust 'could not refrain from asking who created the insects',
says the GFB, which does imply some fear that mentioning the
Creator may be a slight gaffe; but the devils answer cheerfully that
after Adam's fall the insects multiplied in order to plague mankind.
The devils can turn themselves into insects just as easily. Faust
laughs and asks to see them do it, and finds himself tormented by
masses of insects, who actually bite and sting him; but as soon as he
leaves his room they vanish, so the practical joke is a mild one. It is
all very much a children's party, like that too in getting a bit rough at
the end, but quite harmlessly so.

One can argue that it all fits the plan of the story. But this is
practically the only point where the reader meets any devil other
than Meph, and a translator might well be tempted to put a bit more
ginger into them. Also, it comes soon after Meph's explosive
description of Hell, and a reader might naturally suspect that it tells
more truth about devils than that official sermon. Of course, the
palace servants are not the same as the torturers in Hell, but a
translator likes to present a coherent picture.

Visit of the seven principal devils: P. F.'s version

His first step is to turn the visit into a punishment to secure
obedience, with only a transparent pretence that it is an honour or a
treat. Meph (EFB, chapter 19) comes and asks Faust why he is
moping: 'say on boldly, what is thy will and pleasure?' Faust says
'tell me how and after what sort God made the world, and all the
creatures in them, and why man was made after the image of God?'
(EFB, p. 23). P. F. has left out a great deal here. In the GFB
(chapter 21) [o]Meph readily says that God created the world,[12] [p]but in
chapter 22 he says the world has always existed: 'The Earth had to
nourish itself and the Sea separated itself from the Earth, but they
made an amicable settlement with each other as if they could talk.

---

possibly require a book to enable him to do what he could do inherently; though, as
to turning himself into a midge, one can imagine that some brief practical advice
might be helpful.

[12] Sp. 71.

. . . But the creation of man and the heavens they conceded to God so that ultimately they were made subservient to him.' [Sp. 75f].[13] ⁹Faust does not believe him. Lucifer, when he arrives in the next chapter, shows no sign that he has heard of this conversation and the entertainment is quite genuine. [But P. F. makes Meph respond to Faust by] ʳthreatening to tear him in pieces, apparently regarding the question as an insult, and vanishing away; Faust is left weeping bitterly. Then the Devil comes with all his train, and says he knows the thoughts of Faust. He knows that Faust has broken his promise. Hideous forms appear,[14] and the Devil says he will show 'some of our hellish pastimes' to make Faust 'more steadfast'. Here is a bold consistent set of changes, which one might presume to be demanded by the censor. P. F. himself might well protest that it is absurd to present a devil if he is not allowed to speak in character. He would not want the changes himself, but he may have felt sure the censor would demand them; this does not prove that the demands were actually made.

The 'hellish pastimes' which the Devil says he has come to show are presumably tortures, and after seeing them Faust will be too afraid to repent. There is nothing about pastime in the GFB; the

13 [130; E6]'as if they could talk' is more central to the Renaissance view of the natural world than anything P. F. has to offer (he leaves out the whole passage, but probably he had to). A scientist must not *avoid* being anthropomorphic, or he loses all insight into nature; this was why a sober practitioner like Gilbert could say that the earth was a living being. Meph has just said also that men always existed, and perhaps this is a textual error, but more probably, as he is quite casual here, he forgot at first what the doctrine was. It entails that God did not create the angels, or devils, or any other spirits one would expect; and this belief was the actual cause, in *Paradise Lost*, of Satan's revolt against God, so we may expect that it has remained a tradition among spirits. Surely we need not suppose it to be invented, at this point, as part of a plot to throw Faust into despair? [See also chapter 4, p. 114, n. 38: ed.]

14 P. F's translation of the descriptions of the seven principal devils has one remarkable deviation from the original which would seem to be clear indication of censorship and it is surprising that Empson missed it. (I had not recognized the significance until it was too late to alert him.) In the GFB, Satan is listed among the seven principals, but P. F., while retaining the description, refuses to name him as Satan and calls him *Chamagosta* (EFB, p. 24). No commentator mentions this name, and indeed, it is probably a unique occurrence. It clearly derives from the Greek *chamai* and *agostos*, and a likely meaning is 'bowed (or cursed) to the earth', presumably referring to the serpent of Genesis 4. Satan, the adversary, is nowhere mentioned in the EFB; as God's servant in the Book of Job and Christ's tempter in the wilderness, he is too sacred for ridicule. If this change is not the result of ecclesiastical censorship, P. F. must have been an exceedingly pious man.

Devil merely says that, seeing into the mind of Faust, he knows Faust wants to meet the leading devils; and this of course is true – Faust is insatiably curious. Most of the detail is translated tidily, but P. F. adds a joke about Lucifer. He is: 'in manner of a man, all hairy, but of a brown colour like a squirrel, curled, and his tail turning upwards on his back as the squirrels use. I think he could crack nuts too like a squirrel' (EFB, p. 24). Only the last sentence has been added, and one might take the nuts to show the careless gaiety of P. F., but they may also hint at some form of torture. Solemnity is added when the junior devils file in 'until they had filled the whole Hall'[15] – how has Faust's study become so big? Then a great thunderclap shakes the house 'as though it would have fallen to the ground, upon which every monster had a muck-fork in its hand,[16] holding them towards Faustus as though they would have run a tilt at him'(EFB, p. 25). Faust remembers how Meph told him, in the Hell chapter, that he would have 'thy whole carcass tossed upon muck-forks from one devil to another'.[17] Fearing that this may be done at once, he asks the Devil to remove these playful types, and he readily orders them away, leaving only the top seven. Faust calls for Meph, and a dragon flies up, spitting fire about the house, but, after a reverence to the Devil, turns into the usual friar. Faust asks Meph to teach him how to transform himself ⁵like the others, but the Devil himself is in command here; he 'put forth his Paw, and gave Faustus a book, saying hold, do what thou wilt, which he looking upon, straight ways changed himself into a Hog, then into a Worm, then into a Dragon, and finding this for his purpose, it liked him well' (EFB, p. 26). The GFB does not tell us of any changes that Faust achieved, let alone that he picked on bad ones. In the EFB, as he comes out of them, he asks the Devil 'how cometh it that all these filthy forms are in the world? Lucifer answered, they are ordained of God as plagues unto men, and so shalt thou be plagued' (EFB, p. 26). Then the insects come, and Faust in torment calls for Meph, but he does not come, and Lucifer says 'ho ho ho Faustus, how likest

---

[15] EFB, p. 25.

[16] [232; E2]This allowed him to solve his problem about the polite call. What could the servant devils bring with them, which would seem merely habitual and yet a possible threat? Their muck-forks are much the best thing, and so P. F. makes their brandishing of these objects prominent in the large hall which Faust is now assumed to inhabit, until he begs to have them sent away.

[17] EFB, p. 18.

thou the creation of the world?' (EFB, p. 26). And yet afterwards, when they are all gone, he heard 'the sweetest music that he ever heard before, at which he was so ravished with delight, that he forgot the fears he was in before; and it repented him that he had seen no more of their pastime' (EFB, p. 26). It is a very fine chapter, and about half of the English version is added by the translator.

As P. F. adds to the tortures, one might perhaps argue that he is a sadist, but he contrives to take a healthy tone. Even the muck-forks are a kind of sport; all modes of playing catch require skill, and no doubt this one gives the devils a healthy pleasure. Perhaps they were hoping for a game when they brought their muck-forks to the party, as other characters might have brought their tennis racquets. The tone is very different when P. F. introduces the muck-forks into Hell (GFB, chapter 16; EFB, chapter 15); but here he is decently engaged in trying to palliate or shuffle out of sight the most unbearable feature of the doctrine. The GFB twice says in this chapter that the pains of Hell will get steadily worse for all eternity;[18] to go on saying that 'God is love', after that, is enough blasphemy to explode the religion altogether. P. F. does not do much, but he quiets it down. On the first occasion, Meph says that as a stone in a furnace, though it glows, does not burn, so 'the souls of the damned burn for ever without being consumed, their torments increasing day by day' [Sp. 52]. The final clause has nothing to do with the analogy. P. F. gives 'the damned souls in our hellish fire are ever burning, but their pains never diminishing' (EFB, p. 19 [sic]). Of course this is still very bad, but it has not the same lunatic 'horror. On the second occasion, P. F. cannot do much because he is presenting Meph as hysterically excited by his own harangue, unlike the Meph of the GFB, who is always cool like an inquisitor or a tax-gatherer. There he ends the sequence with: 'their hands and feet will jitter. They will bite their tongues in their agony and long to die but in vain; death will evade them and their torments will daily grow harsher' [Sp. 57]. The parallel quotation from the EFB needs to start earlier, to give the impetus of it:

yea, yea, Faustus, thou sayst, I shall, I must, nay I will tell thee the secrets of our kingdom, for thou buyest it dearly, and thou must and shalt be partaker of our torments, that (as the Lord God said) never

[18] Sp. 52, 57.

shall cease; for Hell, the woman's belly, and the earth are never satisfied; there shalt thou abide horrible torments, trembling, gnashing of teeth, howling . . . thy heart crushed as in a press, thy bones broken, the devils tossing firebrands upon thee, yea thy whole carcass tossed upon muck-forks from one devil to another, yea Faustus, then wilt thou wish for death, and he will fly from thee, thine unspeakable torments shall be every day augmented more and more, for the greater the sin, the greater is the punishment. (EFB, p. 18)

The claim that justice is somehow served by this hideous arrangement, though a nonsensical claim, does give a certain judicial calm to the end of the ecstasy, before Meph turns to his victim and says: 'How likest thou this, my Faustus?'. The rest of his speech argues that no one can get out of Hell, and that Faust's sin is already unforgivable. One must allow that P. F. gives his muck-forks a strategic position. He does not manage to palliate the doctrine of eternally increasing torture (which was comparatively new) but at least he has winced at it both times.

Cruelty is an essential part of the book, and the translator's attitude to it is not clear. He adds a whole paragraph to the already long tourist chapter (GFB, chapter 26; EFB, chapter 22) that might perhaps give a hint. It reports a visit to Breslau, and begins as if Faust is for once using his magic powers in solitary freedom; but a horseman readily feels that a willing horse is part of his body, and here Meph has disguised himself as 'a horse, except that it was winged like a dromedary'.[19] P. F. of course will allow nothing ridiculous in his book, and does not even struggle with the dromedary, but may feel that he himself is riding free for a moment:

"From Prague, he flew into the air and bethought himself what he might do, or which way to take, so he looked round about and behold, he had espied a passing fair city which lay not far from Prague, about some four and twenty miles, and that was Breslau in Silesia. . . . In this city he saw not many wonders, except the Brazen Virgin that standeth on a bridge over the water, and under the which standeth a mill like a powder mill. (EFB, p. 41)

It is not a magic object at all. 'Disobedient town-born children', too wild for their parents to manage, are brought to her; she opens her

[19] Sp. 99.

arms, and they kiss her; then she crushes them to mincemeat, and the river washes them away. It seems the good burghers come and appreciate this toy, as a family outing. The insertion cannot be meant as a parody of the rest of the guidebook chapter, which is very unlike it; we find that Faust appreciates public buildings, usually churches, in a civilized manner, and takes an interest in derivations of placenames. At Ravensburg, indeed, the GFB makes him taste the wines of a famous cellar,[20] but this seems to be regarded as one of his regular perquisites. It is only in the EFB that he leaves all the taps running,[21] as a bit of spiteful mischief; and who can decide whether this was put in by jolly P. F. or by the worrying censor? In any case, Faust is not allowed to do any such mischief in Breslau; there he is ᵛcontent to wonder and admire like any other German visitor. This is a bit of sardonic humour, one must suppose, implying that Continentals are quaintly rough; and it implies that he has been to Germany,[22] though probably not to Breslau, because if the Breslau story were already familiar in London he would not need to drag it in. He writes sensitive prose, and 'P. F. Gent.' is usually taken to imply that he held at least a BA degree. At that time, German was not recognized in England as a literary language; such a man would learn French or Italian. His initials do not appear as translator on any other titlepage, though minor reports about magicians and prodigies in Germany had become quite frequent since 1580 in the London press; the popular mind had at last realized that Germany had become the home of magicians. Also, if P. F. were sent there, he ᵂwould have been confronted by incessant public witch-burnings, and might well fear that this assignment as a translator encouraged their introduction into England. He ˣshould not be blamed for introducing a few jovial insinuations against public sadism.[23]

---

[20] Sp. 113.

[21] EFB, p. 40.

[22] For an elaboration of this view, see Richard Rohde: 'Das englische Faustbuch und Marlowe's Tragödie', *Studien zur Englischen Philologie*, Heft XLIII, 1910.

[23] [168; E0]Yet he won't allow Faust at the end to plead that he has been a merciful man, though now to receive no mercy (GFB, chapter 64; EFB, chapter 60); instead, Faust is made to say, for no reason that we have heard, that his pains will be 'more lamentable than any creature hath yet suffered'. [GFB text: 'da ich den ubermässigen schmertzen des Todtes erwarten muß, Ja viel [208] einen erbärmlichern dann jemals eine schmertzhaffte Creatur erduldet hat', 'despite [208] your compassionate nature, suffering more than any cruel creature has ever endured'. Faust is comparing his afterlife with that of, e.g., a wolf: ed.]

Profile of P. F.

These scattered items allow of a fairly confident conjecture. His father was a London businessman trading with Germany, who of course employed translators, but he wanted one of his sons to learn German – when the eldest refused, then the literary one; he would pay for this boy to go to college on condition that he picked up German on the side. Then he was sent to Germany to work for the firm, but was not much good at it. This would be happening shortly before the voyage of the Armada, a time when the English spy network, though amateurish, was very active, and a man with such good cover would probably be asked to help; but he was not much good at that either. Back in London by the end of 1588, he would be rather at a loose end, translating for the firm as required, and sometimes showing round foreign visitors, so that he earned the small allowance from his father; but in need of an opening for his talents. Translation for a publisher was of course badly paid, and not his main object. This picture explains why he feels a certain resentment against Germany, whereas usually a man who has learned a language regards the native speakers as part of his capital.

A depressing picture so far, but he has enthusiasms. While scrapping a lot of nonsense about astronomy from Meph, he inserts (EFB, chapter 18) a splendid paragraph about the powers which a magician could obtain. It is a temptation; Meph in effect says: 'stop fussing about your future and ʸconsider what you can do now'. Perhaps Meph is lying, and anyhow one should not call it a forecast of modern science, because the basic idea of shared knowledge is absent. But he does feel in a rather boyish way, that it would be glorious to enhance the powers of man over nature:

Knowst not thou that the earth is frozen, cold and dry; the water running, cold and moist; the air flying, hot and moist; the fire consuming, hot and dry? Yea, Faustus, so must thy heart be inflamed like the fire to mount on high: learn, Faustus, to fly like myself as swift as thought from one kingdom to another, to sit at princes' tables, to eat their daintiest fare, to have thy pleasure of their fair ladies, wives and concubines, to use their jewels and costly robes as things belonging to thee, and not unto them; learn of me, Faustus, to run through walls, doors and gates of stone and iron, to creep into the earth like a worm, to swim in the water like a fish, to fly in the air like a bird, and to live and nourish thyself in the fire like a salamander; so shalt thou be famous, renowned, far spoken of, and extolled for thy skill; going on knives, not hurting thy feet; carrying fire in thy bosom, and not burning thy shirt; seeing through the heavens as through a crystal . . . Come on my Faustus, I will make thee as perfect in these things as myself, I will learn thee to go invisible, to find out the mines of gold and silver . . . thy time Faustus weareth away, then why wilt thou not take thy pleasure of the world. (EFB, p. 22f)

ᶻIt is rather surprising that the censor let the passage stand (probably the censor had no idea which passages had been interpolated). However, there is no need for P. F. to have read Cornelius Agrippa,[24] who positively claimed not to be original in his views; pious reading alone would be enough; all these powers are claimed by Simon Magus in the *Clementine Recognitions* (Palmer and More, p. 14). What one can say is that the enthusiasm for them shown here belongs to the beginning, not the end, of the sixteenth century. ᵃᵃMaybe P. F. draws here on common gossip rather than wide reading. But he clearly has one great qualification for his work, as has been well recognized; he makes it seem very poetical to be a magician.

The cosmology of the EFB

ᵇᵇOne modern opinion we can definitely ascribe to him, and that not by conjecture but by his own rude assertion. Among the voyages of Faust came the flight to the stars, in a chariot drawn by two dragons, (GFB, chapter 25; EFB, chapter 21). ᶜᶜPerhaps the first readers of the Faust-book seldom realized that it assumes a flat- or saucer-shaped-earth theory, as the careful Spies had omitted W, chapter 31,[25] the only inescapable presentation of this theory, and it would seem almost as barbaric or backwoods then as it does now; in the truncated version, the explanation would not easily occur to them.

[24] Without prejudice to Empson's argument, the information of the first three lines of the above quotation does occur in Agrippa: 'Est enim ignis calidus et siccus, terra sicca et frigida, aqua frigida et humida, aer humidus et calidus' (Agrippa: *De occulto philosophia*, Cologne 1533, I, chapter 2 (facsimile edition, ed. K. Novotny, Graz (Akademische Druck–und Verlagsanstalt) 1967)). Both here and in P.F. the lines sound catechismal.

[25] See introduction, p. 30.

The Venerable Bede, we are told, restored to permitted opinion the rotundity of the earth, and that had been in the Dark Ages. It seemed possible that Spies, acting as a historian, had simply reported any view of astronomy held by his sources; but the main statement by Meph on the topic (GFB, chapter 21), though based on a classical Ptolemaic account (ignoring Copernicus, of course), never actually admits that any heavenly body passes under the earth. Spies manages to say nothing inconsistent with the belief that when the sun 'rises' it is in fact descending from the third heaven; a belief far more starkly opposed to observable fact than anything in Copernicus. ᵈᵈBut P. F. cannot endure this and ᵉᵉhe bounds naked onto the stage:

ᶠᶠYea, Christian reader, to the glory of God, and for the profit of thy soul, I will open unto thee the divine opinion touching the ruling of this confused chaos, far more than any rude German author,[26] being possessed with the devil, was able to utter; and to prove some of my sentence before to be true, look into Genesis, (EFB, p. 32)

and there, in the first chapter of the Bible, you will find the Copernican theory.

This is not as inconsequent as it may seem, because the Faustbook relies tacitly upon Genesis for its flat-earth theory. When the sun comes up, we are told, it is really coming down; it passes the night above the solid cloud-mass, the firmament which 'divides the waters from the waters' (Genesis I.6). P. F. answers with 'the spirit of God moved upon the face of the waters' (Genesis I.2); it means, he would say, the wind of God blows the planets around the stationary sun.

we think that the sun runneth his course, and that the heavens stand still; no, it is the heavens that move his course, and the sun abideth perpetually in his place, he is permanent, and fixed in his place, and although we see him beginning to ascend in the orient or east . . . yet he moveth not. . . . as thou seest a bubble made of water and soap blown forth of a quill . . . even so is the whole firmament or chaos, wherein are placed the sun, and the rest of the Planets turned and

[26] In both original and translation the 'flight to the stars' is presented in the form of a letter by Faust to a former fellow-student; P. F. clearly regards this as genuine and does not doubt that Faust was 'possessed by the devil'.

carried at the pleasure of the Spirit of God which is wind. Yea,
Christian reader, (EFB, pp. 31f)

and so he breaks out of his frame. [gg]Evidently P. F. had not planned
to do so, because he has just meekly translated: 'Then looked I up to
the heavens, and behold, they went so swift, that I thought they
would have sprung in thousands';[27] but this anxiety was already
relieved if you accepted the daily rotation of a fixed earth, as many
people at the time felt permitted to do. [hh]Yet he still seems to feel he
is defying the obvious when he says that the sun remains fixed when
it plainly comes up; even so, that is not nearly as bad as saying it
really comes down. There is no definite statement that the planets
move round the sun, and on the next page he again winces away
from it, as if at the last moment. In between there is a good deal
about God's creation of man, breathing into him his 'wind, breath
or spirit', but then we get back to astronomy: [ii]'even so the
firmament wherein the sun and the rest of the planets are fixed,
moved, turned, and carried with the wind, breath or spirit of God,
for the heavens and firmament are moveable as the chaos, but the
sun is fixed in the firmament' (EFB, p. 32). It seems a hopeless
confusion; the sun is both moved and fixed. Here for the first time it
is plausible that a censor had intervened, and there was a good deal
of censorship against the Copernican theory under Elizabeth, in a
quiet way. In both these passages, very little verbal alteration would
be enough to make sense; and P. F. could allow them to pass in their
muddled form, feeling that anyone whose opinion he respected
would realize that he had been forced but had kept his honour. And
yet, a man who was better informed would hardly have got into such
a muddle. It looks as if, though very keen on the Copernican theory,
he did not know much about it.

[jj]Critics who say comfortably (or did do) that Marlowe had
probably never heard of Copernicus should observe that his chief
source for *Faust* asserts the belief dramatically. But one can get more
from it than that; one can ask: 'Under what circumstances would
this quirk seem an attractive or useful one?' P. F. must be a young
man, new to translation work; but must have been thought well
enough qualified for a fairly important assignment. Also, though he
is not really well informed about astronomy, and only his initials are

[27] EFB, p. 31.

to be printed, he cannot bear to have the public in general think he has even connived at an expression of anti-Copernican views. ᵏᵏThere is only one plausible explanation. He had been attending lectures or hearing talk by a man still young whom he admired, saying that hushing up Copernicus was a great wrong, and he felt himself to be a member of a group. The lecturer could only be Hariot, who published in 1588 his *Brief and True Report* on returning from the first Virginia colony,[28] and was accepted into the household of the Wizard Earl of Northumberland; there would be rooms enough for him to receive disciples. When P. F. first heard him, soon after the defeat of the Armada, he was a figure of immense promise. This is made clear by his enemies. The Jesuit Robert Parsons in his *Responsio* (1592) calls him an astronomer, a necromancer, and an atheist, and elsewhere speaks of 'Sir Walter Raleigh's school of atheism, and of the conjuror that is master thereof, and of the diligence used to get young gentlemen of this school'.[29] They are taught blasphemy there. Of course this is enemy talk, but it is likely that P. F., feeling rather unsuccessful, would go and listen to Hariot. He had already come across wizards abroad.

This is an important result, because the three accusers of Marlowe who have come to light, very different sources, all agree that he was a friend of Hariot.[30] Marlowe also does not seem to know much astronomy, and could hardly be a pupil of Hariot, but it probably means that he and P. F. went to the same parties and heard the same pep talks given by Hariot. To have them meet early, and have P. F. explain to Marlowe the difficulties of his work as translator, and give running accounts of important bits of the original, makes the whole picture much more intelligible. ˡˡOf course, Marlowe in his work as a spy would be sure to meet men who knew German, and could give him running translations of the GFB where he felt he needed them, but such men were unlikely to have studied the occult, and the added paragraph [on the powers of a magus] proves that P. F. had got that interest. One should realize that Marlowe shows no interest in the occult elsewhere, but in this one play is very knowing about it;

[28] Thomas Hariot: *A Briefe and True Report of the New Found-land of Virginia, etc.*, London 1588.

[29] In the English Summary of the *Responsio* (quoted with original spelling in Boas, p. 113).

[30] Baines mentions him explicitly, and Parsons by inference, but I do not find any reference to Hariot in Kyd's testimony, or in Greene's exhortation.

somebody must have helped him to mug it up, especially by telling him to read selected bits of books by Germans available in Latin. Who but P. F.? For that matter the spying connection may have brought them together, or they may have met at college (Corpus College Cambridge has lost the lists of BAs around that time), or indeed they were likely to meet in a London pub, soon after P. F. came home.[31] They would not meet the poet Donne there, because he was being invited to private parties; but P. F. would go there because he was not, and one may be sure that Marlowe enjoyed lording it in pubs, for reasons of his own. Hence they are positively unlikely not to have met, but the scholarly mind does not recognize inverse probability, and the case cannot be pressed.

Finally, there is a puzzling detail in Faust's address to the scholars, shortly before his end. In the GFB he says (chapter 68): 'I despised and denied the baptism, the sacrament of Christ, the human race, all the Heavenly Host and God himself – a God who does not desire that anyone should be lost' [Sp. 220]. The final clause is in apposition, made clear by Jones's dash. As it recalls a text from Ezekiel (Ezekiel 18:23; also 33:11), there can be little doubt that this was the intention.[32] P. F. makes him say, with a slight confusion marking extra agitation, that he has 'denied and defied . . . the Sacraments of Christ's body, God himself, all heavenly powers, and earthly men, yea, I have denied such a God, that desireth not to have one lost' (EFB, p. 79). Perhaps the contortion arose because he could hardly bear to say it. But there is now a separate sentence, definitely not a clause in apposition to 'God', and it has to mean: 'I believed that God *does* desire to send some men to Hell'. One might think that this could hardly be denied, as the Omnipotent actually does send them there, but the thought is treated as blasphemy. There is a parallel sentence by Luther, well known because in the *De Servo*

---

[31] [168; E0]I expect they told each other, in their pub, that you couldn't get any of the plum jobs if you hadn't got influence; but still P. F. could write good prose and would be a lively companion. I hope he was Sir Archibald Partly-Fake, but probably he was Peter Fox.

[32] Text: 'der ich veracht und abgesagt habe der Taufe, dem Sacramenti Christi, Gott selbst, allem Himmlischen Heer, und dem Menschen, einem solchem Gott, der nit begert, daß einer solt verloren werden'. I suspect P. F. found as much difficulty here as myself. He has repeated 'denied' where I have used a dash. I feel Empson's reading of P. F. here is bordering on the perverse, but I was unable to shake his conviction.

Arbitrio, saying that the hardest act of faith is to believe in the mercy and justice of God, because 'he seems to delight in [mm]the torture of the wretched'.[33] It would be natural for the Faust-book to recall the doubts with which the young Luther had wrestled; Faust becomes a Luther who merely happened not to receive the random miracle of grace. That is why Meph told him, in their first conversation, that he could not escape Hell because he was in despair; that is, he could not believe in the justice of God, let alone the vaunted mercy. It does seem possible that the original Faust-book said that, but a tactful editor obscured it; in any case, it was intelligent of P. F. to provide the logical structure of the highly Lutheran story, in so quiet a manner.

Very soon after, the scholars plead with Faust, telling him how to pray: 'yet it could take no hold, but even as Cain he also said his sins were greater than God was able to forgive; for all his thought was on his writing, he meant he had made it too filthy in writing it with his own blood' (EFB, p. 81). [nn]Such a *smelly* thing to do; God might have loved him if he hadn't behaved in such a low-class way. It is a 'brilliant' addition to the German text, one that presumes the original needs polish. [oo]In the GFB, what matters so decisively is to have signed a contract with the Devil, but P. F. invents a point of etiquette which makes Faust seem almost infantile. [pp]The influence of Reginald Scot would be very strong, and he had insisted that magic is always 'slovenly', even when the classical Romans are messing about with the livers of chickens. It is not merely beneath a gentleman, it is beneath a grown man, to toss into one's cauldron a finger of birth-strangled babe. And to be thrown into despair because of signing with one's own blood – it shows the silliness of the whole thing. This makes a startling contrast with the profound reflection just before; but no doubt on both occasions P. F. would claim that he was merely emphasizing something inherent in his original. He was well fitted to advise Marlowe.

[33] Quoted by Aldous Huxley in *The Perennial Philosophy*, London (Chatto & Windus) 1946, p. 270.

a3

The Censor

There are two topics on which the translation fudges, so ^bfar as possible, every time they crop up. One of them has not much doctrinal interest, but had better be taken first; it allows of being carried out very firmly, and is particularly unlikely to be the work of P. F. When Faust demands a wife (GFB, chapter 10; EFB, chapter 9), the spirits punish him for his presumption, but Meph offers afterwards, with an appearance of secrecy, to bring him the 'likeness' of any woman he desires. The spirits were good at imitating, as is clear when they present Alexander and his consort. Faust is to look around the streets wondering which woman to pick, and he 'perseveres' in this procedure for many years, eventually settling for six permanent ones[1] (their relations with Helen, who comes at the end, are left obscure). But in the EFB, an actual woman is always brought. The GFB has Meph saying: 'Just show me anyone you'd like to enjoy, from this town or any other; I shall produce her likeness for you and she shall live with you' [Sp. 34]. Faust is reported to have been very satisfied by this arrangement; 'he would fornicate with one devil today and have another in mind on the morrow'.[2] In the EFB Meph is made to say: 'thou shalt have thy desire of any woman thou wilt, be she alive or dead, and as long as thou wilt thou shalt keep her by thee' (EFB, p. 11). ^cThe idea that he might choose a dead one, from a portrait maybe, does not appear in the German, and maybe P. F. put it in to cover the case of Helen of Troy. Here, at the end, the standard rule breaks down, and it is not denied that he went to bed regularly with the spirit, nor even (except very faintly, perhaps as a legal

[1] GFB, chapter 57.
[2] Sp. 35.

precaution) that he had a son by her. Neither text passes this off as hearsay; the German expresses no confidence in it,[3] the English says: 'to his seeming, [d]in time she was with child, and in the end brought him a man child . . . when Faustus lost his life, the mother and child vanished away both together' (EFB, p. 74). So it is not denied that she was a mother, whatever 'to his seeming' insinuates.[4] [e]Lutherans and Calvinists did not believe in ghosts, so a devil imitating Helen of Troy would be the best he could have. This seems a clumsy introduction for the censor's new plan, but P. F. could tell him that the story was well known, and that if he were forced to omit Helen of Troy his book would not be considered a translation at all.

[f]It was not the policy of the censorship to appear a needless obstacle, suppressing a book very popular on the Continent which was after all a powerful religious tract. No attempt is made, any more in the English version than the German, to explain the status of Helen at the end; maybe the censor could regard her as merely a 'classical allusion'. Faust has summoned seven diabolical *succubae*, using the experience of beautiful women which he has gained on his travels, so says the GFB;[5] but the same rude words might be used of actual human women, summoned when he remembers them, 'and with these sweet personages he continued long, yea even to his last end'[6] (GFB, chapter 57; EFB, chapter 53). P. F. speaks of them with contempt, though they were brought by force, and apparently are left destitute in a remote place; it would be hard to find any moral superiority in the censor's change. Faust at the end loved Helen so much that he could not leave her for a quarter of an hour,[7] so the

---

[3] Sp. 199. W has: 'While she was with Doctor Faustus in his twenty-second to twenty-third year, she puffed herself out as if she were pregnant.'

[4] [132; E8]The orthodox opinion, on the whole, and certainly the Lutheran opinion, was that devils could not have children, and indeed could not have sexual pleasure, though they could deceive men and women into supposing they did. It had been a requirement of faith, though the belief was never made a duty, that sexual pleasure with a devil was the unforgivable sin, and Marlowe seems to accept the ruling of P. F. that Faust has not enjoyed it before. We do not know whether this idea would leap to the minds of a mass audience around 1590, as was assumed by W. W. Greg and his followers. But in the German version he has been enjoying it for a quarter of a century, and this of course (for anyone who knew it) would remove much of the horror from the single kiss on the stage.

[5] Sp. 196.

[6] EFB, p. 73.

[7] Sp. 199; EFB, p. 74.

seven beauties can have had little comfort. It is plain that the authors of the Faust-book are simply reporting all the permissible versions of the story, without feeling any duty to select from them a coherent version. P. F. feels no duty to arrive at one either; he need only obey his censor.

However, he might well feel that real women are the healthier plan. The use of imitation women, even if the powers of Faust are geared up by the Devil, suggests a habit of timid passive sexual fantasy; and P. F. is inclined to take a worldly or breezy tone, which the book needs. On this ground, it might be argued, he could make the change of his own accord. But the actual changes do not support such a theory; Faust has actually less companionship when his concubines are human. The first occasion seems to end the virginity of the scholar; at any rate Meph presents a large magic book to inaugurate the new regime. Faust 'indulged in vile shameful lechery with the Devil',[8] and 'he and his devilish mistress' were amused by the book (GFB, chapter 11). But in the EFB (chapter 10) the book is given separately, and apparently the woman is not allowed to see it.

[8]And then again, what some of these real women said would be alarming. Faust is rather keen on high life, and would see a duchess walking in procession to a state wedding or funeral; surely she would have made some comment, if he had had her fetched? And he could not keep her as long as he liked, a promise which P. F. merely copied from his original; there would be a house-to-house search. It would be easy for P. F. to explain, omitting this extra promise, that the ladies were given a temporary demonic possession, beginning with a trance, before being carried to Faust, and when they woke up at home merely assumed they had had a 'bad' dream. This would make a necrophiliac pleasure for Faust, as though the lady were already dead; surely, if you want his pleasures to be fairly normal, he had better romp with the devil who is occupying her. In short, the mind of P. F. is simply not applied to this annoying demand; he complies with it by a merely verbal change in his text, wherever it is needed. So this is a case of censorship.

This is not because P. F. is shy about women; consider his brief additions to the events in the Sultan's harem. He makes Meph say to Faust: 'Are not these ladies greatly to be pitied, that thus consume their youth at the pleasure of only one man?', thus encouraging

[8] Sp. 35.

Faust to give them what they needed. In both versions, after Faust has gone, the Sultan questions the ladies, wanting to know if he gave them normal copulation (if he did he is not a devil), and they assure him that he did. In the GFB they wish he would come every day,[9] but P. F. invents a tactful wife, who tells the Sultan that he could not have done better himself, and that she hoped the spirit would pay further occasional visits, say two or three times a week.[10] The women who are brought to Faust would at least open their mouths, if P. F. had been writing freely about them.

[h]Some comment is particularly needed towards the end of Part I, where Faust is most especially likely to break away and repent. But, says the German text (end of chapter 16):

> the Devil had taken too firm a hold on him, had hardened and deluded him and had made him captive. Besides, if ever he were alone and inclined to reflect on the word of God, the Devil would come to him in the form of a beautiful woman, embrace him and make love to him; this soon dispersed all thoughts of God. [Sp. 62]

In the previous chapter Meph boasted that he had 'possessed' Faust,[11] and though usually called *the spirit* he can be called *the Devil* here because his behaviour is particularly wicked. Surely Satan himself, though usually meant by the term, would not do anything so undignified. Meph has a skilled piece of nursing to do, and would hardly leave it to other hands. The English says:

> [i]the devil had so blinded him, and taken such deep root in his heart, that he could never think to crave God's mercy, or if by chance he had any good motion, straightways the devil would thrust him a fair Lady into his chamber, which fell to kissing and dalliance with him, through which means he threw his godly motions in the wind. (EFB, p. 19)

Coming just after the appalling description of Hell, this only makes Faust seem an ass; the change could not have been intended to save his dignity.

[9] Sp. 119.
[10] EFB, p. 44.
[11] Sp. 46.

The second requirement

^jThe other main demand of the censor has the same basic intention; there must be no matiness with demi-devils. Meph must be a real devil, from Hell, who inflicted tortures there; whereas the GFB had made him a flying spirit who lived in the storm clouds, and had probably never been to Hell at all. This assignment is more difficult than the sexual one, because when we encounter Meph he plainly isn't in Hell, and there is nothing in the text about how he gets in and out. In the GFB (chapter 11) Faust asks 'What kind of spirit are you?' and he replies 'I am a spirit, a flying spirit, and my realm is here beneath the heavens';[12] this has to be changed (EFB, chapter 10) to 'I am a flying spirit; yea, so swift as thought can think, to do whatsoever'.[13] P. F. invents the story that he is a prince in Hell, ruling the northern quarter (EFB, chapter 5), and this does at least suggest that he sometimes goes there. In the GFB (chapter 21), explaining how he can prophesy the weather for the almanacs, he says he lives in the storm clouds: 'Here in this gloomy air we spirits and devils[14] live, cast out into the darkness';[15] P. F. has to cut this altogether. But he is allowed ^kto translate or echo a phrase used just before (GFB, chapter 19; EFB, chapter 18): 'We spirits who soar through the air under the heavens and who can perceive the divine plan, we can unravel the mystery',[16] 'we spirits that fly and fleet in all Elements, know such . . .'.[17] However, the GFB sometimes makes him talk as the English censor would wish; in his first conversation with Faust (chapter 3) he talks about 'our Government' in Hell, staffed by 'many devils', and the secrets which 'we have never revealed'.[18] But this may be swanking, or a calculated attempt to awe Faust, or again he may speak as a feudal servant would do, loyally identifying himself with his masters. Meph in the GFB is meant to

---

[12] Sp. 36.
[13] EFB, p. 11.
[14] [137; E13]I am assured that, in the style of the author, this does not have to mean that the terms are separable, that there are other spirits who are not devils; but, if you were thinking so already, it would encourage you.
[15] Sp. 73.
[16] Sp. 68.
[17] EFB, p. 23 (sic, for 21).
[18] Sp. 13.

be a puzzling character, who keeps Faust guessing, and the eager readers were kept guessing too. P. F. could not like having this line of interest removed, but he might agree that the change made the book more straightforward and hard hitting; at any rate, he was willing to work for it.

The grand description of Hell (GFB, chapter 16; EFB, chapter 15) requires a skilful bit of fudging. Meph insists that Faust must abandon all hope, saying in the GFB:

> For all those whom God has cast into Hell must burn there eternally in God's anger and disgrace and remain there entirely without hope. For if the damned could share our hopes of salvation (we spirits expect it constantly) then they would rejoice and sigh longingly for the time to come. But they have as little hope of receiving grace as the devils in Hell, and what chance have they after their fall and repudiation? [Sp. 58f]

Obviously the spirits such as Meph, who may hope confidently, have some radical difference from the devils in Hell. Meph is extremely unforgiving towards the men in Hell – 'Why shouldn't they tremble and howl? Why shouldn't they lament?'[19] (not in EFB) – but when he thinks of the devils in Hell, words fail him. They seem to him so alien that he can work up to his main climax with '. . . the unbearable darkness and stench, the remorseless lash and the hideous faces of the devils' [Sp. 57]. This same passage was where P. F. introduced the tossing upon muck-forks, as a substitute for the 'hideous faces', and one can see now that it was necessary, if Meph were to be presented as a devil from Hell. He must also be a prince; so he need not play the muck-fork game himself, and he can admit that his peasantry are brutes, feeling amused so long as they are sporting about it.

¹On the main point, against hope, P. F. gives: 'Even as much it availeth thee, Faustus, to hope for the favour of God again, as Lucifer himself, who indeed though he and we all have a hope, yet is it to small avail, and taketh none effect, for out of that place God will hear neither crying nor sighing' (EFB, p. 18). This is very adroit; it seemed impossible to fudge that very plain statement, but here, as so often, impudence was enough. 'There is no hope, but we all hope' is mere contradiction, and yet it strikes the reader as pathetically true

---

[19] Sp. 56.

to life. And indeed, it was orthodox to admit that God may forgive anyone at the final Judgement, so the residual hope feels pious as well as understandable. But surely it does not fit the character of the devils who have been presented to us, of either type, either the ecstatic sadists with whips or the merry brutes with muck-forks. And all those who are upper-class like Meph must surely be hoping to land a plum job, such as the one he is enjoying at the moment. This version of the story does not hang together, but P. F. has jumped his fence; he has supplied something adequate to the censor's demand.

But also he has humanized Meph as far as possible, and he added that lyrical passage about the intimacy with nature open to a magician. He felt it would be wonderful to become a spirit of the air, and Shakespeare seems to have remembered the passage for Ariel. When he works in the opposite direction, that is decisive evidence for censorship. And yet an opponent might question whether he would submit so readily; a translator who could break out of his frame to speak up for Copernicus was not servile. It seems likely that, as a business man of good standing in foreign trade, he would already have minor government contacts, and would find it sensible to subject the project of this translation to the relevant censor from the start. The question might rather be how the book could have got printed in Frankfurt than whether a London censor would need to have it regularized.

[m]I need here, though feeling I am opposed by an unbreakable wall, to speak in favour of best sellers. An explosive triumph like the German Faust-book, translated into four languages in five years, will necessarily have gone through a special grooming, very unlike what the critics praise during their analysis of a masterpiece. The final editor, a rather sordid type, will have taken his blue pencil over the text saying 'That's out; it's good, but they won't stand it', or 'It's an odd thing, but they can just stand that. So long as it's isolated.' The book needs to be highly spiced, because it is on the edge of voicing the actual problems which face the mass reader, and yet it must have a ready defence against any accusation that it has said anything important. A very large popular mental activity has expressed itself in boiling up the Faust legend, and the text that sums it up must make sure that the fog never clears sufficiently to excite complaint. The editor is by no means a stupid man; he is exercising a habitual intuitive skill which will never again have so large an opportunity. But, in considering the possible influences of such a book, one needs

to consider not only what it says but what it leaves lying about. One should not (I quite agree) ask 'What is the secret message of the Faust-book?', the figure in the carpet or what not. One should ask 'What dangerous subjects did the readers hope to find touched upon, though not taken too far?' ⁿProbably P. F. believed he understood the secret meaning of the author, and meant to help it forward after protecting himself in this way. He could feel sure he was improving the book, for the English reader.

The noncombatants

Who can 'we spirits' be, who for the last 6,000 years or so have hoped 'hourly' for the news of salvation? °*Spies* in Frankfurt did not have to get his publication licensed beforehand, but might find himself in serious trouble afterwards; he would need to be ready with an official reply. Both Luther and Calvin, reviving the view of Augustine, had decided that there were no 'spirits' except angels and devils, and this appears to leave only one reply available. Meph can be one of the pacifist angels mentioned by Dante, who had refused to fight either for God or Satan. They had been thrown out of Heaven with the rebels, but not deep into Hell. Dante puts them into a Limbo just inside the Gate of Hell, which implies that they had no hope, any more than the devils, though not in pain, and he makes Virgil despise them too much to speak about them ('*non ragionam di lor, ma guarda e passa*').[20] They are very numerous ('I had not thought death had undone so many')[21] and may well be camping in the storm clouds, thinking they deserve forgiveness, though presumably they must wait till Judgement Day. However, there is no mention of this legend in the GFB, though there easily could have been; something of the kind is much needed during Meph's halting and embarrassed replies about his past experiences (for example, GFB, chapter 11, 14). To be sure, Meph only once lets drop that 'we spirits' can hope, but it comes at an important point, during his grand description of Hell. And he may be lying but if so why not follow up his lie, and make it plausible? The authors of the Faust-

---

[20] *Inferno*, Canto III, l. 51: 'Let us not speak of these, but look and pass' (tr. Dorothy L. Sayers, Harmondsworth (Penguin) 1949).
[21] Ibid, ls. 56f.

book, it seems fair to deduce, did not much like this explanation of Meph, but held it in reserve in case of a challenge from orthodoxy.

However, there was a recent account of devils not living in Hell, without reference to this legend, which had excited resistance. Aquinas had spoken calmly about devils living in the storm clouds, but he appears to assume that they have been sent on particular missions from Hell, and will return there; whereas these recent ones are afraid of being sent to Hell. The *De Praestigiis Daemonum* of Johann Wier (1563, expanded in later editions) is an enlightened work, opposed to the witch-burning, but it exposed to daylight the full texts of several invocations used by magicians to enslave a demon, as Faust is supposed to do. These tedious rituals had been circulating in secret manuscripts only known to initiates, but would come as a surprise to the public, because they were so determinedly pious and magisterial and unlike the legend. Reginald Scot [p]translated them into English for his *Discovery of Witchcraft* (1584), a fiercer attack on the witch-burnings, which he could express with comparative safety in England as they had not yet come here. His very long book had a second edition under Elizabeth, though of course it was banned by James; but neither edition was registered,[22] which implies that they did not go through the censorship. It shows a flexibility in the English system, and presumably an agreement was reached high up; the Archbishop would not want the witch-burning procedure in England, any more than certain other persons, but could not actually license a book which was probably heretical. (Scot recognizes politely the various spirits and witches mentioned in the Bible, but plainly wants to reduce them so far as he can.) The book came out when Marlowe had just got his BA and probably came under less supervision while working for his MA; he is pretty sure to have read some of it. Though long it is well indexed and contains many good jokes against priests. Marlowe's other writings have practically no reference to the occult, but when he took up the theme of Faust he would long have been familiar with parts of this rationalist attack upon it. So he would realize that modern magicians were not at all liable to sell their souls to devils. Their piety is probably hypocritical, but they expect the angels to give them power over their selected devil, and their chief threat against him is that if he disobeys they will send him to Hell. Scot is delighted

---

[22] See the edition by Brinsley Nicholson, London (Elliot Stock) 1886, p. xxxvii.

by the absurdity of this, as his main aim is to make the whole business ridiculous; he writes in the margin 'how frightened he will be' and such like. Threatening to send a bad child home, he might reflect, is the ultimate recourse of the hostess at a children's tea-party. But in our age plenty of people have been afraid of being deported to their supposed place of origin. The documents take no interest in how these devils became available, or how they escaped from Hell; and Scot cannot have heard of the theory that they had been noncombatants, because he would have laughed at it. Still, the documents tell a good deal, and were in print for readers of English and German as well as Latin. They show that the Faust legend is unjust to magicians, if it implies that they all behave like Faust or like witches. Marlowe makes this point at the start, by bringing on his two older magicians, who treat Faust gingerly.

⁑King James had certainly heard of these authors, since he denounces them both by name in his *Demonology* (1597),²³ and banned the work of Scot when he came to England. Maybe he had learned from there of this popular belief in freelance devils, open to bargains with magicians, living in the storm clouds; but no doubt other sources were open to him. His opinions need not be thought original to him; he writes in a popular or jovial manner, somewhat marred by his implied threat to burn alive anyone who answers back. How can you know that there are devils living in the storm clouds, he asks, unless they have told you so?²⁴ But you know that they are always liars, lying for some bad purpose. It would be rash to ask the King how he knows that they all come from Hell. But he is evidence for a general uneasiness, at any rate among leading Anglicans, at the idea that spirits are so easily available. Of course Scot and King James are slender evidence, but these books were well

²³ King James: *Daemonologie, in Forme of a Dialogue, divided into three Bookes*, Edinburgh (Walde-grave) 1597; see pp. xif for the attacks on Scot and Wier.
²⁴ Empson is interpreting his source very liberally here, although the underlying thought is retained. See *Daemonologie*, p. 10 (sic, misprint for 19): 'all Devils must be lyars; but so they abuse the simplicitie of these [witches] . . . that they make them believe, that at the fall of Lucifer, some Spirites fell in the aire, some in the fire, some in the water, some in the land . . . But the principall part of their fall, . . . the falling from the grace of God . . . they continued still thereafter, and shal do while the latter daie, in wandring through the worlde as God's hangmen to execute such turnes as he employs them in. And when anie of them are not occupyed in that, returne they must to their prison in hel.' There is no specific mention of storm clouds.

known, and they are of opposite tendency. They are enough to make the censoring of the English Faust-book intelligible.

Even so, the procedure was not a great success. Meph becomes much harder to envisage as a character if he comes from the Hell which he describes. It seems obvious that he has not been tortured without hope of escape for 6,000 years; he is rather brash. P. F. tries to deal with it by making him pathetic, but that will not really do either. One must recognize, however, that a careful reserve is maintained 'by both author and translator, because it was not officially agreed in what sense the devils suffered pain in Hell. Meph never actually says that he suffers the same pain as men; P. F. inserts, with apparent frankness, 'thou must be partaker of our torments',[25] but this is delusive, because it might mean 'the torments which we devils arrange for you men'. Hell was built for the Devil, and merely turned out afterwards to be convenient for dealing with men; surely he must be intended to feel the fire. The difficulty is that a purely spiritual being cannot feel bodily pain, but surely the human victims in Hell are also disembodied. Undoubtedly, mental suffering can be very severe, and fit to rank with bodily suffering, as is found in lunatic asylums; but Meph is in no such condition. P. F. wants him to be mysterious and sympathetic, so he is made to hint at sufferings. The tug of war between censor and translator has made the story a bit incoherent, but perhaps that adds to the mystery.

The play gives an interesting bit of evidence here, which presumes that many people in the audience would know what the censor had been up to. There are only two scenes of intimate talk between Faust and Meph before they quarrel (I.iii and II.i, in most editions). Each time, Meph says that he has just come from Hell and is even now suffering its pains; each time, Faust ridicules the claim, reducing him to silence, so that Faust gains an advantage. Many critics have disliked Faust for his bumptious fatuity here, and 'Come, I think Hell's a fable'[26] has been thought playing to the gallery (that is, writing an effective line without bothering whether it fits the character). But this is all right if the author is taking the audience into his confidence, and saying: 'Observe what nonsense the censor has made of the story.' Scoring off Meph in this way twice over

[25] EFB, p. 18.
[26] A: 573; B: 519.

would be excessive unless it had some topical point. Probably the Londoners talked about the censorship all the more because they dared not write about it.

Dating of the EFB

⁸If the intervention of a censor is established, one can reject the argument of W. W. Greg (1950) for a late date to the play. It is argued that Marlowe needed the translation to work from, and Greg argues that the lost first edition of that must have come out in the same year as the second, 1592. (One might argue that Marlowe read it before it came out, but the many translations of the German Faust-book suggest that it would be in demand, and likely to be published soon after it was available.) 'The title page of the surviving edition says:

> The history of the damnable life and deserved death of Doctor John Faustus, newly imprinted, and in convenient places imperfect matter amended: according to the true copy printed at Frankfort, and translated into English by P. F. Gent. Seen and allowed.

'We are entitled to suppose', says Greg rather oddly,[27] that the earlier edition was then recent, because of a minute in the Court Book of the Stationers' Company for 18 December 1592: 'It is ordered: that if the book of Doctor Faustus shall not be found in the Hall Book entered to Richard Oliff before Abel Jeffes claimed the same which was about May last, that the copy shall remain to the said Abel as his proper copy.' Greg comments: 'The ground of Jeffe's claim is not stated, but, no entrance being alleged, it is difficult to see what it can have been if not an edition previous to Orwin's';[28] which must therefore have been printed in May. It is curious that this argument has been accepted for thirty years. To print an edition is not in itself a claim; it may imply a claim, but the claim may be false. If I find your door open and walk in, that does not give me possession of the house. Obviously Jeffes might have real grounds for his claim, such as a contract with the author, or at least a

[27] Greg, p. 3.
[28] Ibid.

letter from him presuming a contract, and might have shown it to a member of the Company without making a formal 'entry'. To publish a rival edition within half a year, with only a moderate claim to have improved the text, could hardly be good business as the London public was quite small; and it would ᵘbe an atrocity in the trade, not to be spoken of so coolly. One might suspect that the tone is cool because the claim of Jeffe was thought absurd; but he was allowed a share in the later editions, which went on selling for most of the next century. And then, why had neither of these publishers registered the book with the Stationers' Company? The next edition is registered (April 1596); that is how we know that Jeffes got his share.[29] 'Seen and allowed' means that the censorship has passed the book though it has not been registered, a process that usually included a pass from the censors.

All this is explained if the censorship had behaved in an arbitrary way. Its habitual demand for secrecy is enough reason why the Stationers' Court Book does not mention it. The translation of the Faust-book had been recognized as needing special attention, but the readiness of P. F. made agreement easy, and the first edition came out in good time, probably combining forces with the ballad about Faust registered on 28 February 1589.[30] Marlowe wrote his play that year, and production was hurried forward; but in 1590 the censors found that it was being interpreted heretically; so they banned both the play and the translation, together with all discussion of them. The play required thorough revision, but sale of the translation was stopped merely to let public excitement about the topic die down. After two years, the censor in charge of the affair casually gave the right of republication to another publisher, wishing to reward him for some connivance perhaps. The original publisher told his wrongs to the Stationers' Company, who were indignant but had to be reticent; however, they saw to it that neither publisher was victimized. The impudent confident tone of an official liar is very plain on the surviving title page.

ᵛMaybe, however, the demand that Faust enjoy human women, not devils, was made during this ban for two years after the suppression of the play. The belief that devils could tempt both men and women into an imitation act of sex was old and accepted, and had

[29] See Greg, p. 4, where the Register entry (5 April 1596) is quoted.
[30] See Greg, p. 6.

become prominent in the witch-trials. All sex outside marriage was sinful, and this kind does not seem to have been more sinful or not much more; it is cited as evidence of a pact with the devils. So far there was no need to alter the translation; but the popular mind had gone further. Theologians said that devils had no sex and were incapable of sexual pleasure, though they took a malignant pleasure in seduction. But the plain man was sure that they were lustful, and deduced that they were homosexuals, which is especially funny on the stage.

ᵂThe clerical censors had an enlightened policy about sodomy. They wished to have it spoken of as something almost incredibly bad, monstrously unnatural, in fact as something that hardly ever occurred; and indeed very few cases were brought forward, so that the death penalty though in force was practically never imposed. Probably this method succeeded in preserving the innocence of many citizens. But meanwhile jokes about the topic went on as usual, and the sexual lives of devils were found particularly absurd, perhaps reassuringly so. This was rather unreasonable, as no sodomy was involved; a devil could turn himself into a midge, so of course he could turn himself completely into a woman; and he had not been a man before. Hence (felt the clergy) this low jeering from the public was ignorant and stupid, as well as disrespectful; they ought to be afraid of the Devil, as on the Continent they were forced to be. Greg and his disciples evidently felt much the same; they could not believe that Marlowe had written or even countenanced stuff like this – he was an educated man, after all. But his family had led a rough-and-tumble life and he might expect this particular line of fun to be wiser than the policy of the bishops. In print, total secrecy was observed about the activities of the censorship, but people talked pretty freely; they would think it very funny to have the Government labouring to protect the reputation of Satan from any suspicion of sodomy. Presumably he was another friendly power, like the Sultan.

ˣThe chief structural use that Marlowe finds for this joke is to lead off a sequence of three raisings of spirits, by which he heightens the status of the last comer, Helen of Troy. First an absurd devil-wife is offered to Faust, then the Emperor is shown exact copies of Alexander the Great and his consort, correct even to the mole on the back of her neck but hardly more than waxworks (surely these cannot be the same *kind* of spirit?), and finally the students are shown Helen, who is a goddess, in person. The more severe experts, at the time, said that a man could never claim he had enjoyed a devil by mistake, thinking it was a real woman; devils were so slovenly that they never completed their disguise, always leaving just the stump of a vigorous tail or what not; (or perhaps they were so vain that they expected the man to be more excited by that procedure). (They were very unlike the meticulous spirits who copy Alexander.) Assuming this to be well known, it would allow of a very knockdown joke not in the words at all, invisible to the censor reading beforehand. The leering female-impersonator, eager to win the love of Faust, raises the side of the farthingale just enough to allow a peep at a great hairy cloven hoof. ʸProbably, as soon as the censors were alerted, a self-sacrificing curate was induced to sit through the whole play, in disguise, and reported that its obscenity was the most offensive thing about it, though perhaps not literally heretical. The devil-wife ogling and yearning at Faust, and Beelzebub preening his monstrous bulk as the favourite of Lucifer, let alone the uproarious scene in the Sultan's harem, were all painful, and the laughter at them took up a lot of the time. But the accusation was true, he would report; the audience did seem to believe at the end that Faust had escaped Hell. The joke that the devils are sodomites might actually come as a surprise to the censors as it was so firmly kept from print; but they would anyhow discourage matiness with devils, who must be kept in their proper place. This further demand, when his book was silenced, ᶻwould be exasperating for P. F., and fully explains the bleakness of his response (though this is not a necessary hypothesis). No wonder he was not inclined to do any further translation for the printers. The whole affair had been tiresome.

P. F.'s mistranslations

Finally, it is as well to consider here a theory often put forward or taken for granted, that many of the variants in the translation are simply due to P. F.'s ignorance of German.[31] Supporters of this theory have had remarkable success in showing that ingenious misreading can often explain them. The Devil alone knoweth the heart of man, but we can observe that these changes are always such

---

[31] For a discussion of the mistranslations, see postscript, pp. 205–7.

as either he himself or his censor wants to justify. One example of each may at least recommend this line of rebuttal. Meph tells Faust at their first discussion (GFB, chapter 3) that we devils will not tell about our government, and nobody (other than the damned in Hell) knows what happens after the death of the damned. Faust becomes '*alarmed*' and says 'I won't be damned',[32] seeming to assume he can laugh it off, and Meph says or presumably sings a riddling poem. The EFB has:

> neither have we given any man any gift, or learned him anything, except he promise to be ours.
> Dr Faustus upon this *arose from where he sat*, and said, I will have my request, and yet I will not be damned. (EFB, p. 3)

The whole sequence in the translation is more hard hitting, cruder one might say, because P. F. wants Faust to be decisive and to be searching for a plan. To mistake 'became alarmed' for 'stand up' was what he wanted,[33] and if challenged he could pretend he had thought it correct.

The other case is more surprising. Faust in his final lamentations says (GFB, chapter 66): 'I could do without Heaven well enough, if only I could escape eternal punishment' [Sp. 215]. At some stage, the censor felt that the more tender lambs in the flock might be unsettled if they read this obvious remark; they must not hear that any man is not always yearning to be in Heaven. The demand would come as a surprise to P. F., as Faust has been allowed to make bold enough remarks earlier on. He put (EFB, chapter 61): 'Ah that I could carry the heavens on my shoulders, so that there were time at last to quit me of this everlasting damnation' (EFB, p. 77) [aa]This too, it has been confidently argued, can be understood as a simple misreading of the German words.[34] If so, it was clever of P. F. to

---

[32] Sp. 13.

[33] Text: 'D.Faustus entsetzt sich darob ...' P. F. interprets *sich entsetzen* as 'desit', i.e. to arise, and this is usually regarded as one of his howlers.

[34] Text: 'ich wolte gerne deß Himmels entberen, wann ich nur des ewigen straffe köndt entfliehen.' P. F.'s translation is based, wittingly or not, on the similarity of *entberen* to the English 'bear', though he must have known *tragen*. This is the sole occurrence of *entberen* in the GFB, so it might have posed a problem but there are other indications in the 'lamentations' that P. F. was tired here. What is strange is that he has to invent a nonsensical rationalization for his variant, and Empson's suggestion that the mistranslation was deliberate is quite plausible.

discover the possibility. He has a sense of reality and a feeling for style; however ignorant of the words, he would know what to look for. But he would rather be thought ignorant of German than be thought capable of originating such stuff as was demanded of him. He is pretty sure to have made mistakes; translating must have been much harder without dictionaries. But a decisive example of one seems to be rare.

a4

The Spirits

If then we suppose that these two types of cut were imposed on P. F. by the censor, what can the censor's purpose have been? Both the beliefs that were cut out had been accepted by Aquinas, at least as fair topics for speculation; we need some local and recent objection. Scot's *Discovery of Witchcraft* gives a powerful case against the witch-trials, and was presumably meant to resist the introduction of the full procedure into England; it certainly received attention, as the title page of King James's *Demonology* says it is written to refute the opinions of Scot, and those of the German Johann Wier. The whole of Scot's Book IV is a detailed report, very coarse and funny, of the stories about the activity of devils, and he ends by solemnly apologizing to his readers for subjecting them to such nastiness. A deliberate working up of hysteria on the subject has been thought to date from the *Malleus Maleficorum* by Sprenger and Kramer (1486),[1] and that book certainly contains a good deal of it. The devils, in the official belief, were incapable of sexual pleasure themselves, only deluding men and women out of malice; but the public reasonably interpreted this as meaning that their pleasures were perverse ones. An Anglican censor, even if in favour of burning witches after a proper trial had proved them guilty, would not care for ribald jeering at their obscene practices – practically a sacred topic; whereas the public, of course, would like it.

This explains the first set of changes, but the second, insisting that Meph comes from Hell and not from the storm clouds, is more of a

[1] The date of the earliest edition of the *Malleus* is uncertain, but it appeared within a few years of the Bull *Summis Desiderantes Affectibus* (9 December 1484) of Pope Innocent VIII.

puzzle. There is a Renaissance development to consider. From late in the fifteenth century till nearly halfway through the sixteenth, there was a strong intellectual movement recommending belief in Middle Spirits, neither from Heaven nor Hell; they could be called spirits of nature, or elementals, or the *longaevi* – they lived longer than we do, but then died completely, like the beasts. They were a very wide group, including both the pagan gods known to the learned and the fairies known to the villagers, and probably also the germs that cause plague. Of course, people had always believed in things like that, and it does not appear that Christian clergy ever made the belief heretical; but of course it would be very wrong to worship them, and the less attention paid to them the better.

ᵇThe basis of the theory was a philosophical one. It is the Principle of Plenitude, which caused the Great Chain of Being;[2] God wants life everywhere, to every degree, in all the niches that could contain it, right up to the sphere of the moon – beyond which all is unvarying and incorruptible. Considering what goes on at the bottom of the sea, a modern scientist can hardly object to this principle, nor yet deny that the gap between men and angels (as they are usually described) is too big not to contain some intervening form of life, playing the role of the duck-billed platypus. And yet maybe this was where the theory broke down.

ᶜProbably the chief attraction of the theory for a Renaissance scholar, devoted to the classics, was that it gave a tolerable picture of the pagan gods. It was disagreeable to believe that they were all devils, solely concerned to do evil, and it would seem atheistical to call them mere delusions (oracles and all); but if they were Middle Spirits, with practically all the powers they claimed, one could read contentedly – also, it does seem plain that they are long dead. If you were a thousand years old, and could expect one or two thousand more, and were accustomed to deal with creatures who are no good after eighty, it would seem natural to call them 'mortals'; and the myth of the ancestors of Jupiter does in effect practically admit that their immortality has its limits – he cannot be holding an infinite number of grandfathers in jail. The death of Pan was also well known. So there would be no obstacle here; and on the other hand

[2] For a succinct account see E. M. W. Tillyard: *The Elizabethan World Picture*, London (Chatto & Windus) 1943, chs. 4, 5, drawing on Arthur O. Lovejoy's *The Great Chain of Being*, Cambridge, Mass. (Harvard University Press) 1936.

the creatures acquired no marks of age until they flicked out like an electric bulb, so Helen of Troy, who seems particularly hard to kill, might really give Faust an heir soon before his end.

ᵈSo Apollo had been a Middle Spirit, and well intentioned on the whole, though of uncertain temper as one could hardly deny; he would have lasted for two thousand years or so, but of course was dead by now. This won solid acceptance, but the releasing trigger was the discovery, and translation from Greek into Latin by Ficino in 1464, of the *Corpus Hermetica* (a part of it had long been available in Latin, but was considered wicked).³ These fragments were probably written by a pious group between 100 and 300 AD, but their supposed author Hermes was widely believed to have been the tutor of Moses in Egypt, teaching how to defeat the magicians of Pharoah, ᵉproving that some kinds of magic are permitted. The writers of the *Hermetica* hold very diverse opinions, some being pantheist and finding illumination in sexual love, others ascetic and other-worldly, but they all take the same tone; this would help to make the supposed one author seem mysteriously wise. There is a lot about spirits, and their effects are considered usually bad; a man should rise above them; but some can be enlightened by priests, and then they can be very helpful (*Asclepius* III). The whole collection was written before, but not very long before, Augustine laid down that all spirits are either angels or devils,⁴ wearing the uniform either of God or Satan ᶠand fighting each other all the time. Surely that was a very Manichean idea; it is surprising that Aquinas put up with it.⁵ ᵍAugustine's arguments must have seemed as flimsy then as they do now, but it seemed more pious to have all spirits earnest in one way or the other. On the other hand, for any study of Nature, at the start of the sciences, it was essential to be allowed a belief in spirits who were neutral; though no one seems to offer a case where belief in

³ For an introduction to Renaissance Hermeticism, see Frances A. Yates: *Giordano Bruno and the Hermetic Tradition*, London (RKP) 1964, and *The Occult Philosophy in the Elizabethan Age*, London (RKP) 1979.

⁴ *The City of God*, Book VIII, chapter 22.

⁵ [389: E0]He does go firmly on record, in *Summa* Q.63 Art.7, saying that the belief of the Platonists in daemons, some of them good, 'living below the lunar sphere . . . yet higher than men in the order of nature', is not 'to be rejected as contrary to faith'. 'There is nothing to prevent us from saying', he goes on with his curious detachment, that the lower angels were divinely set aside for service in this region. [*The Summa Theologica* . . . , English translation revised Daniel J. Sullivan, Chicago (Encyclopedia Britannica) 1952.].

them led to an actual discovery. [h]But the *Hermetica* drop a few hints of the belief, which became important to Paracelsus, that [i]certain spirits have to be at work in us all the time to make our bodies tick over normally. The early development of science is a mysterious thing, but it seems likely that the development allowed one to think about nature with more confidence.

Effect of the Reformation

The Reformation closed this period of freedom, at least on paper; to toe the line became a duty of loyalty. Luther and Calvin positively rejected the belief in spirits of nature, as Augustine had done before them; and at both dates it is hard to see any point of principle behind the confident rhetoric. Probably they just wanted more discipline, and so far their opponents readily agreed; hence there were few places where philosophizing about spirits could still be printed, though fantasies about them, in verse or for plays, were often allowed.

The *De Occulta Philosophia* of Cornelius Agrippa (1533, but available earlier),[6] when it considers these spirits in its third and final book,[7] is a grand compilation of what other people have said about the subject, with an emphasis upon little-known authors in eleventh-century Constantinople. But he has no rule against giving his own opinion; he sometimes names authors who believe that all spirits die, and one can deduce that he agrees with them, but he does not find it of much importance. He does commit himself to the assertion that it is easy to raise nymphs from [j]water meadows by following his instructions, and here one may suspect that (though usually a very adroit man) he overplayed his hand. Of course there is no smell of brimstone about it; he is always very pious and high minded, and he takes for granted that any man would like to raise a nymph from a water meadow. It is natural to suppose that a lot of men tried, and the answer that he had thought best to withhold just a bit of the easy formula would not stand against heavy pressure.[8] Be this as it may,

---

[6] Written *c.*1508–9, the MS circulated and pirated. A manuscript of 1510 is reproduced in full in the facsimile edition (ed. K. Novotny), Graz (Akademische Druck–u. Verlagsanstalt) 1967.

[7] Book III, chapters xvi–xix.

[8] [390; E0]C. S. Lewis, at the start of his survey of sixteenth-century literature

the reason for mentioning him here is that Marlowe had pretty certainly read him. The book was in Corpus College Library when he was up there; indeed, it was in the libraries of ten of the Cambridge colleges. The dons were not hiding the forbidden doctrine from the children. It was in the same position as the forbidden doctrine of Copernicus; no new books giving serious support to either of them could get a licence, but old books which had already been in print could be reprinted, as they did not require one. When James came to the throne he made reprints require a licence (R. F. Johnston and Christopher Hill establish the main facts in this area, but their evidence can be taken a bit further). The method is sufficiently effective where there is no general pressure against it, and yet allows the public an illusion of freedom. The young Marlowe would read it (he read Latin freely though a bit roughly), because after Ovid and suchlike there was not much else in the library amusing to read. He could not afford to go home for the vacations. Of course he would know the folklore on the subject, but this would make him realize early that there had been recent learned support for it. One must realize: he shows no interest in spirits elsewhere, but he has mastered the subject rapidly for this one play. He must have had an advisor, and the most likely person is the translator P. F. It may be objected that the First Part of *Tamburlane* is also well informed about its subject, and yet no shadowy advisor is thought necessary; but the information about Tamburlane was in an available history book, whereas someone would need to tell Marlowe about the *De Nymphis* of Paracelsus.

[*English Literature in the Sixteenth Century*, Oxford (Clarendon) 1954: ed.], writing very well about these matters, [391: E0]remarks that medieval writers treat magic as romantic and remote, whereas writers in his period feel it may be going on in the next street. This tone can still be felt in poetry till the end of the century, but there is a sharp fall in the credibility of white magic about halfway through the century, chiefly of course because of the Reformation, but probably a lot of people had tried out the instructions given by Agrippa and similar authors; they were aggressively sceptical about the fairies. In England, the change seems to have happened to villagers as well as learned scholars, at least in the home counties; it can hardly be the result of Luther.

The *De Nymphis*

This essay or squib had been printed while Marlowe was still a boy, first in German as usual, then in Latin one year later, in Switzerland.[9]Paracelsus had quarrelled with the medical organizations and appeared discredited, and his writings were intolerably hard to read, but a suspicion always remained that they contained the secret of his undoubted cures. A grand edition [k]of all available writings by Paracelsus, in fourteen volumes, appeared in Basel in 1589–91. This situation always means, for a few years before, a susurrus of interest among informed people, with ignorance elsewhere. Marlowe as an international spy would be likely to meet German-speakers, but German-speakers with literary interests were not yet common in London; and Marlowe would be likely to meet P. F., by various routes, but most likely in a pub. It seems clear that neither of them was 'in society', whereas Donne, for example, was. But P. F. would have read the *De Nymphis*.[10] It is only about 5,000 words long, and is the source of several anecdotes which are prominent in later German literature, and applies a powerful analytic mind to the status of such beings. Many dons have argued that Paracelsus here is only reporting, with kindly humour, the superstitions of the miners he worked among (while inventing the subject of industrial disease); but Paracelsus often explained that he despised the opinions of the dons who had rejected him, and thought the miners much more likely to be right. In his technical writings he believes in spirits working for good inside our bodies, with a hierarchical but no harsh political structure; the '*archeus*' of the belly is the chief one, but far from a dictator. Of course, none of this would prevent him from believing in spirits outside of us.

[9] In the *Philosophia Magnae*, . . . *Tractatus Aliquot* Basel (Flöher) 1567, Liber 7, 'De nymphis, sylphis, pygmaeis et salamandris et de caeteris spiritibus'. For the German original (Nissae Silesiorum, 1566), see Karl Sudhoff (ed.): *Paracelsus: Sämtliche Werke* München and Berlin (Otto Wilh. Barth u. R. Oldenbourg) 1922–9, vol. 14, pp. 115–52.

[10] [439; E4]The town house of an Elizabethan grandee usually had a library open to respectably sponsored callers, and surely this book would be recognized as an entertaining curiosity. One would like Marlowe to have read it, because it would alert him to the Gilbertian possibilities of these changes. [Dr Dee would probably have had it but there is no direct evidence that Marlowe was acquainted with Dee: ed.]

The *De Nymphis* begins by saying that the Middle Spirits are not spirits at all, [l]as they have bodies; but of a subtle kind of matter, and a creature who can pass through a stone wall is a spirit for common language. [m]They are of earth, air, fire and water, and perhaps more kinds; and some say that each kind must withdraw into its own element at cockcrow. Presumably the spirits of the air go high up; it is agreed that they can travel very fast. Angels and devils, being pure spirit, do not live in space and can appear immediately anywhere, even inside a prison; whereas Middle Spirits can turn themselves into any animal they like, so they can get through a keyhole, if it is big enough for a midge (the magician's boy is called Midge in *John a Kent and John a Cumber* (1590), and he can enter the castle). Middle Spirits can hear what you say at any distance, but cannot read your thoughts, which probably angels and devils can (I am afraid Ariel can: *Tempest*, IV.i.164). Paracelsus agrees with Agrippa that Middle Spirits are not immortal, though they live a very long time (so that a mage may call up classical gods), and indeed, another name for them is *longaevi*; hence they must have children, though seldom, whereas angels and devils cannot breed, otherwise they would cause a glut. [n]However they die like the beasts; they will not appear at the Judgement. As Robert Kirk said, 'they are far from Heaven, and safe from Hell'.[11] (Paracelsus admits that this is strange, but recalls that many of the acts of God seem strange.) They are so close to us that they can interbreed with mankind, or at least nymphs can, the female spirits of water, and if a nymph is properly married to a man she acquires an immortal soul, as a woman who marries an American gets an American passport. Paracelsus gives an earnest warning to young men that they must not jilt a nymph; there have been several cases where it has led to murder. And really one cannot blame the nymphs, he goes on; human women have no business to do it – what have they got to lose? – [o]but a nymph is fighting for eternity. [p]Marlowe could not read this without feeling that an exalted love between two males, though equally liable to turn disastrous, ought to have the same adhesive power; or at least, ought to entail the power to make a self-sacrificing gift.

[11] Robert Kirk: *The Secret Commonwealth of Elves, Fauns and Fairies* Comment. Andrew Lang, Intro. R. B. Cunninghame Graham, Stirling (Eneas McKay) 1933.

The decline in belief in Middle Spirits

qBy the time of Scot's *Discovery* there had been a change in the public mind which helped the Reformation suppression of these beliefs; at least, Scot mentions it, and he was likely to know. He says in his preface that, in the recent past, many people were afraid of Robin Goodfellow, but now they laugh at him and only fear witches;[12] soon they will laugh at witches too (by the way, the edition by Montague Summers omits both the preface and the final 'Discourse of Devils and Spirits', so that Scot appears only interested in the nastiness that interests Summers).[13] Maybe witches were merely found more exciting than fairies, as bad money drives out good. In any case the collapse of the belief in nature-spirits left a gap, particularly felt by magicians, which was partly filled by the fallen angels of the storm clouds. Maybe the ones whose fall was stayed in the upper air were different and more deserving, but anyhow they were a convenience.[14]

rThe influence of Pomponazzi (1462–1524) was probably important for this change. He was an Italian professor of philosophy who argued that, so far as our knowledge extends, a creature can only learn through its senses; if purely spiritual, it could have no means of acquiring information or even of communicating with its fellows. He died in his bed, at a reasonable age, as he would not have done if he had been born a bit later, and even so, he probably survived because 'the resurrection of the body' comes in the Creed, and that took care of the worst implications; but he seems never to have claimed this escape route, merely saying that the truths of philosophy and theology were independent. Reginald Scot is a plain minded man, though a well-read one, and it comes as a surprise to find him quoting Pomponazzi and giving his name; of course he proves that the devils cannot do what the witch-burners said they did, but Scot does snot seem to realize that he proves a lot more.

---

[12] *Discovery of Witchcraft*, ed. Brinsley Nicholson, London (Elliot Stock) 1886, p. xx.

[13] London (John Rodker) 1930.

[14] [193: E3]It had long been a problem for magicians that devils, though they came willingly to a call, demanded terrible payment, whereas nature-spirits though harmless could not be set to work. ([391: E0]It was only by luck that Prospero won a claim over Ariel.)

The Mortalist Heresy, that the soul is in abeyance after death till the resurrection of the body, which was held by Milton in secret, was clearly a way of coming to terms with Pomponazzi, and would not have been considered so shocking otherwise. When Donne in *The Ecstasy* praises the senses to his mistress, saying:

> We owe them thankes, because they thus
> Did us, to us, at first convay[15]

the platitude is spicy because it recalls Pomponazzi. Henry More's *Philosophical Works* (1662) make an attempt to use light as the matter of which spirits are made, but he does not explain how their senses could work;[16] and Milton more soberly in his epic accepts that angels are material, though their matter is more subtle than ours and is mainly in the form of gas. One might think that this problem, about angels having no sense, must always have been obvious; and so it was to Aquinas, but he performed one of his masterpieces of obfuscation. 'The Knowledge of the Angels' is treated at great length, but perhaps Q.57, Art.2 is all one need master. This was what gave Leibnitz his theory of the pre-established harmony, though in Aquinas it applies only to angels. A part of God's knowledge is extended to each angel, so that he can appear to see and hear what he needs if he is to be thought sensible, though really he is just a puppet (of course Aquinas does not say so). It seems plain that this theory had long remained mercifully obscure, but by 1500 it was putting an intolerable strain upon common sense; otherwise the puncturing of it by Pomponazzi could not have raised such a great echo. 'One can be confident at least that the objections to the position of Aquinas had become much more obvious during the sixteenth century, so that all spirits were allowed a subtle kind of matter. It was thus possible for a character in a play to become uneasy about whether he had been turned into a devil or a pagan demigod. And surely Marlowe would want to dramatize this situation if the possibility occurred to him.

[15] *The Poems of John Donne*, ed. H. J. C. Grierson, London (OUP) 1929, p. 47, ls 53f.

[16] *Henry More's Philosophical Writings*, ed. Flora Isabel Mackinnon, New York (OUP) 1925.

The status of Meph in the Faust-book

ᵘ"If Marlowe made an important change in his treatment of the legend, he would need to claim that he was returning to the original, which had been obscured by some form of censorship. ᵛIn this way he could avoid any reference to the English censorship, which indeed he contrived to obey. He would claim (especially in talking to officials) that Meph in the German text already sounds very like a nature-spirit, whether or not he does it in order to deceive. This would not annoy the officials, because the point had already occurred to them; that was why they had insisted that Meph in the EFB must come from Hell. It is time to survey the reasons for suspecting him.

ʷFaust summons the Devil, and after much difficulty 'a diabolical spirit' appears,[17] approaching Faust at last in the shape of a grey friar. Faust does not ask its name till chapter 5, when he has struck the bargain with it – he signs away his soul in the next chapter. We are told that Faust himself formulated the deed and drew up the letter of contract, but he receives no corresponding document signed by the other party, and asks for no evidence that he is dealing with a qualified agent. (In the play he calls for Meph by name when he conjures, and surely one of the lost fragments must have explained how he knew the name.) In the early chapters, he does ask some questions, and Meph is very evasive. He never once says he has himself actually been in Hell, or even in Heaven. Faust tells him to describe Lucifer before his fall, and he demands three days' grace to study the subject (GFB, chapter 14); when he returns he gives only the standard propaganda against Lucifer, available from any pulpit. Even if he were a pacifist angel, who refused to fight on either side, he would surely have heard Lucifer trying to win the pacifists over. Of course, one can invent explanations; perhaps Meph has been pleading with Lucifer, without success, for permission to release a more favourable account, or perhaps he thought the demand of Faust a good excuse for a holiday (it is hard to believe that he needed a special permission for so clear a case, and he needed none to accept the only startling demand of Faust, who asks after the return of Meph to be changed at once into a spirit). But surely this process of

[17] Sp. 10.

explaining must be what the author of the Faust-book wanted us to engage upon; the quaint stiffness of these early replies of Meph is pointedly unlike the offensive familiarity of his talk later on. One might argue that very different documents had been fitted together into a long consecutive account, and probably they were; but the final editors were evidently prepared to alter the text where they thought good. And we are often told that Meph is working very subtly to confuse the judgement of Faust, so that everything he says may be discounted, but this is not the way anybody considers the report of an untrustworthy but unique witness in a novel. If he is not worth attention, one had better stop reading the book. He plainly gives Faust a good deal of frank warning. Even a strict Lutheran had ˣprobably heard about Middle Spirits at his mother's knee, and to watch whether the book ever slipped over into letting Meph admit that he was one of them would be one of the points of curiosity.

ʸAt the start, when Faust has decided what demand to make in his pact with the Devil, he puts first the demand to become a 'spirit' ('*geist*')[18]. Why does he want this?[19] ᶻMeph says he will immediately perceive that he has become a spirit, as soon as he has signed and sworn (GFB, EFB, chapter 4); but we hear no more about it. It should at least mean becoming able to fly, as Meph does, and Faust could test this quickly;[20] but in all his journeys he is merely carried

[18] Sp. 16.

[19] [170; E0]For completeness I shall add my own explanation, though I realize I have no standing here. The mystery of the demand to be made a spirit did no harm to the Faust-book, which fed on mystery, but it had fallen into its place from some actual story. This would be a play, performed in Latin in a college, and the wicked magician thought he would be safe if he were turned into a devil, because then he could enjoy Hell; instead of being tortured, he would do the torturing. It is the invention of Belsen. But he is gradually induced, by a series of harangues, to recognize that the devils in Hell are tortured even more than their victims. Collapse of smart Alec, and what more could be required? But the mysterious activities of history were even then deciding that Faust was a splendid character because he had eaten a cartload of hay for three farthings, and it would be a blasphemy to say that he had ever really meant any harm. This bit of the story could be left in all right, so long as nothing was made of it. But of course something would be made of it, and I do not pretend to know what went on in the mass mind as the bestseller swept across Europe. [For the possibility of a Latin play of Faust, see John A. Walz, 'A German Faust Play of the Sixteenth Century', *Germanic Review*, III, 1928, pp. 1–22: ed.].

[20] [401; E7]On the scheme of Paracelsus, Faust could also have found out at once whether he had been turned into a Middle Spirit or a devil: a spirit of the air can fly at immense speed, but an angel, not really living in space, can appear anywhere as if at infinite speed.

about, either by Meph or by a dragon. Is he afraid to mention that he has been flagrantly and immediately cheated? But he speaks up about other things quite readily. And why is the word used at all, if there are no spirits other than angels and devils, not even ghosts? Meph is regularly called 'the spirit' in the narrative, and not the 'familiar' of Faust;[21] this is pointless unless it implies a mystery about his status. Unless the author was a highly sophisticated novelist, there have been cuts.

Faust presents two sets of demands (chapters 3 and 4); after the first, Meph says he will have to refer them to the god of Hell. He returns later in the same day, and Faust is ready with the new set, which are accepted without any need for further reference, though they are very different. He had first made three demands, which are hardly distinguishable, as they are almost solely concerned with his thirst for knowledge; however, the first says Meph must be his servant, 'obedient in all things bidden, asked and expected of him',[22] and he may of course ask for power and pleasure, when they occur to him. But the next two demand that Meph shall answer *any* question and answer it *truthfully*, so his mind is at present on knowledge only. Meph answers at length, with an indirect warning against damnation: aa'we have never revealed the true foundation'[23] of Hell to a man, but the damned will learn about it by experience. Faust became alarmed, and said fatuously 'I won't be damned for that, nor for your sake'.[24] Meph answers with a jeering riddling poem, which ends 'Your heart's despair has brought you there'.[25] Faust was 'irresolute from that time on',[26] but told Meph to come back at evening, when he would have proposals. He then said, 'albeit with some misgivings',[27] that he wished to cease being human and 'to become a devil incarnate, a member of the Devil himself'.[28] This explanation is added by the GFB editor and is not found in

---

[21] Widman, in his *Warhafftige Historie* Hamburg (Hermann Moller) 1599, Part I, chapter 10, makes Meph's status explicit. Meph tells Faustus: 'You should not fear me, for I am no devil but a *Spiritus familiaris*, happy to dwell amongst men.' Widman avoids any discussion of this distinction in his otherwise exhaustive commentary.

[22] Sp. 11.
[23] Sp. 13.
[24] Ibid.
[25] Sp. 14.
[26] Ibid.
[27] Sp. 15.
[28] Ibid.

manuscript W; however, in both 'to be a Spirit' is put first among the formal demands.

bbMeph knows all the standard doctrine about Hell, without claiming to have been there; but he is actually short of information about Heaven (chapter 3). ccThere is also an odd detail in the first account by Meph of his relations with Lucifer. Meph tells that ddhe [Lucifer] was thrown out of Heaven for his arrogance and presumption, but he established a government here.

> Now because the fallen angel Lucifer has his dominion and princedom beneath the heavens [that is beneath the sphere of the moon], and *because of the change in him*, we are obliged to transform ourselves, negotiate with human beings and become subservient to them. Otherwise, no human being, no matter how skilful and powerful, could ever bring Lucifer into subjection. And so our Master sends a Spirit, and such am I. [Sp. 13]

Spies omits 'because of the change in him' (from manuscript W), perhaps feeling it too elaborate for an initial speech; but the change adds its mite to the pervasive suggestion that Meph has never seen Lucifer before his change, and never been in Heaven at all. How could he say 'the fallen angel'[29] if he fell himself at the same time? The effect is now: 'we Middle Spirits never bothered with men until these devils came down and forced us to be go-betweens'. And the next sentence is so odd that it might be a slip of the pen, if the whole text had not been scrutinized at least twice. P. F. cuts it out, however. Meph seems to be *hoping* that some man will eventually bring Lucifer into subjection; but how can he hope that if he is 'a limb of Satan', lacking distinction from him, as if merely one of his appearances? The sentence might pass as meaning: 'No man could use the powers of the Devil for his own purposes without a Middle Spirit to act as go-between'; but even in this mild form it assumes that Meph is not a real devil, although he speaks here of 'our kingdom' and 'our habitation'. He may be boasting, but he may speak of 'the family' as a feudal servant would do – this is where he says he is a servant.[30] We need not assume that Meph knows a great

---

[29] Sp. 13.

[30] [452; E11]Probably Oberon would consider him a traitorous quisling, but their relations are not considered; perhaps Oberon is a leader of an Underground, hiding from the devils, and that is why he has to live permanently in the dawn.

deal about the First Things, and only gets them wrong to deceive; if he only lives for two or three thousand years, it was his grandfather or greatgrandfather who saw the arrival of the devils, and the attempt at happy lives of the earlier Middle Spirits, before they were dispossessed, will be a family tradition "among Middle Spirits, which they dare not tell to the Devil. Meph can afford to let it out in a grumbling way to Faust, because he could always explain to his masters, if exposed, that he was only trying to bemuse Faust, and thus damn him with greater certainty.

Thus the informed reader, in 1587, when the book was new, would be interested in the status of Meph, and how much he really knows. There has been a regular type of best seller ever since, one might say, which appears to bring news about some topic of great current interest but evades committing itself. Here the reader is tantalized; the next chapters seem deliberately badly written, with Meph letting drop his standard answers like an unwilling schoolboy. When asked to describe Lucifer before his fall he demands three days off to mug the subject up, and then reports only what could be heard in any human sermon (GFB, chapter 14; EFB, chapter 13). The book suggests very strongly that Meph did not know, and of course a Middle Spirit would be likely not to. Puck and Ariel would also be found, if one could set them a paper, much below par at general knowledge. As to Hell, he says very firmly that no one can get out of it, and never says he has himself been there (though he once, early on, calls it 'our habitation').[31]

Such are the points which a suspicious reader might have noticed before he arrives at the fierce sermon on Hell (GFB, chapter 16; EFB, chapter 15), where Meph says that the devils in Hell, as well as the human sufferers, have no hope of salvation but that 'we spirits expect it constantly'.[32] This brief aside is the only firm bit of evidence for the pacifist angel theory, because Middle Spirits died like the beasts; if salvation means going to Heaven, they had no hope at all. So at least Paracelsus reports from a very widespread popular opinion; but female nymphs could get there by a human marriage, and one can well believe that male ones resented the distinction. Negotiations at a high level would be in progress. It becomes clear at the end of Part I, a firmly marked stage because Faust now

[31] Sp. 13.
[32] Sp. 59.

recognizes that he is doomed, that Meph wants earnestly to get to Heaven (GFB, chapter 17; EFB, chapter 16). ᶠᶠFaust asks him: 'Suppose you were in my position, a human being created by God, what would you do to please God and mankind?' [Sp. 63]. (This at least carries a hint that God did not create Meph.) Meph says, with no mention of the rest of mankind, that he would do anything whatever to please God, so as to gain 'eternal happiness, glory, and splendour'.[33] Faust agrees that he has been foolish:

> 'But tell me, Mephostophiles, do you wish you were a human being in my position?'
> 'Oh, yes' sighed the Spirit, 'and small question of it. For even if I had sinned against God I would bring myself back into His grace.' [Sp. 65]

Faust says, then surely he can repent too; even now, but Meph says it is too late now that he has committed his heinous sin. It is an insolent contradiction, presumably telling Faust that he has not enough staying power; and it feels intimate and poignant, far more so than the casual remark let drop in the previous chapter, the Hell sermon, that 'we spirits expect constantly'[34] to win salvation. So it is good evidence that Meph is a Middle Spirit, born without the capacity for eternal life, either in Heaven or Hell. If Meph is a pacifist angel, he is in the same position as Faust, hoping to win back the favour of God; and surely he is not trying so hard as he says he would, if he were in that position? Bullying Faust till he feels too weak to attempt repentance does not seem the best way to please God. But theology is always in a cleft stick here; God is not to be blamed for what the devils do, and yet nothing can happen which he does not want to happen. Some might argue that even here Meph is doing the work of God; but it would be a desperate position. Maybe Spies realized that this chapter presumes Meph to be a Middle Spirit, but thought it too good to lose and expected that if challenged it could be explained away. P. F. is all in favour here, and expands the passage enthusiastically.

Faust has next to become an almanac-maker, needing to earn his living apparently; P. F. says (EFB, chapter 17) he 'forgot all good works, and fell to be a calendar-maker',[35] no longer speculating

[33] Sp. 64.
[34] Sp. 59.
[35] EFB, p. 22 (sic, for 20).

about scientific discovery perhaps, whereas the GFB (chapter 18) had never accused him of such thoughts. ᵍᵍTo live where he does, says Meph, makes one good at astronomy; he is too high up to get any earthshine (GFB, chapter 21; not in EFB): 'Here in this gloomy air we spirits and devils live, cast out into the darkness. Here we dwell amidst violent storms, thunder, hail, snow and the like, so that we may tell the seasons of the year and know what the weather should be' [Sp. 73].[36] It is not quite such nonsense as the summary in the GFB; but P. F. was right to make large cuts here and insert his splendid description of the powers of a magus. But what are 'spirits and devils'? The phrase need not mean two different groups, and might be a rough way of describing the pacifist angels, who are demi-devils. They have been 'cast out' from Heaven. But the muddled passage just before, about their not getting the earthshine, implies that they have been cast out from earth; they used to be spirits of nature, but the aggressive devils drove them into hiding – the devils were still an army, and it would be irritated by defeat. They of course had been cast out of Heaven, and no one denied that they sometimes camped in the storm clouds while on business. It seems a neat case of intentional double talk, implying that Meph is a Middle Spirit but keeping an escape in reserve. Even so, Spies need not have realized it.

ʰʰThe brief period of intimacy between Meph and Faust here is part of the story; after recognizing that he is damned, he must be sufficiently comforted not to break out and repent, and then must be flattered by being allowed his great voyages, where he treats Meph curtly as a servant. The high point of the intimacy comes when Meph explains, after being coaxed to tell, that God did not create the world (GFB, chapter 22; not in EFB). In the previous chapter, while lecturing on astronomy, he has said as part of the routine that God made the world; he is not in the least offended, as in Marlowe, when Faust also assumes it. Indeed, he seems to regard the true story as only fit for the men's locker-room, so that he tells several milder versions before he blurts it out.[37] As a plan to delude Faust it is totally ineffective; Faust disbelieves it at once, and never thinks of it again. There was a tradition that proud Satan had denied his

---

[36] The source of this is Hartmann Schedel: *Weltchronik* ('Nuremburg Chronicle'), tr. George Alt, Nürnberg 1493, folios 6af.

[37] Sp. 45, 71.

creation by God,[38] and had offered the same freedom to all other angels, perhaps to win their support, and had thus caused the War in Heaven; but Meph has an entirely different story, calculated as what a Middle Spirit would tell. The earth and sea have always been there, but

> [ii]The Earth had to nourish itself and the Sea separated itself from the Earth; they made an amicable settlement with each other as if they could talk ... But the creation of man and of the heavens they conceded to God so that ultimately they were made subservient to Him. [Sp. 76]

This has been ascribed to Greek philosophers, but it is a bit like central Africa too. It has the wisdom of the primitive. Of course, when God made Heaven, he did not make empty halls; it would not be Heaven without all those angels singing and dancing in his praise. And when some of the angels revolted he made men, a strictly selected few of whom will fill the vacant places. But, when all this fuss is over, the spirits of nature may hope to get back their rights. It is a very clear picture, but the last sentence quoted suggests that Earth and Sea merely allowed God to pretend he had created men and the heavens; if so, the future is still dark. Surely, it is absurd to say that Meph invents this myth merely to unsettle Faust, because it doesn't. It is a secret which the dispossessed Middle Spirits tell to one another, and the devils would be much angered to hear it; Meph yields to pressure from Faust when he tells it, and may have a dim hope of winning a disciple; but he is snubbed, and then passes long years as a servant to the exacting Faust. It is not surprising that he taunts Faust spitefully at the end (GFB, chapter 65; not in EFB); he does not claim to have plotted against Faust, as in the corrupted version of the play. P. F. was right to cut this whole chapter from his translation if he wanted to present Meph as grand and mysterious.

Spies appears to have been in favour of the jeering, perhaps on some theological ground; this final chapter he merely reproduces [from the MS], but he inserts a whole paragraph in chapter 2, when Faust tries to summon the devil, saying 'the Devil must have laughed

---

[38] [156; E0]The heresy, that God did not create any of the spirits, is important to the Satan of Milton and had been propounded by the Satan of St Avitus, Bishop of Vienne, in a Latin poem of about 500 AD.

to himself . . . Faust was fooled to an astonishing degree',[39] and there are some bits of the same coarse fun. He might feel that this tied the story together; the appalling practical joke of the Devil must always be felt behind the jolly pranks of homely Faust in the middle. P. F. was quite right to leave out this insertion too, though so far as we can tell he had no means of knowing it to be an insertion.[40] The merit of the book is to present the two views of Faust, and it is useless to try to unify them; though of course different methods of smoothing over may be needed for publication.

Other spirits in the Faust-book

A detail from the magical performances should be added. [When Faust was asked to present Alexander the Great and his consort before the German] ʲʲEmperor (GFB, chapter 33; EFB, chapter 29), he explained to the Emperor that their mortal bodies cannot literally be revived, but that 'very ancient spirits [*die uhralte Geister*] who have seen the living Alexander and his queen are able to assume their shapes' [Sp. 135]. The word '*ur*' literally means primeval but is often used to mean merely antique; however, this makes little difference. If all the spirits are immortal, and all were created about 6,000 years ago, it is ridiculous to say that a few of them are so old as to have seen Alexander (say 2,000 years ago). The devils are military aristocrats, and would be ashamed to do copying work; the slaves who do it, like the ones who copy the women Faust desires, are drawn from the conquered Middle Spirits. A coherent picture of the relations between devils and Middle Spirits gleams out from these successive hints.

Or rather, this tactful arrangement seems the natural one to presume, but it is thrown into doubt by a brief sentence near the end of the book. Helen of Troy, during the last year of Faust, gives birth to a son, and Faust is his father (GFB, chapter 59; EFB, chapter 55). So she cannot be a devil; even the witch-burners, though very credulous, agreed that devils cannot produce children. The boy told prophecies to his father, who was dead within the year, so he is definitely said to be a magical child. Helen cannot

---

[39] Sp. 7.
[40] Unless he met *Spies* in Frankfurt. See John Henry Jones: *The German and English Faust-books: Parallel Texts* (forthcoming) introduction.

be simply ordered up (GFB, chapter 49; EFB, chapter 45); she must be coaxed, whereas the spirits imitating Alexander and his consort could be called up and behaved like slaves. The contrast is made very plain, and yet nobody says, either in W or in Spies, either in the English text or in the play, even that Helen is royal, let alone that she was the daughter of Jupiter and had been hatched from an egg, thus proving herself to be a demigoddess;[41] though they had all been taught it at school, with whatever degree of disapproval. Poor Alexander had failed to become a god, though he was arranging it when he happened to die in his wild courses, but Helen was born with that status, and Pausanias mentions seeing a shrine to her in her native town of Sparta, around 150 AD. [kk]Though never quite unworshipped, she had had to pass some rather lonely centuries, and need not be blamed for making an arrangement with the devils. In fact she *is* Helen of Troy, one of the kinds of Middle Spirit. Presumably the censors felt that one bit of classical fantasy, just before the horrific end, could not really delude anyone. Manuscript W hedges, saying: 'while she was with Doctor Faustus in his twenty-second to twenty-third year, she puffed herself out as if she were pregnant' (W, chapter 60), and P. F., whether on orders from his censor or anticipating them, puts 'and to his seeming in time she was with child, and in the end brought him a man child' (EFB, p. 74). This is pretty flimsy; where did she get one that prophesied? But Spies does not blench: 'During the final year she became pregnant by him and bore him a son ... This child revealed many future events to Doctor Faustus' [Sp. 199].[42] It seems possible that Spies considered this a genuine part of the legend, in the sense that the historical Faust had said it himself. We have a glimpse of him in Wier, building up his legend by a dangerous joke (calling the Devil his brother-in-law).[43] Anyhow, he or another probably derived it from the legend of Simon Magus (p. 12 of the invaluable Palmer and More); but Simon had said that his Helen, before her many reincarnations, was the Wisdom of God, so this

---

[41] [204; E3]In the play, the speech of adoration by Faust to Helen is almost all about Jupiter, but the connection is not pointed out.

[42] There is a Latin margin note at this point in the GFB, probably the astonished query of a manuscript reader which Spies neglected to delete: '*Quaestio, an Baptizatus fuerit?*', i.e. 'Was it baptized?'

[43] See Palmer & More, p. 107.

detail needed picking out as the suitable one. It was an important step.

^{II}Helen is not romanticized in the Faust-book, any more than in Euripides; she was tops for beauty, so she did a lot of harm. She is a suitable companion for Faust because she is above the law. But she is not viewed with any reverence, even as a human queen; she might be a barmaid. After dinner in his house, the students ask Faust to raise her,[44] and he says he will do for them what he did for the Emperor, perhaps not realizing that this will turn out entirely unlike raising the puppets who imitated Alexander and his consort. Or perhaps he has an inkling, as he uses a different phrase: 'I will present her to you so that you may see her spirit [*geist*] in person exactly as she was in her lifetime' [Sp. 172]. They must not speak or leave their seats. It is Spies who adds the rather bold phrase 'I will present her to you.'[45] When he comes back from his study he leads in Helen, who behaves extremely unlike the previous zombies: 'She looked all around the room with such a shameless and mischievous expression that the students were inflamed with love for her, but since they took her to be a spirit it was not hard for them to forego their passion' [Sp. 173f]. All that prevented a mass rape, apparently, was that the students judged her not solid enough for the purpose. The author titters discreetly here; the ignorant students thought her a spirit, but Faust, leading her back to his study, realized that a pagan goddess is adequately solid. The idea that she might be a devil, an absolute spirit, does not occur to either of them. P. F. as usual feels that the treatment lacks social tone; she is royalty. Her dress becomes 'sumptuous', and

> she looked round about her with a rolling Hawk's eye, a smiling and wanton countenance, which near had[46] inflamed the hearts of the students, but that they persuaded themselves she was a Spirit, wherefore such phantasies passed away lightly with them; and thus fair Helena and Doctor Faustus went out again one with another. (EFB, p. 65)

But at first 'the students were all amazed to see her, esteeming her rather to be a heavenly than an earthly creature'.[47] This is the first

---

[44] GFB, chapter 49: EFB, chapter 45.
[45] That is, it is not present in W.
[46] Text: 'neere hand'.
[47] EFB, p. 65.

suggestion that she is a goddess in person, but it is easily absorbed into admiration for her royal finery and posturing. ᵐᵐThe last sentence of the chapter in the GFB says that the Devil often blinds a man with love, and it is hard to break oneself of a bad habit;[48] P. F. endorses this with added splendour: 'the Devil blindeth and inflameth the heart with lust oftentimes, that men fall in love with Harlots, nay even with Furies, which afterwards cannot lightly be removed' (EFB, p. 65).[49] But he has made her more splendid too.

Marlowe's audience; changelings

ⁿⁿOne thing does emerge from this confusion: the pretence that all men who raise spirits deserve Hell, as Faust is presumed to do, cannot be sensible. It is probably propaganda for witch-burning. Such is what most of the audience would think, not only the author, whose opinions they would probably reject, if they had been told. An attempt to gauge the opinion of the first audience, though necessarily flimsy, must therefore be made.

ᵒᵒIn the main, the first audiences of Marlowe could regard Middle Spirits as suited only to light fantasy, for which they were often employed; in a preface to Greene's *Menaphon* (1589), the supercilious young Nashe mentions trailing a play about Oberon round the provinces as the most hopelessly old-hat thing an actor could get reduced to. But there was an aspect of them which most hearers would have to take seriously, because someone else in the family did. The doctrine that fairies are always trying to steal human babies, leaving something very inferior in their place, was still prominent among midwives and nurses, and made babysitting a more responsible job than now, hardly to be allowed to a man; nurses would insist upon the unhealthy practice of keeping the tiny windows shut, because the fairies came in that way. It frequently gets mentioned in the plays. Probably it was retained as a means of soothing a mother who is gradually discovering that her baby is an imbecile; the story that ᵖᵖher real son has been taken by the fairies, because they thought him so promising, and that he will be having a long life and a fine career, is at least a tempting pacifier. A man who

---

[48] Sp. 175.

[49] The ambiguity of the final statement suggests that P. F. may be writing from bitter personal experience.

denied the belief might incur guilt. Only a cad would remind the mother that her son might have escaped Hell. These intimate commitments would allow the first audiences to feel a salty kind of satisfaction in the absurd plan of Faust: 'Well, there's many of them might do worse than settle for that', and 'he'd be a fool not to stick to it'. This kind of sympathy is all that the play requires, and probably no one responsible for putting it on expected the audience support to be so disastrously warm.

There is a point which seems out of line here but should not be ignored. M. W. Latham, in *The Elizabethan Fairies* (1930)[50], reported that there is no evidence for the full superstition, an imbecile considered as something left in the place of the kidnapped child, before 1560.[51] If so, it appeared just about the time when the other beliefs about Middle Spirits fell into ridicule. The idea that an adolescent may be seduced by the fairies, and that he (or sometimes she) will be lucky ever to escape, and then cannot tell what happened, is very widespread in legend; but why should it become prominent, for babies only, just then? One feels it must have something to do with the witch-burning, because it arose when that storm of terror was boiling up on the Continent and in Scotland, and yet they seem far apart. At any rate, no one can say that it was merely a survival of out-worn superstition, attractive to literary men because so quaint. The Elizabethans were active thinkers even when foolish ones, and the crosscurrents between the various opinions were probably complex.

The censor's anxieties

It is now possible to appreciate the statesmanlike anxiety of King James and the censor of the EFB, granting that such anxiety usually looks absurd when it has turned out to be needless. The effect of admitting that the devils were made of subtle matter, so that they were practically indistinguishable from the Middle Spirits, or for example the pagan gods, and of allowing certain types of devil to live permanently in the stormclouds, was to encourage a very

---

[50] Columbia University Studies in English and Comparative Literature, New York 1930.

[51] [251; E7]She also reports that in Scotland the fairies were believed to pay a fixed tribute of souls to Hell, and to kidnap human babies for that purpose.

undesirable degree of intimacy between mages and devils. The offers of love, in ᵠᵠthe play, between Faust and Meph, made in either direction at different times but never fully accepted, were meant to be very poignant, and would strike a theological listener at an early performance as fully justified satire (of course, he would be sure that all apparent Middle Spirits were devils, with no sex). Quite apart from this dark suspicion, mages had no business to romp with devils, as Faust is plainly doing in GFB, chapter 23. The play has a corresponding attempt at a romp, but it arranges that Faust has just before been thrown into terror, suddenly realizing that his associates are devils. Probably the Queen's censor Tilney, whether aware of Marlowe's trick or not, took the precaution of asking the advice of the censors of print, under the Archbishop, and this text would go to the man who had handled the translation. He would think the play calculated to meet the points he had raised; otherwise rather free, of course, but there could be no theological objection. The reaction of the audiences to the production was what produced the scandal.

The Play

I have next to reveal what was once so carefully hushed up; it should have become fairly obvious. ᵇFaust must have a scheme to escape Hell; this is needed anyhow, if the play is to have its feet on the ground. In the Christian scheme such a thing is impossible; but in popular belief to be stolen by fairies, which involved loss of one's immortal soul, was a well recognized danger, especially for babies. Although belief in Middle Spirits, the philosophical term for fairies, was no longer a reigning intellectual fashion as it had been fifty years before (a university wit in 1590 was likely to express contempt for it), the ideas were still very familiar – only the upside-down use of them, presuming a man who was keen to lose his soul, would come as a surprise. It would readily provoke laughter. The devils were much more powerful than the Middle Spirits, and also had much more incentive to share their powers with a magician, because that might prove a means to damn him; such at least was the standard view.

To explain the original story, Marlowe supposes a Middle Spirit who is a quisling or rather a double agent, professing to work for the devils, and actually inducing them to grant their powers to Faust, but on condition that Faust gives his immortal soul beforehand to ᶜthe quisling. Faust is at first delighted by the results but before long the intense experience becomes too much for his nerves; he decides to repent, supposing he may yet go to Heaven. Meph regards this as a cheat, and counters it by saying that he really is a devil, so that Faust has really sold his soul. To prove it he calls up the Devil and his whole court, at the end of act II (they are a charade put on by his Middle Spirit friends). Faust, after a brief crisis of horror, decides to live bravely for his time on earth, and the play mentions that he does grand things that are useful for his countrymen,[1] but he only feels at peace when playing practical jokes (incidentally this also satisfies the devils, who imagine he is carrying out his promise to be an enemy of mankind). But at the end, when Meph has succeeded in bringing him to the agreed hour of death without having repented, so that Meph gets his immortal soul, nothing happens except that his old friend advances upon him with open arms and a broad smile. The last two words of Faust are 'Ah Mephastophilis', and the censor could not rule how the actor was to speak them. He dies in the arms of his deceitful friend with immense relief, also gratitude, surprise, love, forgiveness, and exhaustion. It is the happiest death in all drama.

[I have already considered the obvious gaps in the surviving texts (see chapter 1) which I have argued to be cuts by the censor.] dThe purpose of these cuts was to keep the audience from even hearing a rumour that one might escape the Judgement by joining the fairies; the act I Chorus and the act II scene with the magicians, both quite short, were all that really needed to go. A plain statement by Faust that he had been deluded, and never intended the Devil to have his soul, would come well at the start of act III; but the situation would be plain without it.

[As I have shown in chapter 4, Faust's plan is hinted at in the Faust-books. Thus] eFaust, when he first talks to Meph in his study, asks only for knowledge, truthful answers to his questions; but Meph says he must pass the request forward, and it may entail Hell. Faust is much more masterful in the English text than the German here, saying 'I will have my request and yet I will not be damned';[2] Meph agrees to return with the answer at twilight, and Faust is left 'pondering with himself how he might obtain his request of the devil without loss of his soul'[3] (not in the German). When Meph comes back, Faust has prepared a list of demands, and the first is that he must be made a spirit, in '*Form und Gestalt*'. Evidently he has decided this will solve his problem, but nothing more is said about it, though it is accepted with the rest. Both the German and the English authors comment that it means becoming a devil, but the word in the pact is merely *geist*, fand Faust wants not to become a devil but a

---

[1] A: 1408f; B: 1943f.

[2] EFB, p. 5 (sic, for 4).

[3] EFB, p. 4 (sic, for 5).

Middle Spirit, because then he will die like a beast, and escape Hell. He hopes therefore that Meph is himself a Middle Spirit, only pretending to be a devil. Faust can make a good offer to such a character, because the Middle Spirits were indignant at being excluded from eternal bliss, and Faust can give Meph his soul. When, in the play, he says, with aching pathos, 'Stay . . . and tell me; what good will my soul do thy Lord',[4] and receives a hideous though hypocritical answer, he is trying to coax Meph into giving the real answer.

Meph need hardly be ashamed of it; indeed one has to ask, if these were their intentions, why did they not reach agreement at once? Because Lucifer will not allow this plan to succeed if he gets to hear of it, and he probably has universal powers of telepathy; but it may be assumed that he does not pay attention universally, so there is hope if Faust and Meph behave in the standard manner for all the twenty-four years. Probably it would be safest to have no showdown at all. Also, Meph would have no more control over Faust, once he had admitted the truth; knowing that he had not, after all, committed an unforgivable sin, Faust could safely perform a grand repentance in his last hour, leaving poor Meph deprived of the soul he had worked so hard for. Indeed, there is a risk of this anyhow, and one can understand that Meph tries to drive him to suicide when he threatens it. Meph is not a good friend, but Marlowe expected male friendships to lead to betrayal; and perhaps Meph is taking the surest way to give his friend what he most wanted. At any rate he is not betraying him into eternal torment, as in the B-text.

Evidence from the play

[g]As the best evidence for this theory of the play is that it gives point and thrust to so many of the details, I will now go through the text picking out some examples.

A number of threats of death in the New Testament have to be interpreted by theologians as threats of Hell, though it seems queer to talk about eternal peace if what you mean is an eternal torment of inconceivable intensity. This point was familiar to the various sects of radical reformers, and the passage quoted by Faust at the start of the play gives a specially clear example of it.

[4] A: 478f; B: 426f.

> ʰThe reward of sin is death; that's hard. . . .
> If we say that we have no sin
> We deceive ourselves, and there's no truth in us.
> Why then belike we must sin,
> And so consequently die.
> Aye, we must die an everlasting death.
> What doctrine call you this? . . . Divinity, adieu.
>   (A: 72–8; B: 69–75)

'The reward of sin is death' is followed (Romans 6.23) by 'the gift of God is eternal life', and the doctor of divinity has the text before him, even if he has forgotten it – Meph could hardly hide it from him by 'turning the leaves' (V. ii, l. 95). Every hearer would know that much had been said to oppose this summarized decision; but the choice of a text might also recall points in its favour. One might naturally suspect, as the Anabaptists had been saying for two generations, that the New Testament writers who speak of 'death' in this way did not all mean 'eternal torture', leaving their commentators to explain what they meant. An Anabaptist Synod held at Venice in 1550 had agreed on ten points of doctrine, among them: 'Only the elect resurrect; . . . the souls of the wicked perish with their bodies'; and two Socinian missionaries who held similar views were expelled from Holland in 1598, after publishing books there (see D. P. Walker: *The Decline of Hell* London (Routledge and Kegan Paul) 1964, pp. 73f, 78). Faust, I submit, is meant to recall this belief, early on in the play, by frequently saying 'death' when he might be expected to say 'Hell', though admittedly his own ideas are very confused. He ends this first scene with the line:

> This night I'll conjure though I die therefore,
>   (A: 199; B: 198)

though surely he knows that he is risking worse than oblivion. His first words to the returning Meph are:

> I charge thee wait upon me whilst I live,
>   (A: 281; B: 262)

an untroubled phrase with no sign of horror for what will come next. Soon he is answering a warning from Meph:

> This word Damnation terrifies not me,
> For I confound Hell in Elyzium.
>> ((A: 303f); B: 284f)

Commentators usually take this to mean that he mixes them together, as one might dilute vitriol with lemonade; a possible meaning for the verb, but not with '*in*' to follow, since it would require 'with' (NED 7). He says he destroys Hell, or brings it to ruin, by putting it in a bath of Elysium; a foolish remark perhaps, confessing 'that he still thinks about Hell, but at least a firm one. (He is still using the same procedure, comparing the views of different societies on the afterlife, in his final despairing speech.)

Within thirty lines of this recall of Elysium he is dictating his message to Lucifer, which has been so firmly avoided by the busy commentators:

> Go bear these tidings to great Lucifer:
> Seeing Faustus hath incurred eternal death
> By desperate thoughts against Jove's deity,
> Say, he surrenders up to him his soul
> So he will spare him four and twenty years . . .
>> ((A: 332–6); B: 312–16)

Surely, this implies an acceptance of the Socinian Belief, that anyone out of favour with God merely fails to receive eternal life. But then, how can he make a bargain with the Devil, who is not going to get his soul anyway? ʲIt does not seem sensible, but the promises to hurt Christians, destroy churches and what not, never carried out, may help to pass it off, for most of the audience at least. Some of them, I submit, must be intended to realize that Faust does not believe what Meph has been telling him – surely his retorts make that very plain – and pretends to send him on an embassy merely to save his face, while hoping for more frankness later. It may well be that Faust, like some Socinians, believed in a period of punishment for bad men before they were allowed the mercy of oblivion; and if Faust thought this he might be consistent in expressing terror when alone but a joking manner when his Spirit is present. It may well be that he is uncertain between different beliefs, so that he has to gamble; that is the usual situation of mankind. But, even to a merely possible Lucifer, he would not send a message saying: 'Because I will have to come to your Hell anyway, if you and your Hell exist, therefore I demand from you beforehand a large reward for agreeing to go there'. It must be Meph that he doubts; he does not believe that Meph can really take a message to Lucifer; and he would just as soon have Meph know that. At the same time, as soon as Meph has gone, Faust assures the audience that he believes Meph at any rate to be real, and able to give him great powers.

The lost Chorus before Act II

It may be answered that this detail is typical of the flippant casualness of Marlowe, finding a dashing piece of poetry for Faust ᵏwithout considering whether it makes sense. But there is no other mere contradiction in the play, and this one comes (in my view) just where it is needed, to make the audience want an explanation. They had to wait during a brief comic scene, also about a struggle for power over men and spirits which is likely to fail, and then should come the Chorus before act II, which is admitted to be 'lost'. The censors demanded to have it cut because it told the secret; that Faust does not believe Meph to be a devil at all, only a Middle Spirit telling lies as usual, and as usual wanting some man to give it his immortal soul. Faust does believe in Hell, and also believes he has already incurred Hell by his desperate thoughts against God (which we are never told, but can easily imagine); or at least, he is afraid of it and thinks it worth guarding against. If he can become a Middle Spirit, and this is his first demand in the pact, he will die like a beast, just as they do: an immense relief. (Consider, most of the audience would have been earnestly warned when young against going with the fairies, who were nice to children only in order to steal their souls, and would have heard much fuss about watching over babies, lest they become changelings. The plan of Faust would strike them as a 'good idea'; why had nobody thought of it before?) One might think then that Faust and Meph could agree on the deal at once; but it is an illicit operation – one cannot expect God to be pleased at the escape of a sinner; and also, these characters work under much greater difficulties than we think usual, because everything they say can be overheard – though it may pass without notice, we must presume. The Chorus needs to explain to the audience, with particular care, that they are not to believe everything Faust says; he thinks of himself as surrounded by a number of invisible listeners, and often speaks with the intention of deceiving them.

The warning is very timely. Nothing in the first act is likely to excite hatred against Faust; except perhaps his saying, as he starts to conjure, that he has 'prayed and sacrificed' to devils,[5] which we may now reflect is probably a lie, known to be false by devils but a bait for Middle Spirits.

Act II

He next has a soliloquy expressing terror, and this need not mean any change of heart; [1]he would not be sensible if he did not recognize his gamble as a very dangerous one. He expresses no desire for Heaven. It is useless to go back, because God cannot love him, he decides, and the speech ends:

> The god thou servest is thine own appetite,
> Wherein is fixed the love of Belzabub.
> To him I'll build an altar and a church
> And offer luke-warm blood of new-born babes.
> (A: 448–51; B: 398–401)

The note of Greg decides that only two lines in the speech 'carry any suggestion of Marlowe', and that the two lines last quoted 'read more like parody'.[6] They do, but why was the parody accepted? Was it the standard custom among Pembroke's Men to destroy their own dramatic effects? The disgust of Greg is no explanation. But if Faust says the lines leering blindly round at the listeners whom he imagines will be pleased with him as a result, a thing they have just been told to observe, that is a dramatic effect, as well as being funny. We never hear of his doing any of these things he promises the *soi-disant* devils he will do, nor do they ever ask him to; surely it is rather gratuitous to assume that the omission has no point.

Another change with the second act is that Faust now says he is acting only for love of Meph, and avoids acknowledging the claims or perhaps the existence of Lucifer. He really is wooing Meph, but in the interest of an unmentioned business deal; it is a wonderful scene,

[5] A: 250; B:233.
[6] Greg, p. 321.

but the audience needs to be given the clue beforehand. Meph
arrives at midnight and says Lucifer has agreed to his serving Faust,
'So he will buy my service with his soul';[7] the words by no means
exclude the idea that Meph, not Lucifer, will get the soul. Faust
answers 'Already Faustus hath hazarded that for thee',[8] still ignoring
Lucifer; but he is told that Lucifer demands his signing a deed of gift.
'Tell me, what good will my soul do thy Lord?'[9] he asks, pathetically
but idly – they both know it can bring Meph eternal bliss. Meph
uses Latin because his answer is feeble (as when asked about
astronomy, later in the act); to have companions in pain is a solace,
he says, and it might be true of himself, but Lucifer has shown no
sign of wanting Faust as a companion. Still, it is a loving reply; he is
particularly Mephasto here, a tender baa-lamb, and claims to suffer
as much as the men he tortures.

> [m]Meph   But tell me, Faustus, shall I have thy soul?
>   And I will be thy slave and wait on thee,
>   And give thee more than thou has wit to ask.
> Faust   Aye, Mephastophilus, I give it thee.
>   (A: 485–8; (B: 433–6))

('I'll give it *him*' says the B-text, as dogma requires, but the effect is
an absurd jolt.)

> Meph   Then, Faustus, stab thine arm courageously
>   And bind thy soul, that at some certain day
>   Great Lucifer may claim it as his own,
>   And then thou be as great as Lucifer.
> Faust   *No*,[10] Mephastophilus, for love of thee
>   I cut mine arm, and with my proper blood
>   Assure my soul to be great Lucifer's,
>   Chief Lord and regent of––perpetual night.
>   View here the blood that trickles from mine arm,
>   And let it be propitious for my wish.
>   (A: 489–98; B: 437–45)

The Bad Angel in the first scene has said to Faust:

---

[7] A: 472; B: 420.
[8] A: 473; B: 421.
[9] A: 479; B: 426f.
[10] See below, (p. 129)

Be thou on earth as Jove is in the sky,
Lord and commander of these elements
(A: 108f; B: 405f)

and Meph, just after he has been summoned has called Lucifer

Arch-regent and commander of all spirits.
(A: 308; B: 289)

It would be impolite of Faust not to echo this formal praise of the absent monster in a ringing line; but he has only to pause before saying 'perpetual night', and we remember that escape is all he is bargaining for. The last two lines are a half-playful addition, as he watches the blood drip into the saucer; *bloodshed* is a term for murder, and he welcomes the demand for a little blood if it is in earnest of real death in the end. Looking back in the quotation, at least two details become more sensible after the praise for 'perpetual night'; Meph may well (as a gentle tease) think that Faust lacks wit if he does not realize that Lucifer is this only; and it is thorough mischief-making for him to insinuate that Faust plans to become as great as Lucifer, except as Death itself is no better than a dead man. I have presumed to put '*No*' instead of 'Lo', because that is plainly what the sense requires, and likely to be removed by an early censor, and also because 'Lo' is entirely outside the vocabulary of Marlowe, who would think it an affectation. All this part is so brilliant when restored that I feel I cannot have gone wrong, though other parts are of course debatable.

Such is the high climax of the series of puns confusing eternal torture with eternal peace, though they are occasionally used again till the grim end of the second act. The two Faust-books have nothing comparable in language, but they do present the mind of Faust as ⁿsomehow unable to believe in an eternal life. His second contract with the Devil (GFB, chapter 53; EFB, chapter 49), made when the terror is coming near, takes for granted that his afterlife will have a natural period, whether in Hell or the grave. Later editors insert a negative here, but whether they are right or not makes little difference; the presumption of Faust in the sources would appear sensible to Marlowe, and is inherent in the tone of outrage which can be heard in the final speech.

What happens next in the play is the congealing of the blood, by an obstacle which Marlowe invented,[11] together with the impossible means of melting it again. The purpose seems to be to make clear that Faust when irritated is unable to keep up the pretence; he is now evidently giving his soul to Meph.

> Why streams it not, that I may write afresh?
> Faustus gives to thee his soul; ah there it stayed.
> Why shouldst thou not? Is not thy soul thy own?
> Then write again, Faustus gives to thee his soul.
>   (A: 506–9; B: 453–6)

Meph fetches a chafer of coals, which melts the blood again, and while Faust is busy he comes forward and speaks to the audience one of those ringing lines which one carries away from a performance of a play by Marlowe:

> O what will not I do to obtain his soul?
>   (A: 514; B: 461)

The next words of Faust admit that the deed has in form given his soul to Lucifer, but surely the cry of Meph, exasperated by the interruption, leaves no doubt that he is the person who expects the use of this soul. Of course we know nothing about the money arrangements of Lucifer's empire; likely enough, unless Meph wins for Lucifer this DD, a worthy prize, the debts of poor Meph will close on him and send him to Hell for the first time. But this, I readily agree with L. C. Knights and his school, is irrelevant conjecture because there is nothing to support it in the text. Both Faust and Meph use the language of passion about their different needs, and this gives a positive warmth to their relations while they are working together. It was the nearest thing to a happy marriage in Marlowe till it was dirtied by the censor.

°The writing which appeared on his hand after he had signed the pact is mentioned rather remotely in the GFB, as if a reader is permitted to find it too much, perhaps making God too specially interested in Faust: '. . . pierced a vein in his left hand – and we are reliably informed that such a hand shows the blood-red impress of the words: *O Homo fuge*' (GFB, chapter 5).[12] *Any* such hand? The

---

[11] Perhaps Marlowe's own pen dried at this point.
[12] Sp. 20.

EFB accepts it outright with a smart addition: 'a vein in his left hand, and for certainty thereupon, were seen on his hand these words written, as if they had been written with blood, *o homo fuge*, whereat the Spirit vanished, but Faustus continued in his damnable mind, and made his writing' (EFB, chapter 5).[13] He is braver than the Devil. Marlowe uses it to drive home the rationality of the plan of Faust:

> Whither should I fly?
> If unto God, he'll throw me down to Hell.
> (A: 518f; B: 465f)

In fact, there is no real distinction between God and the Devil, and a man should try to escape both. The document he is signing, as we hear in a moment when he reads it out, leads off with the demand 'that Faust may be a spirit in form and substance';[14] and this really does provide an escape, if 'a spirit' means a Middle Spirit.

PAfter Faust has read out the pact, Meph demands a formal confirmation:

> Meph Speak Faustus, do you deliver this as your deed?
> Faust Ay, take it, and the devil give thee good on't.
> (A: 558f; B: 504f)

Greg's note says merely 'One is glad to be able to relieve Marlowe of this line'.[15] He has done very little indeed to give himself the power of absolution. The text of the pact is copied from the EFB,[16] so he expects it was on another piece of paper, which ought also to have contained the companion list of demands, from the side of the devils, saying for example that Faust must be an enemy of all Christians. I think Marlowe wanted to leave this out anyway. His [Greg's] real argument (p. 104) is that 'the devil give thee good of it' 'lacks Marlowe's dignity'. But obviously a dramatist does not have to make all his characters dignified, and any Elizabethan might use this phrase if occasion arose. Greg feels something ᵠdifferent: that Faust is made to appear like a delinquent child, cheeking the beak before

[13] EFB, p. 7.
[14] A: 541; B: 488.
[15] Greg, p. 329.
[16] EFB, chapter 6.

being dragged off to punishment; he sounds pathetic and, even worse, silly.[17] But he is within a few lines of making his most famous utterance: 'Come, I think Hell's a fable',[18] and soon afterwards he is assuring Meph that only old women believe there is any pain after this life. He cannot be holding to this rejection consistently, as he has already spoken in the same scene of hazard and torture; but it is a satisfactory form of cheek if he believes he has found a way to escape Hell, so that Meph will never get any good from the bond. In fact, unless a tolerable ground for such a belief had already been presented to the audience, earlier in the play, the whole scene would be simply bad. (A modern audience does not feel this, but only because they think Faust happens to be right.) Such is my main reason for believing that a plan for escape had been presented, and had been cut out fiercely by the censor, causing the immense confusion through which we must pick our way.

ʳMeph continues to pretend to be a devil, and indeed to claim that, even while he speaks he is still in Hell:

> Where we are tortured and remain for ever.
> Hell hath no limits, nor is circumscribed
> In one self place, for where we are is Hell,
> And where Hell is, there must we ever be.
>
> (A: 566–9; B: 512–15)

This is the point where Faust makes his most revolutionary comment: 'Come, I think Hell's a fable'. It is commonly assumed that this was an impudently fatuous thing to say,[19] to a devil whom Faust had himself raised from Hell; but, when you realize that in the genuine Faust-book Meph has never been to Hell either, but talks about it with the excited ignorance of a human preacher, it is not so plain that all the good sense is on his side. This use for *come* appears in the NED (though one would like more information) as a new development, so that it would be 'modern slang'; the speaker

---

[17] [96; E0]Perhaps he disliked in such comments what Bernard Shaw said was the theme of *Ulysses*, 'the fatal habit of low jeering', boasting that you see through the imposture of society without having any plan to make things better.

[18] A: 574.

[19] [40; E5]James Smith, in an influential article ['Marlowe's *Doctor Faustus*', *Scrutiny*, VIII, i, (1939), p. 54: ed.], said that he behaves there 'with a coxcombry which may arouse either hatred or contempt'; yes indeed, or quite different feelings instead.

appeals to the good sense of the hearer, or rather the common background which he can presume that they share – 'Be yourself', he says, 'Remember, we are living in the sixteenth century'. Like many other ᵇdetails that give life to the dialogue, this 'come' is in the A-text but not the B-text, and Greg thinks they are all vulgar 'actor's gags'.[20] Probably the copyist of B thought the same, and also took a gruff attitude towards the charms of Faust, as did Greg and his allies, but we need not suppose that their procedures 'restore the original text'. Christopher Hill, whose work I greatly revere, regards this speech of Meph as a hint of agreement with the Family of Love, who also maintained that Hell is only a state of mind;[21] but many earlier theologians had believed it was both a place and a state of mind, and considered how this was possible. Aquinas explained that devils when sent out on missions were afraid all the time, knowing they must go back, but a later theory said that they had to go on sinning all the time, though they did not want to (rather as Faust is prevented from repenting). But Meph suggests no qualification, and perhaps most of Marlowe's audience would think his belief modern and enlightened. No wonder it irritates Faust; we should remember that, according to the Faust-books, he has just had himself made into a devil, and he has been promised that on signing the deed he will be able to test his condition by immediate trial (GFB, EFB, chapter 4). It seems obvious that the Meph we encounter has not been enduring for thousands of years the tortures he describes, but we cannot be sure what creatures with no bodies may be capable of;

[20] [19; E4]Surely an actor, when given an impressively emotional part, with a lot of fat in it as the phrase goes, does not usually labour to make himself and the author ridiculous – least of all an Elizabethan actor. He might do it to curry favour with the audience, if they were already laughing at the story, but the gossip tells us they were thrilled. And this detail is consistent with many others in the first two acts; the player of Faust must have added his gags steadily. The process ends at the Masque of the Seven Sins, when Lucifer appears in person (for the first time) and puts on a mediocre cabaret entertainment; Faust suddenly loses his nerve and becomes grimly terrified. We in the audience need not blame him, but meanwhile we are being forced to laugh – all the devils are doing 'actors' gags'. Surely it is useless for a critic to think: 'How can I cut down this text so as to make it sufficiently unvulgar for mandarins such as myself?'; he ought to be thinking: 'What can the author have intended by this very odd treatment of the story, which we know to have been found satisfactory by his audiences?'

[21] Christopher Hill: *The World Turned Upside Down*, London (Temple Smith) 1972, p. 140.

Faust, however, can speak from direct experience, reporting that he himself is not at present being tortured. No critic seems to admit that Meph has been fairly caught out here. Faust does not insist upon it, but uses the occasion to demand a wife; he is already sure that Meph is a Middle Spirit, and does not want to force an immediate admission. He was already assuming it just before, when he said:

> Thinkst thou that Faustus is so fond, to imagine
> That after this life there is any pain?
> Tush, these are trifles, and mere old wives' tales.
>   (A: 580–3; B: 525–8)

Talking to a strictly immortal being, it would be bad manners to say 'after this life'; but a Middle Spirit, such as Faust had just become, did have an end to its life, and could be sure of dying like a beast. Of course Faust is talking presumptuously, assuming that the trick has worked, while secretly terrified that he may go to Hell after all; but he is not talking such nonsense as is usually thought.[22] (Of course, an opinion about human experience, which Faust may sometimes entertain but cannot hold consistently, comes out when he calls the belief in Hell an old wives' tale.)

'He blames Meph for robbing him of Heaven, and Meph says it is his own doing. Besides,

> Thinkst thou Heaven is such a glorious thing?
> I tell thee, tis not half so fair as thou,
> Or any man that breathes on earth.
>   (A: 632–4; B: 574–6)

Earlier he had said that remembering the loss of Heaven was as bad as ten thousand Hells, so his supposed knowledge of it is not very consistent. It seems plain that he is making love to Faust here, however insincerely; the betrayal, if there is one, is thus made more terrible. (The final half-line is added after a pause, as if out of shyness, or fearing a rebuff; if Heaven is twice as ugly as the ugliest man, it must look remarkable. The B-text makes this nonsense more prominent by ignoring the delivery and trying to tidy the scansion.) Faust twists the argument round, and one might suppose he has made a firm decision:

[22] See appendix 1, pp. 182–4: 'Debunking'.

Faust	If Heaven was made for man, twas made for me.
	I will renounce this Magic and repent.
	(*Enter the two Angels*)
Good Angel	Faustus repent, yet God will pity thee.
Bad Angel	Thou art a spirit, God cannot pity thee.
Faust	Who buzzeth in my ears I am a spirit?
	Be I a devil yet God may pity me,
	Yea, God will pity me if I repent.
Bad Angel	Ay, but Faustus never shall repent. (*Exit Angels*)
Faust	My heart's so hardened I cannot repent.
	Scarce can I name salvation, faith, or Heaven,
	But fearful echoes thunder in mine ears,
	Faustus thou art damned, then swords and knives,
	Poison, guns, halters and envenomed steel
	Are laid before me to dispatch myself:
	And long ere this I should have slain myself,
	Had not sweet pleasure conquered deep despair.
	Have I not made blind Homer sing to me
	Of Alexander's love, and Oenon's death,
	And hath not he that built the walls of Thebes
	With ravishing sound of his melodious harp
	Made music with my Mephastophilis.
	Why should I die then, or basely despair?
	I am resolved Faustus shall ne'er repent.
	Come, Mephastophilis, let us dispute again,
	And argue of divine astrology.

(A: 637–63; B: 579–603)

Greg's note says that, of course, 'Be I a devil' may mean 'If I were a devil' or 'Though I am a devil', but that 'spirit' means 'devil' anyhow, as is shown by 'the other passsages in which the word is used'.[23] Does Cornelius mean that when he says

> The spirits tell me they can dry the sea,
> And fetch the treasure of all foreign wrecks?
> (A: 177f; B: 166f)

He would not admit being on such easy terms with devils, even if he were; and Valdes expects to be served by 'the spirits of every element'[24] (earth, air, fire, and water), which could only mean

[23] Greg, p. 335.
[24] B:144; A (155) has 'subjects' not 'spirits'.

Middle Spirits. Besides, Faust is accustomed to logical argument, "by his training, and he enjoys it by his nature; he means here, quite fiercely, 'Nay more, even if I were a devil'. To read the passage the other way makes it elegant variation, absurdly out of place. The view that God could not pity the devils, because he was just, had been much discussed but was admissible; whereas it might seem blasphemous to say he could not pity Ariel or Puck. In any case, a devil might be expected to blaspheme; but the position here is quite a standard one, though ruthlessly phrased. God could not accept a Middle Spirit into Heaven, because they had no souls but died like the beasts; in this sense, he could not pity them, or not without a special miracle. The Bad Angel means 'You cannot under the arrangement which you have ingeniously made'. Of course, Marlowe might use Greg's interpretation as a defence when attacked by the censor; but it could not seem obvious to the first audiences, who were accustomed to hearing about fairies and pagan gods. If Marlowe had wanted to impose the clerical use of the word, he would not have left so many loopholes. A spectator who accepts the earlier opinion of Faust, that the devils on the stage are only Middle Spirits, should regard the two Angels as merely products of the unconscious mind of Faust, like the dagger of Macbeth.[25] He may think the same of the nightmare voices and insinuating weapons in

---

[25] [59; E0]Hence they never appear again after the end of the second act, because from then on he is no longer in doubt, but convinced (perhaps wrongly) that he is damned. Some modern critic has objected to the usual view, arguing that the audience could not guess, when other devils were running around, supposedly real, that this Evil Angel was supposed to be imaginary. The audience would not find it hard, because the two Angels (one at each ear) would seem an absurdly old-fashioned theatrical device, from their first appearance ('medieval', as modern commentators dotingly explain). They come just after Faust has ordered the rival magicians to be shown in, and he seems robustly confident; it is his most intellectual or scientific moment, which of course includes feeling public spirited, and he wonders whether he had best use his power to 'resolve me of all ambiguities' or to 'wall all Germany with brass'. He shows no sign of having heard either Angel, but he would consider the Evil one to have given him highly moral advice. Modern debunkers often say that Marlowe's Faust has none of the high motives of the original one; but Marlowe had to concentrate on making Faust popular with his audience, though of course shocking, so the egg-head side of Faust, though firmly expressed, was not made prominent. The next time the two Angels appear, one from each of the big side doors, each heading firmly to one ear, Faust hears what they say, and answers. They are no longer a ridiculous theatrical device, because it is plain that his judgement is deeply torn. This is the start of act II.

the speech that follows, but most of the early audience would think that Meph had sent them. I thought at first that no one could be supposed to kill himself *because* he was afraid of Hell, surely a reason for staying alive, but I found it was accepted as a regular cause for suicide, even in early Christian times, and much more in the sixteenth century. Thus 'when determined to make Meph tell him about Hell (GFB, chapter 16; EFB, chapter 15), Faust says 'ragingly, I will know, or I will not live.' (EFB p. 18 [sic, for 16]). P. F. adds 'ragingly', but that is hardly needed; Faust here is not always irresolute, as we were told in chapter 3.[26] He regards the threat of suicide as a means of getting what he wants. When he is granted a vision of Hell (GFB, chapter 24; EFB, chapter 20), which he finds disagreeable, he tries to kill himself, shouting to the devils: 'Hold, you infernal hags, take here this sacrifice as my last end; the which I justly have deserved'.[27] (It is reported that Swift only laughed once in his life, and it was at the end of the *Tragedy of Tom Thumb*, where the Ghost of Thumb happens to get killed in the general holocaust. He would have enjoyed the Faust-book, but no doubt despised it too much to read it.)

"One must conclude (I still think) that the unconscious mind of the sufferer felt certain that the belief was mere nonsense, so that only the living fear needed bringing to peace; but at least Marlowe's treatment would not seem curious. Whether he is a devil or a Middle Spirit, Meph has a good reason for trying to frighten Faust into suicide as soon as he threatens to repent; Meph is (in our terms) spending a great deal on his expectations from Faust, and may up to the end be cheated by a sanctimonious and highly applauded Faust who welches on him by repenting. One must avoid making Meph too bad, though of course he is rather bad. Marlowe always expects love to work out as betrayal, especially love between two males, but he assumes that the love is real. Meph initially felt that he was saving Faust from eternal torment, and he may still expect that this would be the eventual result if Faust repented, as God is so very unreliable, and Faust too. But also he wants to get his money back (if we may use human language); Meph himself is quite pure, and may be sure of immortal bliss if he takes over this contraband soul, even if by rather rough means. It is the great merit of Marlowe as a dramatist,

[26] Sp. 14.
[27] EFB, p. 28.

though here he only carries a usual trait of Elizabethan drama to its limit, that he always makes his bad characters feel justified by their own standards. So we need not worry about whether Meph sent the nightmares, or the buried half of the judgement of Faust is thrusting its way to the surface; which is fortunate, as there would be no way to tell.

The B-text, in the above quotation [p. 135], gives:

> And long ere this I should have done the deed,
>   (B: 593)

avoiding a repetition of 'kill myself' or thereabouts; and Greg's note says: 'The actor has substituted the more natural phrase, which the author avoided on account of duplication with the preceding line'.[28] The refined author provided an elegant variation, but the coarse actor did not appreciate it. Surely it is plain that the B-editor, when he made this change, showed the same bad taste as Greg. The boyish directness of Faust is one of his few charms; and the slight jolt of the repetition here has the very accent of innocent confession. Even Greg admits that the A-version is 'more natural', and why must the author be forbidden to be natural? (This type of argument, repeated hundreds of times, is what is held to have proved that the B-text is the original one.) Faust then explains that he has not killed himself because of the great pleasure he takes in recovering the arts of the ancient world; it would be 'base' or low-minded to stop living while he can do that. (Meph can join the music easily because the Greek gods were Middle Spirits, just as he is; Marlowe would not want to suggest that they are devils.) Faust is still taking for granted that he can die when he pleases, with no threat of Heaven or Hell, though the other view ˣbeats at the doors of his mind when he sleeps. At the end of this speech, he turns to arguing about astrology, as if it were the same kind of classical pleasure as telling Homer to sing; and yet it rapidly proves fatal. ʸThe dramatic thrill, as in Thomas Hardy, depends upon Meph arriving just too late to hear Faust pronounce his change of mind [that is, his resolve never to repent]; but probably Meph did hear it, and thought it too untrustworthy to alter his plan. The decision was a misfortune for us; the Renaissance might have done much better otherwise; but Meph can hardly be blamed, as the mind of Faust is so plainly ill-prepared.

[28] Greg, p. 335.

ᶻMarlowe's Faust shows very little interest in the advance of knowledge; this has often been pointed out and yet he is commonly accepted as a type case or symbol of Western Man, selling his soul to get hold of the atom bomb. Goethe's *Faust*, though much more concerned with this question, tends to be regarded as a palliation of it, but that of Marlowe as thrusting upon the raw horror. I think this instinct is correct, though Marlowe did all he could to avoid the grisly praise. The 'crude old German chap-book' is highly intellectual here; the initial demand of Faust, when he raises a spirit, has three parts, but all three concern his craving for total and certain knowledge. The spirit warns him of his danger, and after a pause for thought he puts first the demand to be made a spirit, thinking that will make him secure, but his later demands are still mainly for knowledge. This is weakened by the English translator, who feels that power and pleasure have also to be demanded, but the main bones of the story are still clear. Marlowe omits the idea altogether;[29] his Faust only demands to have Meph as his slave, answering questions of course but only as they arise. It is not easy to see why he did this; perhaps he thought it would be boring for the audience to have a donnish Faust, or liable to excite censorship if he started off by threatening to produce advanced opinions. One must realize that he was inherently in a dilemma there, unable to present his spirit either as in favour of Copernicus or as against him; if Marlowe wanted to recommend Copernicus, either procedure would do harm to his cause. What he can present is the break in the mind of Faust, mysterious to most of the audience but decisive when

[29] [151; E5/3]The books given to Faust by spirits should be noticed, as Marlowe has Faust mention them in his last words. In the EFB there are two presentations, after each scene of threat (chs 10, 19), presumably as a mark of forgiveness though it is not said; the first given by Meph, an all-purpose treatise on 'devilish and enchanted arts', the second by Lucifer himself, for transforming himself into an animal. P. F. invented the [152; E5/4]earlier gift of a magic book, perhaps to make him seem more dependent, but also because it was a normal element in such tales which had got left out. Greg, on the other hand, clearly thought that one or other of the two presentations of books in the play, ending II.i and II.ii, must have been added by the ubiquitous hack; we know this because he expresses astonishment at finding that they are both present in the EFB. I find it quaint and queer that so many men whose salaries are paid by universities, and who are themselves genuinely eager to promulgate their views, have insisted (during this century) that Faust could not possibly have wanted knowledge, and that to imagine he did is unhistorical sentimentality. He is presented in the play as a bookworm; it is one of the several comic aspects of him; also his learning is always viewed with earnest respect.

properly acted, which follows on hearing the ignorant replies of Meph about the stars in his shuffling Latin, obviously meant to cover up. Poor Meph, if you accept him as a Middle Spirit, may easily not have read up on this abstruse and tiresome subject, whereas if he were a genuine devil, automatically knowing everything, he would answer like clockwork. Such is what Faust ought to have thought; it was a good opportunity to laugh at the claims of Meph and make him ᵃᵃconfess his real status. Instead the terrors in the mind of Faust, of which we have been warned, overwhelm him; he becomes convinced that Meph really is a devil, and is deliberately cheating him about astronomy. From then on he believes he is doomed to eternal torment.

So there is a reason for holding back, in the play, any mention of his thirst for knowledge, well known from the book; it is being reserved for the crisis of the drama. This scene takes a good deal of acting, to bring the points out; but as usually viewed it is just dismally pointless. To take a minor detail, consider the difficulty of making an audience feel the expected reverence when Meph says:

> Nor are the names of Saturn, Mars, or Jupiter
> Feigned, but are erring stars.
>
> (A: 671f; (B: 612f))

It is true that the names themselves had been supposed to contain inherent magical powers, and poor Meph is trying to cash in on that, but surely the first audiences would find this as ridiculous as a modern one does. The lines only go over well if Meph is presented as struggling to make do, while Faust is already in the grip of an irrelevant delusion. At the breaking-point there is a typical bit of deflating by the B-text. In the A-text, Faust says:

> Well, I am answered. Tell me, who made the world?
>
> (A: 694)

Meph refuses to tell him, and says he is damned, and goes out to fetch help. The B-text has 'Now tell me, who . . .',[30] as if it were just the next step in a lesson, and Greg prattles about the superiority of this reading. '"A" omits *now*, but the word is significant as

---

[30] B: 636.

introducing a new subject, and it also has a spice of sly malice in it.'[31] The word *significant* almost always introduces fatuity in modern criticism, but I doubt whether it has ever introduced greater fatuity than it does here. The challenge to Meph needs to be spoken coldly and abruptly; if it is treated so, an audience, then as now, can grasp at once that he intends defiance. I grant it is not obvious what they are quarrelling about, but that Meph has been answering fishily (or like an official) is plain to all. Retreat into Latin was an obvious means for attempting dignity, but here the Latin is simple enough for many of the audience to realize that the answer is empty, as Faust tells them. I thought at first that [bb]a sentence or two by Faust must have been cut, saying 'then they really are devils', but there is nowhere for this deflating prattle to be inserted; the sequence is extremely tight, and after all he says that the devils have come to take him to Hell before his time, and prays for Christ to 'seek to save' him,[32] and admits that he is damned – all of it a complete break from his earlier talk. And the reason for the change is something prominently mysterious about astronomy, which Meph has failed to tell. The first audiences would have no difficulty in understanding that this meant the scandalous doctrine of Copernicus. Incidentally, the fiery and crystalline spheres were not, as Greg says, usually considered the abode of God and the angels, and when Meph says they have been exploded (which is not in either Faust-book) he is merely trying to use a recent bit of gossip he has heard about astronomy. Donne when he wrote in 'The First Anniversary' 'The element of fire is quite put out'[33] had clearly no idea that this theory was a blasphemous one, however upsetting; and yet, some people in the first audiences may have thought what Greg did – it is a suitable thing for Meph to say. Of course it is unlikely that an intelligent Middle Spirit should not have heard of the Copernican theory, and Marlowe is merely following his text there, as he does conscientiously; but the sudden conviction of Faust that this proves Meph to be a cheat, and a devil, is presented as a kind of madness.

[31] Greg, p. 338.

[32] A: 712; B: 653.

[33] 'An Anatomy of the World: The First Anniversary', l. 206 (*The Poems of John Donne*, ed. H. J. C. Grierson, London (OUP) 1929, p. 214).

Act II: The visit of the devils

Lucifer and Belsabub and their attendants are friends of Meph, pretending to be devils for fun; the main evidence for this is in the sex joke: ^{cc}a parade of devils arrives, quite expensively dressed and speaking in a top-class manner, and we find at once that Belsabub is the female consort of Lucifer. Oddly enough, the B-text is the one that spells it out; all the words are in the A-text, but with none allotted to Belsabub. The explanation seems plain; the words were what the Queen's censor Tilney must be induced to let by, and a slight rearrangement of the speakers would be beneath his attention. So the intended delivery need not be written into the text passed by the censor. Here for once at least a knowledge of actual performance may be allowed to glimmer into the mind of the B-text editor. He gives:

Faust	O what art thou that lookst so terribly.
Lucifer	I am Lucifer, and this is my companion Prince in Hell.
Faust	O Faustus, they are come to fetch thy soul.
Belsabub	We are come to tell thee thou dost injure us.
Lucifer	Thou callst on Christ, contrary to thy promise.
Belsabub	Thou shouldst not think on God.
Lucifer	Think on the devil.
Belsabub	And his dam too.
Faust	Nor will Faust henceforth; pardon him for this,

(B: 657–65)

and then, to return to words only present in the A-text, ^{dd}Faust in his terror promises Lucifer

> Never to name God, or to pray to him,
> To burn his Scriptures, slay his Ministers,
> And make my spirits pull his churches down.
> (A: 726–8)

^{ee}(The presence of a ready throng of slave spirits is taken for granted, and surely they are not all veterans who date back to the War in ^{ff}Heaven?)

^{gg}Lucifer Do so, and we will highly gratify thee, Faustus,
     We are come from Hell to show thee some pastime; sit down,
     and . . .

(A: 728–30)

In the B-text, this has been cut and expanded:

  Lucifer So shalt thou show thyself an obedient servant,
      And we will highly gratify thee for it.

(B: 667f)

Of course a real top devil would have to express satisfaction at being obeyed, but no devil ever asks Faust to act on these promises, ^{hh}and surely this makes the reply of the A-text Lucifer, the bogus one, much the more convincing. It is a great feature of Faust that he refuses to be downed (very properly, as he lives next door to Punch) and as soon as he is convinced that he is doomed to Hell, in spite of his earnest precautions, he becomes fascinated by Hell, demanding to know all about it. ('I will know or I will not live', GFB, chapter 16).[34]

ⁱⁱWe may expect the Lord of the Flies to be large and a bit monstrous, looking hardly less terrible than Lucifer; but just now he is decked out as a consort, and simpers and bridles when he introduces himself as the Devil's dam. This forces the audience to laugh. No doubt a modern producer might gloss it over tactfully, but I doubt if an Elizabethan one even could, and anyhow why should he want to? The author plainly wanted a laugh here. But a subtle distinction needs to be made. Lucifer himself is shown as wanting to be playful, giving indeed a firm instruction but feeling sure it will be obeyed, and meanwhile providing a light entertainment; gentlemanly ease is his note, while hoping to convey an appalling threat behind it. Faust of course grasps this, and it makes him discount any apparent comedy in the scene. But the joke about the sex-life of Lucifer and Belsabub is like a political cartoon; it would only be presented by a fierce opponent. The audience might be tempted to think that dramatic illusion has been abandoned; they are only looking at human actors, jeering at devils. They will not think so if they have followed the story, as explained in the missing Chorus before act II; they are looking at genuinely supernatural beings, with

---

[34] Sp. 50ff.

alarmingly great powers; but these creatures are only pretending to be devils, while feeling a good deal of hatred for them, so that the imitation falls at moments into crude farce, just like what human actors would do. I submit that this allows some genuine interest to be taken in the Masque of the Sins, which is otherwise a rather flat cabaret show (one should realize that Theophrastus had given classical authority to the knowing thumbnail sketch of a familiar type, so that it would appear absolutely standard to the first audiences). Also they can feel comfortable about Faust, as well as wiser than he is. He has suddenly become convinced that his plan has failed, and that he is doomed to eternal torture; but they are confident that he has not signed a pact with the Devil, and should therefore be pretty safe even if he has failed to become a Middle Spirit.

ᵗⁱWhen Faust regards the Masque as a preview of Hell he separates himself from the audience; and this should be particularly clear at the end, when Lucifer asks jovially:

> Now, Faustus, how dost thou like this?
> Faustus   O this feeds my soul.
> Lucifer   Tut, Faustus, in Hell is all manner of delight.
> Faustus   O I might see Hell, and return again, how happy were I then.
> (A: 796–800)

In the B-text he is made to say: 'O how this sight doth delight my soul',[35] removing him from his mad absorption only at the cost of making him sound fatuous. A few recent critics have blamed him for his vice of 'curiosity', and he does show it in this craving to grasp Hell before he arrives; but he only does it after he finds himself doomed to Hell, as a means of handling life while certain of Hell. I feel an almost personal dislike for critics who accuse Faust of cowardice.

At the end of this scene, which means Hell to him but not to the others, Lucifer gives him a book and says he will have him fetched at midnight to see Hell, since he would like to. Faust says he will keep the book 'chary as his life';[36] ᵏᵏthere should be a shudder on the key word 'life'; he means 'as carefully as I will avoid going to Hell before my time'. At the end of his previous scene with Meph he was also

[35]   B: 731.
[36]   A: 806; B: 739.

given a book, and they were innocently happy being bookworms together. The point of the repetition is to drive home the contrast of feeling: the first time, he felt safe from Hell, the second time he is sure of his doom. (Of course, unless you recognize the suppressed story, the repetition is footling; that is why the B-editor left the first part out, and Greg thought it had been added by a producer.) Here then Faust touches rock-bottom,[37] and the exhilaration of the Chorus to the third act comes as an astonishment. "It says that Faust was taken up to the stars, so that he has made sure about astronomy, and was then given a thorough tour of the civilized world. Of course a modern reader knows that Faust couldn't learn whether Copernicus was right by any amount of ""peering from a spaceship, but this was probably not clear to Marlowe and his audiences.[38] However, it would no longer matter to Faust, whose mind has now become settled; he is certain of eternal torment, but can arrange during his life to publish very much the best almanacs (or prophecies). That is the old picture, and Marlowe accepted it, at least in the praise of Faust for his learning after his death. But Marlowe's character had received much more of a jolt than the old Faust, because he had expected more important items of knowledge. But though he had been fobbed off, and his future prospects were appalling, still it would be base to despair. He would at least have fun, while he yet could; and this has won him permanent regard, except among modern literary critics.

Act III

Granting that this was the intention, it must be admitted that act III starts very badly. Faust talks like a guide book for twenty-four lines. Maybe, as Greg suggests, the A-text had been altered from the old prompt-book to suit productions where there was no balcony; and quite possibly there was a first draft available, actually written by Marlowe before the right use of the balcony had been suggested. But it must be Meph who talks like a guide book. Faust is still sulking furiously, though they have been on tour for some time; Meph is

37 [84; E0]The actor should interpret him as immensely knocked back, and of course the comic scenes are removed; they are very much out of place here.
38 See appendix 1: 'Astronomy in the play'.

tirelessly coaxing. We know the decor from Henslowe's *Diary*: 'One
dragon for Faustus, One city of Rome'. First then we have the
Chorus, out on the apron stage, saying that Faust has been taken to
the stars on a dragon to satisfy his craving for knowledge, then the
curtain above is opened to show a backcloth of clouds, and this
dragon appears, pulled slowly across the upper stage, with Faust
sulking and Meph praising Trier, Paris, Naples, Venice, Padua. It
rounds the corner while he is still talking, and the upper curtain
closes; servants carrying dishes may perhaps cross the main stage.
The upper curtain opens again to show the city of Rome, and the
dragon reappears, with its passengers – Meph pointing out the seven
hills and the Tiber, and Faust refusing to look. Then they appear,
probably at one of the big side doors, with a grand tapestry behind it
and a bust on a pedestal. Faust says with calculated insolence 'Have
you brought me to Rome, as I told you?' and Meph says 'You are in
the private withdrawing-room of the Pope.' Faust then makes the
speech that Greg[39] considered an obvious parody of the style of
nnMarlowe, because it is ludicrously pompous, when he is only
saying he doesn't mind seeing the sights:

> Now, by the kingdoms of infernal rule,
> Of Styx, of Acheron and the fiery lake
> Of ever-burning Phlegethon, I swear
> That I do long to see the monuments
> And situation of bright splendent Rome.
> Come, therefore, let's away.
>   (A: 862–7; B: 848–53)

But the decision to sympathize with the works of man, instead of
doing harm as he promised to the Devil, is what turns him into a
rogue-demigod, immensely popular; and he has only just arrived at
the belief that he is certain of Hell. It is a very dramatic speech, given
the proper setting for it. So in its way is the reply of Meph, who says
in effect, 'Yes, but you'd better have some lunch first, and you know
you wanted to box the Pope's ears, so take some part in holy Peter's
feast'.[40] Then the main back curtain opens on the Pope's long dinner
table, and we return to the existing text with

[39] Greg, p. 349.
[40] A: 868–71.

now, Faustus, to the feast;
The Pope had never such a frolic guest.
(B: 1071f)

The table only has guests on the far side, and Faust as he advances is in front of it, on the wrong side, but it would be a good thing to have him jump over the table, just next to the Pope. (The reason why everything about Pope Bruno ought to be omitted, as not added till 1602, is that it is irrelevant to the central interest of the story, which is otherwise followed closely.)

°°After he has boxed the Pope's ears, and Meph has foreseen that Faust will be damned to Hell by the Pope's officials, he becomes rather jolly, with two lines more of it in the A-text[41] (and Greg (p. 356) picks on this tiny extra bit to bemoan the crudity of the anti-papal sentiment). One should remember that the anathema of the Pope would give the Protestant audience strong reason to feel that he could not really go to Hell in the end. Of course nobody wanted a comic scene after this big joke, so the placing of the comics is wrong as usual there; what you were pleased to see was the cool serene flight of the dragon over Constantinople, with Meph pointing out St Sophia and the Bosphorus. This painting of a city from the air was of course not on Henslowe's list, because the Sultan scenes had already been forbidden when he bought the text and its extra.[42] Then the back curtain opened upon exactly the same banquet scene again, PPexcept for oriental robes over papal uniforms, but this time Faust is visible, dressed as 'a pope', and heralded by fireworks (in fact the scene is again copied from the Faust-book directly).[43] He says he is Mahomet, and all escape except the Sultan, who is fixed to his chair. He demands the keys to the harem, which are handed over; and he goes to the recommended door, with some pious phrase about how he will edify the inmates. The curtain closes, and the two noisy comics run on outside with a silver goblet, chased by the innkeeper;[44] Robin is gasping out an incantation. Meph after a

---

[41] A: 912f.

[42] [86; E0](It was revived very clumsily after the Restoration, when the incident with the Pope was forbidden.) [See the 1663 edition 'in which the Roman scenes are replaced by one at the court of the Soldan of Babylon' (Greg, p. 14): ed.]

[43] GFB, chapter 26; EFB, chapter 22.

[44] [86; E0]Here, after all, is where a lapse of time needs to be marked, six busy days for Faust, and an outside scene is convenient at this point, to allow for [87; E0]some

suitable pause bursts out through the curtains, furious because he has been summoned from Constantinople. While the comics are hiding from him in the folds of the curtain they have animal heads fitted onto them (these have disappeared when they join the indignation meeting against Faust near the end of act IV), but they are somehow unable to escape through the curtain, and they run off sideways. The middle third of it opens for an intimate harem scene, with soft brightly coloured cushions, where the six wives assure the Sultan that the god Mahomet was quite normal, for all six days, and faintly insinuate that he did the work better than their husband. The Sultan rebukes the silly girls, and says that we Moslems know how to give supreme honour to our prophet without confusing him with the Creator (it is hard to see under what head the author could be punished for giving him this orthodox comment, but it would add to the distaste felt by the censor). I hope he added what was invented for him by P. F., that any children born of the visit would be brought up as heroes.

⁹⁹Even after restoring the Sultan, the third act would still be rather short in lines, but would not feel so, as there is so much action; indeed it probably would not be shorter than the fourth in time. However, the first two acts contain at least half the lines of the play, and a modern production should have its one interval there.

Act IV

The Chorus before the fourth act survives only in the A-text, which reports what was left after the cuts, because for practical use the third act had now become ridiculously short (and the B-text aims at giving an actable version). Faust is now on his way home, wanting to be accepted fairly quietly, and his friends are glad to receive him; the idea that his visit to the stars has made him useful at astrology gets a mention here. He needs first to have a success with a grandee on his own side (after the shocks for two grand enemies), so he is at once shown with 'the German Emperor'.⁴⁵ In the A-text, the Emperor says he wants a sight of Alexander, because

---

decoration of the harem on the inner stage. The comic characters are really worthwhile here, greatly adding to the bustle of the whole affair – the fun of the harem ladies needs to be rather quiet and reflective.

⁴⁵ B: 1234.

> when I hear but motion made of him
> It grieves my soul I never saw the man.
>
> (A: 1067)

The B-text makes him say

> We would behold that famous conqueror,
> Great Alexander, and his Paramour,
> In their true shapes, and state majestical,
> That we may wonder at their excellence.
>
> (B: 1264–7)

It seems to me astonishing that Greg could prefer this, but at least, if it is an imitation of Marlowe, it is done by a hack with a good ear. All the same, the brevity and dignity of the A-text is much needed to make the magic feel tolerably real.

I have now to consider how this scene is joined on to the next. Greg, arguing that a good deal of the B-text is original, says that any production needs here a scene about the knight who is given antlers and raises an army for revenge. He agrees that the scenes that survive were not written by Marlowe, but maintains that Marlowe planned for them and farmed them out.[46] It is ᵣtrue that both Faust-books give two chapters to this fight for revenge, far apart;[47] the insult rankles, in the mind of the aristocrat, and the effect is to give Faust the credit of a military commander, as he calls up his devils. I don't deny that Marlowe's Faust in his speech to Helen of Troy shortly before death imagines himself as fighting for her in the Trojan War; but one could take that argument backwards; Marlowe (while otherwise ignoring that side of him) felt that this rather pathetic expression of willingness was enough recognition of it. He is plainly not a military type, and the added scenes are a slight distraction, though sensibly chosen when the censor's cuts created a need for fill-ups. Also, Greg might say that Faust needs to be off the stage here, partly as a relief to himself and the audience, partly to mark lapse of time. But he is off the stage for quite a time both before and after (as I agree to restoring the tavern scenes from the B-text). As to the lapse of time, it is a very different thing from the flurry of the revenge scenes; what has to be suggested somehow is the passing of twenty

[46] Greg, p. 116.
[47] GFB, chapters 35, 56; EFB, chapters 31, 52.

years. I suggest that the A-text makes a fair attempt, and the B-text none at all.

After releasing the knight from the window by telling Meph to remove his antlers, adding a sufficient farewell, 'hereafter speak well of scholars', Faust says:

> Now, my good lord, having done my duty, I humbly take my
> leave.
> Emperor   Farewell master Doctor, yet ere you go, expect from me a
> bounteous reward.
>
> (A: 1131–3)

(The B-text absurdly makes him say 'Thou shalt command the state of Germany'.)[48] Faust bows himself out to the front, and the back curtain closes. A servant comes out from the side with Faust's travel bag which Meph takes over, and then a more grandly dressed servant with a bag that evidently contains the reward; Faust tips him. He sighs and stretches himself. He says:

> Now, Mephastophilis, the restless course that time
> Doth run with calm and silent foot,
> Shortening my days and thread of vital life,
> Calls for the payment of my latest years.
> Therefore, sweet Mephastophilis, let us make haste to
> Wittenberg.
> Meph   What, will you go on horseback, or on foot?
> Faust   Nay, till I am past this fair and pleasant green,
> I'll walk on foot.
>
> (A: 1134–42)

(None of this is in the B-text.) Meph goes off to the other side door carrying both bags, evidently to the stables; Faust walks ˢˢslowly round the outside of the apron stage, as is often done by processions. Like the men in a procession he is impassive, not looking about. The audience should be curious to know what will happen next. When he comes round to the back of the stage the curtain opens on the usual pub set (having changed from the reception room of the Emperor); there is an easy chair, and Faust sinks into it, apparently to sleep. The horse trader comes fussing in, and it becomes clear that Faust was ready to play a trick on him (there seems no advantage to

[48] B: 1369.

us in calling him a 'horse-courser' as in the stage direction; surely, as he is simply a trader, the term is misused).

We must now suppose quite a bit of time to pass, while the trader collects the horse, tries him out in the nearest sheet of water, and comes indignantly back; Faust meanwhile sleeps, or so the direction assures us. We last heard him say:

> Away, you villain; what, dost think I am a horse-doctor?
> What art thou Faustus but a man condemned to die?
> Thy fatal time doth draw to final end;
> Despair doth drive distrust into my thoughts,
> Confound these passions with a quiet sleep:
> Tush, Christ did call the thief upon the Cross,
> Then rest thee, Faustus, quiet in conceit.
>
> (A: 1168–74; (B: 1546–51))

This is allowed into the B-text, but it is intensely resented by Greg, who says in his note: '*Tush* is not it itself un-Marlowan (introduction, p. 51), but I hope and believe that its use here is';[49] and in the introduction: 'Nothing could be further from his manner than the combined piety and bad taste' of this line, 'a vein of rather sentimental piety' which is probably 'intruded' by Rowley rather than Decker (p. 118). But it is no use pronouncing about the style of a dramatist unless you understand what he is doing with his characters. Faust is not belittling the religion here so much as blaming himself for stupidity. Marlowe might agree with Greg that it was vulgar of Faust to become cosy as he settled down, and yet claim that such was the story in the Faust-book. When the horse trader clamours to reproach Faust, Meph refuses to let him approach, saying 'he's fast asleep, come at some other time'[50] . . . 'I tell thee he has not slept this eight nights',[51] and yet, whether asleep or not, he is clutching the false leg ready to be pulled away. The B-text omits the whole ten-line section of defending his sleep, and Greg has no comment there, and yet it is clearly relevant to the story; people certain they were going to Hell really did find it hard to sleep. The Faust-book in its third part has a lot of horseplay of this kind, and Marlowe uses only one such incident, the one in which Faust

---

[49] Greg, p. 372.
[50] A: 1192.
[51] A: 1196.

appears to be asleep ᵗᵗso as to play his trick; and it is Marlowe who inserts the idea that Faust would have difficulty in sleeping. Surely it cannot be argued that he did not intend this sequence.

We know he does not need the money that he gets from the horse trader, because we have just seen him win a large reward. The social jump is also meant to be startling, and we lose both effects if he has to appear, in between, as commander of a platoon of devils. The horseplay, we are to gather, is a part of his coming home, a return to his origins. ᵘᵘBoth Faust and Marlowe were low-class boys sent to university for their brains, expected to make good priests; Marlowe could not go home for the vacations, and his family led a fairly rumbustious life in Canterbury, at least they frequently went to law. Under the discipline of Corpus, Marlowe could imagine himself doomed to Hell, but not when among more familiar types; and he would regard the psychology of Faust as a thing he could easily understand.⁵² ᵛᵛHorseplay, in fact, is homey; and the comfort arises not chiefly because it makes Faust popular, though that is an incidental result, but because a low comedian obviously does not go to Hell – he would seem out of place there. After all, Faust has now turned himself into the likeness of Robin, who has also raised a devil by magic, and nobody supposes that Robin will go to Hell. What is arresting about the Faust-book is precisely this, that it presents side by side the giant rogue and the tragic martyr to knowledge; perhaps simply because the readers enjoyed both, but they had somehow to feel (and the censor of the book too) that the joint pleasure was not forbidden. Probably Marlowe thought he had explained the original intention of the Faust-book, but I suppose one would have to say it was an unconscious intention, even if he did. A best seller, aimed at satisfying a crowd, is rather more likely to have an unconscious intention than a masterpiece.

To go back a bit, Greg speaks with some contempt of the Chorus to act IV, as it is not in the B-text, saying that it seems 'to have been drafted with little regard to the play as it stands. It represents

---

⁵² [286; E5]There is no reason to [287; E6]think Marlowe of lower class than Shakespeare, who made friends among landowners near Stratford (and was lucky not to get involved in the Gunpowder Plot that way), but Canterbury was probably more stratified, being so much bigger. Still, their temperaments are probably the chief cause of the difference. The point is merely that Marlowe felt himself well able to express a working-class point of view, and had no duty to stick to a middle-class one.

Faustus, instead of passing from Rome to Innsbruck via Constantinople, returning home and spending some time among his friends before his fame reaches the Emperor'.[53] But the Chorus here simply reports the Faust-book, and then the play jumps forward to the meeting with the Emperor; there is no contradiction ʷʷat all between the Chorus and the scenes that follow. Of course the comic scenes are misplaced as usual, but nobody supposes that this was planned by the author. And there is a later detail from which we could deduce that Faust has been home for some time, before meeting the Emperor. In the last scenes of act IV, there is a carter indignant with Faust because he ate up a whole load of hay, having only paid three farthings; the horse trader is also complaining, and Robin and Dick though they have only Meph to blame (and they no longer have the faces of a dog and an ape, so his punishment was very mild), and finally the Hostess is worrying about who pays for the ale. They sound like a crowd, but Marlowe has managed to present only one of these rough incidents which critics find so bad and so frequent, and his Faust has only been responsible for one other, off stage. Still, if you consider when Faust did this to the carter, he must have done it after returning to Germany and before meeting the Emperor, because the later scenes are continuous. The comic scenes are all short, and if the dead wood of the later additions were cut out the play would run smoothly. Of course I agree that horseplay is not fun; I feel with my colleagues there; but consider how much we have to suffer from Shakespeare, and in *Faust* the supposed fun is more to the point.

Faust gets no sleep after defeating the horse trader, as his servant Wagner comes in to say that the Duke of Anhalt wants him, and he sets off at once. The anti-Faust indignation meeting arrives at the pub, expecting to find him there, and he transfers them (by magic, of course) to the castle of the Duke. He is off the stage here for about sixty lines, while they denounce him to one another outside the curtain; we may suppose them in a kind of porch, waiting till the Hostess has an inner room ready for them. (The chair on which Faust slept was shown within this curtain, which was briefly closed while Meph was trying to fend off the horse trader, so we are not surprised to have it closed again when Faust leaves.) Then the angry party are let through the curtain, saying they will drink a while

[53] Greg, p. 358.

before they seek out the Doctor; and Faust enters on the outer stage by a side door with the Duke and Duchess. They are in the open, as Faust is congratulated on making an enchanted castle in the air; then the back curtain is drawn, and another ^{xx}grand reception room is shown, with a tapestry and oak chairs; it is here that Faust sends Meph to fetch the grapes for the Duchess. The clowns then bang on the door at the back of the inner stage, and Faust asks for them to be let in; they are dimly conscious that they are somewhere unexpected, but too drunk to behave accordingly, so they are noisily absurd till Faust strikes them dumb, one after another. The act ends with the Duke, ready to reward Faust, saying (before the curtain closes):

> His artful sport drives all sad thoughts away;
>
> (B: 1266)

and at once we have Wagner as Chorus on the open stage saying:

> I think my master means to die shortly.
>
> (A: 1267; B: 1777)

The technique is not intended to deceive; the audience is meant to realize that the fourth act has jumped over twenty years, and that the amble of Faust over the pleasant green covered 300 miles, and yet feel that the essential truth was told by this untroubled procedure. Greg says he gets an impression that an already written scene is being adapted for a new purpose (p. 119), and it is true that there are logical fissures, but this is not the reason why. You might indeed save appearances by a theory that Faust just went, by his power as a spirit, from a pub near Innsbruck to a pub near Wittenberg, where the horse trader expected him, and that the two lines just quoted are assumed to be spoken twenty years apart. But this is not what the scenes feel like; the walk round the apron needs to be accepted as a kind of incantation, if only as an earnest that the twenty years were all pretty like the offered sample. Any plan for turning the story into a play would need to offer this earnest somehow. And a few minutes of sheer peace, considering the incessant racket of the play, are likely to stand out. The act is a fragile structure, though so boldly designed, and it is completely destroyed by admitting any later addition.

Modern critics often express intense contempt for Faust because he had grapes brought for the Duchess. The crawling toad-eater! A decent man would have brought them for the wife of the socialist district planner. This would be a foolish attitude even now, and it is irrelevant to the time of Faust. He plans a peaceful retirement in his own district; the frontier of the Principality of Anhalt was about five miles from Wittenberg, though ʸʸno doubt the Duke's castle would be as much as twenty miles away. The sequence of receivers for his main shows of magic seems carefully planned in the Faust-book, and Marlowe follows it exactly. The Pope and the Sultan are positive enemies of his own people, and treated as such; the Emperor is a Roman Catholic, but after all he is 'the German Emperor', as Marlowe's stage direction calls him, and Faust is willing to perform for him. The Prince of Anhalt, in the time of the book and the play, was a leading Protestant ruler and an ally of Elizabeth, so no wonder Marlowe makes Faust say of him 'an honourable gentleman, to whom I must be no niggard of my cunning'[54] and the Faust-book makes him do a series of wonders at the castle. Finally the 'glorious deed' of raising Helen is done for the students out of friendship alone. It is not a contemptible record. But he had once proposed to dress all the students in silk, and wall all Germany with defensive brass; what has happened to prevent him?

The Faust-book does not tell us what he had hoped to learn, when he first raised Mephostophiles and demanded nothing but knowledge; but it is clear that an important landing place has been reached at the end of the first part, when Faust has been beaten down into realizing that he is doomed to Hell, and that spirits are tormented there as well as men; and the second part begins (GFB, chapter 18) with the words 'Since the spirit would no longer answer any questions concerned with divinity Doctor Faustus had no option but to make the best of it'.[55] So he sold his soul to the Devil only to gain further knowledge of theology? This is obviously a hush-up, smudged in for fear of persecution, or anyhow Marlowe would have thought so at once. The EFB makes it less absurd, saying that the spirit refused to answer any more of 'such like questions' so Faust 'forgot all good works, and fell to be a calendar-maker',[56] but even

---

[54] A: 1234f; B: 1575f.
[55] Sp. 66.
[56] EFB, p. 22 (sic, for 20).

here one may reflect that Faust has not asked any questions relevant to good works. Nor yet to bad ones; it is only the EFB that says he became 'an enemy to all mankind' (EFB, chapter 4), but the GFB makes him swear to 'be an enemy to all professed Christians',[57] and he himself has strong lines about it in the play, yet he never does any harm till right at the end. Marlowe as a dramatist hardly ever explains things, knowing the advantage of leaving them open; but he would be sure to realize these gaps in his story, and very likely to check [zz]his source. What we can observe is that he does his best to ride over the gaps by giving opportunities for the actor, and that he reports the third part of the Faust-book exactly when he makes Faust in later years deliberately settle down in Wittenberg, as a popular and often useful eccentric, needing only minor outbreaks of horseplay to make him cheerful, who is astonished and indignant when he finds himself due for eternal torment. He had found that he was not allowed to do anything grander, so the modern critic need not be spitefully contemptuous of him. [aaa]There is no need to deny that he achieves less than he set out to do, but his placid comic-uncle later life, greatly admired in his time, should not be jeered at if it is part of a heroic endurance. The poet Cowper, also convinced he had incurred eternal torment, and at his best when writing about heroes, could more fairly be jeered at for his mufflers and his pet hares. The astonishment of Faust at his release, though the audience has been led to expect it so firmly, his delighted gratitude at finding that the false friend has deserved his love after all, his eager acceptance of annihilation – nothing less than this unique death scene could be adequate after the fierce rapid contrasts of the fifth act.

Act V

[bbb]Given the basic clue, the textual problems of the last act become straightforward. One must realize that, even on Greg's theory, the editor of the B-text had a printed edition of the A-text before him when he destroyed the poetry and printed instead a debunking version of the students' comments on Helen of Troy.[58] Whether or

---

[57] Sp. 17. It is interesting to note that Widman's Faustus (*Warhafftige Historie*, (1599), Book I, chapter 9) refuses to be an enemy to *all* mankind, agreeing only to hate his own enemies.
[58] See appendix 1: 'Debunking'.

not he was printing the first draft of Marlowe (an enormously improbable theory) he was printing the text he preferred, another element in a pietistic treatment of the ending of the play. Then Old Man speaks up, with entirely different speeches in A and B, and Greg finds practically no difference between them, except that the style in A is shockingly vulgar. He can find no explanation, except that perhaps a greedy actor might have written A for himself, as more exciting. Surely they have one basic difference; A recommends ^{ccc}the pleasures of Heaven, whereas B says 'No mortal can express the pains of Hell'.[59] But also, rather by contrast, whereas A seeks to convert Faust by infecting him with loathing for his sexual pleasures:

> Break, heart, drop blood, and mingle it with tears,
> Tears falling from repentant heaviness
> Of thy most vile and loathsome filthiness,
> The stench whereof corrupts the inward soul
> With such flagitious crimes *or* heinous sins
> As no commiseration may expel,
> But mercy Faustus of thy Saviour sweet
> Whose blood alone must wash away thy guilt.
>
> (A: 1306–13)

The grammatical complaints of Greg are I think trivial except for 'crimes *of* sins',[60] where I have written in the emendation which would readily be granted to Shakespeare. It is of course an excited speech, and would be deliberately cooked up as such by Marlowe, who would admit no sympathy for it. But he intended it seriously, because he aimed here at a radical opposition of moral judgements. Old Man in A has two speeches, for the two appearances of Helen of Troy, and in both he gives no sign of knowing she is present; but this is the less surprising because, at this stage of the play, hardly anybody pays attention to anybody else, and probably he just refuses to look at her. He agrees with Greg and Dame Helen Gardner that to love Helen will mean certain damnation for Faust, because she is a devil; but Faust thinks she is a Middle Spirit, being undoubtedly a daughter of Jupiter (hatched from an egg); and after all those years of sex with devils, to love a real lady will mean turning over a new leaf, perhaps with some effort. The opposition is made

[59] B: 1822.
[60] Greg, p. 383.

more basic by the refusal of Old Man to notice Helen; he says nothing at all about devils, and would obviously feel the same about human women – love is what he expresses this intimate loathing for, though perhaps by accident; he might just as reasonably say it about the earlier pleasures of Faust. Indeed, the hysterical tone rather suggests a confirmed sodomite, upbraiding a disciple who has played truant and had a woman. However, it certainly needs to be acted; the grander the appearance of Helen the more it needs an opposition. Her silence must be admitted to be a weakness in the play, but it would be very hard for her to say anything ^{ddd}without making it plain whether she was a devil or a goddess. Of course the story would be well known among the audience, that she had lived with Faust and had a son by him shortly before he died; so they would know that she was able to speak.

Now this behaviour of Old Man, which did not make a good impression upon Greg, would be especially exasperating to Faust who was discovering true love at the very gates of Hell. He remarks in the Faust-book that he has always been a merciful man, but it was a well-known part of the story that he once fell from grace and ordered punishment for Old Man, shortly before his end. Marlowe set out to present this incident firmly, thinking it lifelike, but he needed to show Old Man as an extremely tempting victim, and Faust as merely striking back. In the 1594 version no such palliation was to be allowed; Old Man must be presented as entirely sympathetic and deserving, so as to put Faust firmly in the wrong. But even the first version of the speech (in the A-text) was enough to make Faust threaten suicide, and then give serious attention to some more inviting remarks by Old Man. No wonder Meph decides to intervene fiercely; but there is no need for him to hold out a dagger for suicide fifteen lines earlier; the audience could hardly even be sure what he is doing, as he remains silent, though apparently he bars the way out. Anyhow the deduction of Greg from the text, that the offer of the dagger is a second thought of Marlowe himself, is plainly wrong; the adjustment on the printed page (to fit in the stage direction) could have been done in 1601. This leaves us with no reason to think it early, and the scene is already crowded; it fits the real story all right, but probably it had better be omitted.

^{eee}Faust in his address to Helen plays with the idea that she may cost him his soul, but there is no reason to think he fears any truth behind the words. Of course some of the audience may find

'dramatic irony' here, but there is no need for it; the idea that she may help to keep him from repenting has just been said plainly to Meph, as an inducement for him to fetch her.

> Sweet Helen make me immortal with a kiss:
> Her lips suck forth my soul, see where it flies.
> Come, Helen, come, give me my soul again.
> Here will I dwell, for Heaven is in these lips,
> And all is dross that is not Helena.
>   (A: 1359–63; B: 1876–80)

The opposition to the sex-horror of Old Man is as sharp as it could be, and the audience should feel that; but it does not require the discovery of Greg, that kissing a devil was considered the sin against the Holy Ghost, unforgivable. This was quite a silly superstition, only heard of as part of the anti-witch campaign, and it is not even in the background of the German Faust-book, where Faust has more serious grounds for doubting whether he can be forgiven, and yet can still envisage repentance even after years of bedding with devils. I do not see why the English should invent it if it was not known to the Germans. P. F. actually hunts round for a silly fear to ascribe to Faust, and supposes him to think that signing the pact with his own blood was unforgivable – it was so messy. Even then, P. F. does not stumble upon the Greg theory. And surely the reverence with which Greg talks about this belief is a bit sanctimonious; like so many neo-Christians, he assumes that heretic-burning is the essence of Christianity, no longer tenable perhaps but still to be viewed with loving regret. The figures in Henslowe's *Diary* do not suggest that the audiences felt the same;[61] and it is known that James could not revive burning as he wished – there were times when the crowds pulled away the faggots.

The last soliloquy of Old Man, after Faust has led Helen away, is one of the few passages that are in A but not in B. Greg explains that 'to have the Old Man sneaking in to eavesdrop' would 'impair the theatrical effect' (p. 125); and 'the shift from moral implication to poetical appeal would, I think, be inevitable in representation', so the editor of B might well have 'authority' for cutting these nine lines, because they had been cut from later performances. Clearly Greg thinks there are two moral codes, one called moral, the other

---

[61] See chapter 6, p. 174.

poetical, and this has much truth; but it is not enough to ᶠᶠᶠexplain the decision. Perhaps it was merely overlooked in the first suppression, as Old Man begins by saying;

> Accursed Faustus, miserable man,
> That from thy soul exclud'st the grace of Heaven,
> And fliest the throne of his tribunal seat.
>
> (A: 1377–9)

The devils as well as mankind are to appear before God on the Day of Judgement, so that even if Faust has become a devil he has still not escaped from this tribunal. But he has done if he has succeeded in his real plan, becoming a Middle Spirit, so that he will die like a beast. However, the censor need not have minded having him accused of this intention; probably the eager hacks who wrote the additions demanded to have the speech out, because of its later part, in which the devils torture him. The actor would welcome the opportunity of acting pain with no visible cause, and I suppose with the closing line:

> Hence Hell, for hence I fly unto my God
> (A: 1386)

he would stumble behind the back curtain, followed by the devils of the stage direction. Greg says that Marlowe cannot mean him to be killed, because he survives the attack in the Faust-books; but Marlowe anyway differs from them, because they say that he could not even be hurt, being 'armoured by prayer';[62] also the question is unreal, because the stage performance cannot show whether he dies after his exit. Marlowe would be likely to find the Faust-books too pietistic here; it is well known that religious characters can get painful diseases. As to the promise of the Good Angel, who says that if he repents the devils 'shall never rase thy skin',[63] we need not doubt that the Good Angel was telling a lie, to encourage Faust; the Faust-books leave us in no doubt that they could hurt him. Marlowe would want to hold the balance even, and leave no doubt that Faust behaves badly to Old Man (though with the palliation that he has

[62] Sp. 188.
[63] A: 710; B: 651.

been exasperating), committing his first real sin, one might say, in his last action.

ᵍᵍᵍThe last words of Faust seem to me decisive for the interpretation of the play, so far as they go, because there is only one effective way to say them. Of course one might be confronted by a still more effective interpretation hitherto unthought of, but there is not much margin for this; and at any rate an inferior one, within the terms of reference of the author, can be rejected with confidence. When the clock has struck, or presumably while the twelve strokes are going on, the A-text gives:

> O it strikes, it strikes, now body turn to air,
> Or Lucifer will bear thee quick to Hell:
>> (*Thunder and lightning*)
> O soul, be changed to little water drops,
> And fall into the ocean, ne'er be found:
>> (*Enter devils*)
> My God, my God, look not so fierce on me:
> Adders and serpents, let me breathe awhile:
> Ugly Hell gape not, come not Lucifer,
> I'll burn my books, ah Mephastophilis.
>> (*Exeunt with him*)
>>> (A: 1500–8; (B: 2084–92))

ʰʰʰSome critic has said that 'Earth gape'[64] and so on are very theatrical; but Faust is trying to escape by using the magic he has commanded since he became a spirit, immediately upon signing the pact; it has only at this moment been withdrawn from him. Next he gives further useless orders, this time to enemies who are closing in upon him; he may intend to make humble pleas, but the grammar is still imperative. Then he thinks of a just possibly effective offer, the ultimate sacrifice; he will return the knowledge for which he sold his soul. Only extreme terror would wring the proposal out of him, and it gets no reply. At last, with great resilience, he emerges from the cocoon of horror-fantasy which he has spun round himself, and looks at Meph, who has come to fetch him. (Of course in this version he has not been looking at an actual fire.) He can read in the eyes of Meph that it is all nonsense; he need only enter peace, which is what he has been pleading for. With a passion of love and gratitude, he

[64] A: 1473.

dies in the arms of the killer, who can then be seen filching from him his soul.

iiiThis is a magnificent ending to the play, and its abrupt calm is merely rounded off by the epilogue (which even its present form does not actually say that Faust has gone to Hell). It is so much what Marlowe would have wanted, being both exalted and sardonic, that I cannot envisage anything else – most of this essay consists of scouting round for evidence, or thinking up supporting detail in plot or production, though the main interpretation already seemed to me certain. The B-text is clever at making it invisible; even in the last line, it adds to the difficulty for the actor by putting '*oh*' for 'ah', which has a surprisingly great effect. Greg is percipient as usual about this difference (p. 91), and agrees that the A-text is usually right when it says 'ah' against an 'oh' in the B-text (often they both say 'oh') but he does not explain it. 'Oh', I think, marks an outburst of personal emotion which is imposed upon the listener, whereas 'ah' (as well as being more unusual, solemn or high-faluting) assumes a community of sentiment – it expands into an audience ready to welcome it. That is why its use before the last word of Faust makes us certain that he has not found Meph to be a betrayer.

In my first book, *Ambiguity* (1930), I used this passage as an example of corruptions of the negative, part of the 'seventh type';[65] the divided mind of Faust includes a craving for the last curiosity to be satisfied, and that is why the negative is almost inaudible in 'Ugly Hell gape not'. There may be some truth in this, but it has nothing to do with what happens at the end, with 'Ah Mephastophilis' – there, I said: 'he has abandoned the effort to organise his preferences, and is falling to the devil like a tired child.'[66] This was much praised when the book was new, being felt to show a kind of theological insight; as part of the same vogue, there was a heretical saint in *The Bridge of San Luis Rey* by Thornton Wilder, I think, who 'leaned against a flame and died'. I thought this was a disgusting way to talk about officially approved torture, and each time I came across another bit of praise for my 'tired child' I felt ashamed at having got mixed up with the neo-Christians at their most typical. But my ear had been right; one can hear, in those last two words,

---

[65] William Empson: *Seven Types of Ambiguity*, London (Chatto & Windus) 1930, p. 261.

[66] Ibid., p. 262.

that he is no longer terrified but has arrived at an exhausted peace. ⁱⁱⁱSome critic answered this line of talk, rather hearteningly, by saying that it does not matter about the inner ear, because the actor is expected to scream the house down. Well yes, that was what he did in the Rose of the pious Henslowe, from 1594 onward, and it is a comfort to observe in Henslowe's *Diary* that his production rapidly emptied the house. The point about the inner ear is that it ought to tell us how the author wanted the lines to be spoken, and presumably how they were spoken in the first production, when he was alive and among friends; a thing which the audiences of Henslowe at first imagined was going to be revived, so that they packed the house, but were disappointed.

It may be thought that this ruins the tragedy, providing instead a complacent comedy of enlightenment. But Faust still dies at the end of the play, and during his life he suffers as much as ever. Also the dramatic ambiguity imposed by the censorship, therefore plainly necessary even in the lost first version, makes a great difference. It is a dangerous technique, liable to excite impatience, but here it is doubly justified – apart from any government, we never do know where a recently dead person has gone. Even on the orthodox view, we do not know what God will decide on the Day of Judgement; the exultant confidence of Henslowe's devils, that God will confirm their capture of Faust, rather invites a rebuff; but Faust would have a long time in Hell first. One way and another, the bold plan which I suggest for Faust would strike the first audiences as absurd but not painfully upsetting. On the other hand, Greg and his allies, thirty years ago, felt that anything in favour of Faust was false sentiment, especially bad because it was the false sentiment of a later age. The texts are often in favour of Faust, on minor points, but in all such cases a neo-Christian had a duty to misread them. This movement dates from the 'nineties', and recalls the poet Lionel Johnson, declaiming in his pub against the frightful *vulgarity* of disbelieving in Hell (with much truth, as until the machines came the belief in eternal punishment was regarded as a social duty, to maintain the essential work in the fields). But for Marlowe, the decision had been taken before he arrived on the scene. In a part of the sources for the Faust legend, it seems clear, the magician had been hated and denounced, mainly on doctrinal grounds, but in ᵏᵏᵏanother, more vulgar part, consisting of anecdotes about his triumphs, he had become a 'rogue demigod', a type almost universal in human legend, and always viewed (though he is rough) with tender admiration. In the German Faust-book the split is already plain, and both sides are treated with excellent firmness. But a play is different from a book; to end a play with enthusiastic damnation would mean coming down on that side much more decisively. Indeed modern audiences, when they put up with the play, do so because they feel confident that God did not really commit this gross injustice. It is my sanctimonious opponents, and not I, who show flippant indifference to moral reality here; and they cannot claim evidence that Elizabethan audiences were on their side. I maintain that an inherent doubt in the story needs recognition in the plot, and that the first audiences were well able to feel so; once the historical obstacle is removed, that is, the presumption that they were all suckers, there is any amount of evidence for what really happened.

a6

The Sadistic Additions

The fifth act in the B-text contains about eighty lines not in the A-text, mostly concerned to make all the spirits reappear so as to jeer and exult over Faust, aiming to increase his mental torments; the audience is incited to feel that he deserves the utmost punishment which is coming to him, and that they hate him and rejoice at this prospect. It is sometimes implied that he had never any choice, being already doomed, or already tricked into his fatal error, before he even approached the devils; but this is felt to imply that he inherently deserved damnation, so that the audience has even fuller permission to rejoice at his torments. A stage direction requires an actual view of Hell. Also, at the end, the students come in and point out his limbs torn asunder, while reporting his shrieks.

It seemed to me obvious that these passages, since they are out of touch with the play that has gone before, were added at the command of a censor, who was indignant at hearing that the audiences took the play to mean an escape from Hell, a last-moment triumph for the secret plan of Faust. I still think it obvious, but realize now that a full treatment is needed to satisfy an opponent. Few critics present themselves as actually believing that Marlowe wrote the lines, but most of them assume that Marlowe ordered them to be written, or made himself responsible by not forbidding a plan to do that. As the law stood, after selling the play, he had lost all power to forbid rewriting of it; all the same there is no need to think that the doctored play appeared before he had been murdered. Greg said (as part of his proof that the B-text was the original one) that Marlowe first wrote the dirty parts, merely as a theological exercise, and then, after he had written the final soliloquy, felt that this more human treatment had made his earlier bits unsuitable.[1] Even so, Greg went on printing the parts that he thought Marlowe had rejected, and seems to have assumed that they would always be treated as part of the end of the play. Bernard Shaw said that Marlowe was a nasty young boy trying to make our flesh creep with a Hell in which he no longer believed;[2] and he had in mind chiefly the passages now in question. This view of Marlowe does, I think, make him a bad author, not merely a nasty one; so it needs to be considered.

ᵇIt may be thought absurd to try to rescue Marlowe here: 'But of course he would end *Faust* with screams and torture. All his plays end with a horrid thrill; even Dido throws herself into a bonfire; and this play gave him the biggest opportunity.' I don't deny that he is a sensational author. But he can more plausibly be accused of self-pity than craving to torture others; he was himself accused of two things for which he might (just possibly) receive a painful death, atheism and sodomy,[3] and these two provide the two most ghastly ends in his plays; very likely he was also fond of plots, like Barabas – at least, he is clearly in sympathy with that grotesque villain. It is the source of his dramatic power. He reverences the outlaw who defies the world; if he pretends indignation, there, it is only as a means of boring from within. The mood could be expressed plainly about Tamburlane, partly because he was felt to have saved us from the Moslems (he was not much further away in time than Napoleon is now);[4] he is ruthless in war and thinks it fun to torment the defeated kings, but they probably deserved it, and he is a shepherd who has won

---

[1] Greg, p. 132

[2] G. B. Shaw: *Our Theatres in the Nineties*, London (Constable) 1932, vol. II, p. 182 (in a review of a production of *Doctor Faustus* by members of the Shakespeare Reading Society at St. George's Hall, 2 July 1896).

[3] [416; E7]We have a good deal of evidence about his beliefs, from friends, enemies and spies, and it is remarkably consistent. He seems to have talked rather wildly – probably the spies followed him into his pubs; but the basic position is what was later called Deism; his 'atheism' meant not believing that Jesus was God. Among such heretics it was very unusual to believe in Hell, though some believed in temporary punishments for the wicked before oblivion, and some in eternal bliss as a reward for the good. Marlowe would thus not feel personally involved in fears about Hell; but surely it is plain that he had fears on earth. A Fellow of his college was [417: E8]burnt as an 'Arian', his own heresy, and Henry VIII's death-penalty for sodomy was still on the statute-book – apparently never applied, but they could fish it up as soon as they wanted to, and it was his habit to boast about that topic.

[4] Tamerlane: 1336–1405 AD (*Chambers' Biographical Dictionary*, 1974).

through by merit alone. He is allowed to die with dignity, almost without pain; perhaps he dies as a result of blaspheming Allah, but anyway that is unlike blaspheming God the Father. On the other hand, boiling the Jew in his own cauldron is felt as hardly more than a practical joke; he dies briefly, with vigorous curses proving that he would have done worse things if allowed to live on. The death of Ithamore is meant as dreadfully sad; Marlowe always grieves over young outcasts who are plucky and resourceful, and of course doomed (that is what his homosexuality amounts to) – the anxious yearning can be made prominent because it is disguised as tough humour. The play makes evident that Barabas loved Ithamore, and became a rogue elephant after Ithamore had betrayed him; his outrages then reached a political level. Of course, Barabas could not bear to hand Ithamore the money that he kept promising; but he would have done if Ithamore had shown the sense, or perhaps the baseness, to coax him for it. So all the middle of the play, which critics have agreed to find rather mysteriously bad (perhaps the author was drunk) is full of tender sentiment. Well then, such are the plays which had made his name before he wrote *Faust* (if you accept the earlier dating), and they are not stuck in a groove; if the death of the Jew affected him at all when writing *Faust*, he would want his new play to be notably different.

He only wrote two plays after it, granting that *Dido*, whatever its date, is an elegant exercise after Vergil. *The Massacre at Paris* does ʿnot seem to me so bad as is usually said; the young French nobles have been brought up to such wrong opinions that they are entitled to the charity usually reserved for teddy boys. They are brisk and proud and they are all fatuously doomed. It has less depth than the other plays, and is obviously planned to gratify the audience; but morally it makes no concession. *Edward II* copies its terrible ending from Holinshed, and the play undoubtedly tries to make us sorry for this king; a grim feeling that he deserved it may be assumed from the old story, but the pathos is what is laboured or underlined. One may suspect that Marlowe, whose career was in effect ruined by the suppression of his first *Faust* and the suspicions which thereafter hung around him, came to take a grimmer view of his audiences; the producer of *Faust* would be sure to say to him, after the disaster, 'Oh, if only you had stuck to straight torture of Faust at the end, there wouldn't have been any of this bother, and they'd have lapped it up just as well.' Marlowe might well come to feel, two years later, that he could not be blamed if he cashed in on this interesting bit of history. So I grant that the two final plays, after he had been treated savagely, do feel a bit savager. But even so they are not in the least like the additions to *Faust*. The petty, spiteful, cosy and intensely self-righteous hatred worked up against Faust here is a very recognizable kind of nastiness, not found in his work elsewhere.

However, one should not deny that he might have done it. For example, he might be afraid, anxious to show he was not an 'atheist'. But in that case, he would have had different plans from the start; the B-text introduces inconsistencies. For example, it makes the devils witness a crucial event of the play, the conjuring by Faustus, in grim silence, and Greg explains that this was omitted from the A-text merely to suit performances on tour, with no balcony. The direction merely says: '*Thunder. Enter Lucifer and four devils, Faustus to them with this speech*' (B:225f). Surely, in any large hall, they could be set up on a table at a side of the stage, perhaps with a curtain to cover their exit; and the same applies to their appearances gloating over Faust at the end. Here they speak freely; and why do they not speak earlier? We may find the silence terrifying, but Marlowe would think he could do ᵈbetter than a silence, and the audience would think so too. But in the A-text the devils appear only once, and briefly, to show Faust the pastime of the Masque of the Sins; surely the costume manager would complain. Their dresses and make-up would be expensive and time-consuming, and are still demanded for the performance on tour; why are these exciting objects used so grudgingly? There is only one answer; it was necessary for the plot. Their appearance is only a charade, put on by other nature-spirits who are friends of Meph and think it fun; this is a help, as it means that the human actors need not work hard to be convincing. The friends of Meph will realize that he wants to frighten Faust, but not that his plot is so far-reaching; they too are fond of horseplay. The B-text editor not only wants the devils to be real but also wants Faust to be doomed from the start, long before he has signed his pact; whereas the Meph of Marlowe keeps having to do something resourceful to hold Faust's repentance at bay.

The same backward look is taken by the new Meph, now frankly an enemy:

Faust   O thou bewitching fiend, twas thy temptation
         Hath robbed me of eternal happiness.
Meph   I do confess it Faustus, and rejoice.
         Twas I that, when thou wert i'the way to Heaven
         Dammed up thy passage, when thou took'st the book,
         To view the Scriptures, then I turned the leaves
         And led thine eye.

(B:1986–92)

A number of modern critics have pointed out, with the confidence of a teacher correcting an essay, that Faust was very ignorant not to know the rest of the sentence, immediately following the passage that he quotes.[5] But Faust, and Marlowe too, had gone through a thorough course of study in this subject; and it is quite unnecessary to suppose that they did not know the cover-up or fob-off clauses at the ends of these sentences (two of them). They would also remember what Luther had said, in the *De Servo Arbitrio*, as the whole Faust-book is so Lutheran:

> This is the acme of faith: to believe that God, who saves so few and condemns so many, is merciful; that he is just who, at his own pleasure, has made us necessarily doomed to damnation, so that he seems to delight in the torture of the wretched and to be more deserving of hate than of love. If by any method of mine I could conceive how God, who shows so much anger and harshness, could be merciful and just, there would be no need of faith.[6]

For a thinking man with genuine belief, to accept the promises of God requires a miracle, and it had been vouchsafed to Luther but not to Faust; 'Faust is hardly to be blamed for this, and he tells us early in the play that he is doomed for 'desperate thoughts' against God. It seemed to me quite certain that this bit of the B-text had been added by one of Henslowe's hangers-on, obeying a high but

---

[5] Empson is referring to Faust's first act I soliloquy. (A:i, l. 70): '*The reward of sin is death*' . . . 'but the gift of God is eternal life' (Romans 6.23); (A:i, l. 72f): '*If we say that we have no sin, We deceive ourselves, and there's no truth in us*' . . . 'If we confess our sins, he is faithful and just to forgive us our sins and to cleanse us from all unrighteousness' (I John 1.8, 9).

[6] Quoted by Aldous Huxley in *The Perennial Philosophy*, London (Chatto & Windus) 1946, p. 270.

general instruction, when I realized that he is just as ignorant of the theological layout as our modern literary critics themselves. ʿIf Marlowe wrote it he was playing to the gallery very coarsely, and the procedure would be almost as painful to him as having to betray poor Meph. A man who was accustomed to meet government spies might be led far astray, I cannot deny, but as they had already murdered him before the crucial production we can have no need to smear upon him so much shame. In fact, the Oscar Wilde idea, that it is all right to tell any lie for the sake of art, was very remote from his circumstances. Considering that P. F., though only a translator, and only allowed to print his initials, and shockingly ignorant of astronomy, could not bear to have any reader think that he did not support Copernicus, we need surely not attribute a more shameless indifference to Marlowe. It is not a matter of the opinions expressed by the characters; he would not want one of his plays to be twisted round so as to imply false sentiments. If Greg did not know this he ought to have done, and indeed could have found it readily enough by searching his heart.

ᵍOne other point can perhaps be snatched from this new enemy Meph; he says, jeering at Faust, to curry favour with Lucifer:

> his labouring brain
> Begets a world of idle fantasies
> To over-reach the devil; but all in vain.
> (B: 1908–10)

Old Man during his last speech had also said that Faust had 'tried to flee' the Judgement Seat,[7] but this had been cut out from the B-text version. What seems astounding, in the texts remaining to us, is that Faust never does plan any means of fleeing or overreaching at all. This hack knows what he has been paid to combat, the idea of a Faust who plotted to join the nature-spirits, but has forgotten that he is not allowed to recall it. However, as the whole audience (in 1594) were recalling it already, there seemed no need to correct this slight failure in tact. For that matter, at the other end of the play, the Prologue was still allowed to announce that it would survey

> The form of Faustus' fortunes, good or bad,
> (A: 9; B: 9)

[7] A:1379.

though this hesitation could hardly seem relevant, if his fortune was certain to be the very worst thing possible.

I must not deny that the Faust-book has a whole chapter (GFB, chapter 65), towards the end, of Meph jeering at Faust in an oafish manner, and this P. F. sensibly omitted; it was not what he wanted, nor Marlowe either, but it was all right for the debunking hacks needed by Henslowe to satisfy the censor. Of course they were all within reach of the original German. The Meph of the Faust-book is a rather soured but sturdy character, willing to do what is assigned but no more, and interesting chiefly in what he lets drop. The Meph of Marlowe is intelligent and insinuating; he longs for love, or at least can pretend to; but there are obstacles before he can speak frankly. To return him to the Faust-book version at the end is a severe shock; very dramatic of course, but not rewarding on second thoughts. Faust when he conjured would have taken anyone who came; there was no need to have a tender friend come. To make him turn sour at the end is a deliberate muddying of the story.

I should also recall, in collecting this argument, that the [h]complete change in the speech by Old Man, from a hysterical expression of sex-horror to a warm friendly piece of advice, not at all blaming Faust for his manhood but saying he will now need to take care, can only be intended to make the audience hate Faust for demanding (as soon as Meph drags him back) to have Old Man tortured; it is the first sin of Faust, anyway, but in Marlowe's version he had been unbearably exasperated. The spectacle of Old Man being tortured to death, standing untouched but with devils at the sides of the stage pointing 'influence' at him, would have been an extremely welcome assignment to any Elizabethan actor, let alone the audience. The reason why it had to be suppressed is very plain, though hard for us to appreciate. What is being worked up is a craving to see a wicked person tortured, and to get a saint tortured just before (having to feel sorry for him) would be a severe break in the mood. To give up the extra torture was rather a sacrifice, but this was a very wholehearted bit of hackwork, based upon religious conviction one need not doubt.

Coming now to the dirty bits: the Good and Bad Angels have not appeared since the Masque of the Sins, when Faust became certain that his plan had failed, and he was in the hands of the devils, so that he was no longer in doubt. In Marlowe they represent his own divided mind, and cannot be seen by other characters; now the representatives of God and the Devil are quite solid, and so frankly in cahoots that they finish one another's sentences. The suspicion of the young Luther, that God simply *is* the Devil, gets a powerful expression here.

Good Angel	O Faustus, if thou hadst given ear to me
	Innumerable joys had followed thee.
	But thou didst love the world –
Bad Angel	gave ear to me,
	And now must taste Hell's pains perpetually.
Good Angel	O what will all thy riches, pleasures, pomps,
	Avail thee now?
Bad Angel	Nothing but vex thee more,
	To want in Hell, that had on earth such store.
	(*Music while the throne descends*)
Good Angel	O thou hast lost celestial happiness.

(B: 1997–2006)

So Faust has to watch the throne going up again empty; it was brought down only to torment him with regret. As has been pointed out, it is very unlike the style of Marlowe to break a blank verse line between two speakers;[8] but this does not seem decisive – he was quite capable of finding a new method for a special effect. But what he would not want is the mean-mindedness of the whole procedure, which is also unimaginative. No one subjected to overwhelming pain would think 'what frightfully good champagne the Pope had – why, I might ibe drinking it in Heaven now.' Presumably it is intended to excite the jealousy of the audience, and thus feed their hatred.

---

8 [105; E0]Miss Roma Gill remarked in her edition of the play (The New Mermaids (1965), p. xviii), as part of her evidence that Marlowe did not write these passages:

Instances of a regular verse line divided between two speakers are rare in Marlowe's work as a whole, and of the nine in this play, five occur in obviously non-Marlovian scenes . . . and the other four in these doubtful portions of V.ii. . . . The whole nature of the play is changed by this addition. Without it we have the tragedy of an individual who wilfully seeks his own destruction; with it, Doctor Faustus is a more medieval play where man is a puppet manipulated by external powers.

Yes, indeed, and also it is particularly absurd to make these two complete each other's sentences, as if in connivance. Faust had long suspected that Satan only carried out the plans of God.

The Good Angel rubs in the loss of Heaven for ten lines, and then 'Hell is discovered', and the Bad Angel takes over. He seems to be pointing out a lot of detail, as when Meph pointed out the seven hills of Rome; most of it of course a pretence, but a glimpse of real fire would be needed, dangerous in that theatre though it was. Three braziers would be discovered on the back stage, rigged so as to give out a good deal of smoke through which flames could be dimly seen.

> Now Faustus, let thine eyes with horror stare
> Into that vast perpetual torture-house.
> There are the furies tossing damned souls
> On burning forks: their bodies broil in lead;
> There are live quarters broiling on the coals
> That ne'er can die; this ever-burning chair
> Is for o'er-tortured souls to rest them in.
>
> (B:2018–24)

Actually suffering these tortures would surely be worse than hearing about them; this preview while yet alive cannot add much to the pains of Faust. No doubt there is spite among the devils, but a burning spite among the audience is what it is concerned to excite and relieve. There is the same feebleness of imagination; a body that could take rest in an ever-burning chair must be totally unlike our own, and what can be meant by 'over-torture' – too much for what purpose? A human body has to be allowed times for recovery before further torture is applied, but why should these paradoxical bodies, also called 'souls'? The absurdity of the description seems to be intended, for an effect upon the audience; so perhaps I was wrong in calling it feeble – it is like the 'wit' of metaphysical poetry. It is almost flippant, but that does not make it any less nasty. The purpose of this intimate half-playful tone is to remove the inhibitions or resistance of the audience, so that they feel free to indulge the pleasure of hating and despising the victim of an official torture – in communion so far, though each of them is itching to savage the eyes or genitals of the scapegoat himself. It is skilfully done, as a lead-in to the great soliloquy; perhaps a connoisseur at the time would remark that, though of course no imitation could approach the real thing, the new *Faust* gave the atmosphere of a witch-burning better than any other play.

jIt is to the credit of the Elizabethan public that they did not care for Henslowe's new *Faust*. Luckily we have the figures during those years for his share of the daily takings, from named plays;[9] and it looks as if he had promised the censor, as part of a bargain, to revive Hell every few months even if it meant emptying his theatre. There is no other play which he kept on reviving after the figures had sunk so low. His first night was on 30 September 1594, and he does not mark it as a new play; it brought in a record figure (72 shillings),[10] only once surpassed, by a new Shakespeare play two years before; and curiosity continued to bring a fair audience for the next two performances (44s., and 33),[11] but then it goes pretty steadily down (there is an eccentric 52s. just after Christmas that year, which calls for a special explanation).[12] Meanwhile other plays by Marlowe keep on being revived with respectable success, though of course new plays get bigger houses. The final sequence for *Faust* in the *Diary* is 4 November 1596: 17 shillings, 17 December 1596: 9 shillings, 5 January 1597: 5 shillings.[13] On 11 October 1597 he tried again, but perhaps could not be bothered, or could not bear, to write the figures down on his new system of accounting; the entry appears to mean that the house was quite empty.[14] Undaunted, he paid hacks to add the Pope Bruno material, which does at least give a new interest and a further opportunity for spectacle; and he led off with it at the opening of the Fortune Theatre [k]in 1600, with Alleyn returning from retirement to take the name part. [l]We do not hear about the reception of the play then or later, but the B-text went on selling for the rest of the century. Still, for at least five years, the audiences remembered that they had been fobbed off.

Greg has some humane and interesting reflections about these additions, which his theory requires him to regard as derived from the first draft, handwritten by Marlowe, but excluded from the original prompt copy. Marlowe set out to imitate 'the old religious and moral drama' (as would be natural for a scholarly man, after accepting an assignment to dramatize the Faust-book), and

[9] See *Henslowe's Diary*, ed. Walter W. Greg, London (Bullen) 1904.
[10] Ibid., f. 10.
[11] Ibid., ff. 10, 10 verso.
[12] Ibid., f. 11.
[13] Ibid., ff. 25, 25 verso.
[14] *Henslowe's Diary*, f. 27 verso; the takings entry is a single 0 in the tens of pounds column. 'Joroneymo' and 'the comodey of Vmers' were both played on 11 October and the receipts are noted as £2 in each case. Perhaps there was no performance of 'docter fostes' that day after all.

regarded them as 'allegorical' or somehow 'at a remove from the level of actuality' (pp. 131f); but after he had written the final soliloquy, 'entirely satisfying the requirements of the human situation', he felt that, for his literary effect, it was necessary to cut these 'abstract' passages out. Sure enough, says Greg, the soliloquy is wholly out of key with the 'morality' element, and seems indeed irreconcilable with such a conception. ᵐIt is tempting to suppose that he meant rather more than he said here. Greg was much accustomed to committee-work, and would almost automatically avoid exciting the resentment of his pious colleagues, always liable to surge up in a rancorous manner. Why, it seems fair to ask, did he find the despairing speech 'irreconcilable' with these expressions of the official doctrine? Because it denounces that doctrine, even though covertly; there seems no other possible answer. We must deduce that, if Marlowe set out to preach Christianity, merely as part of the professional work of a man of letters, he found it too disgusting, and then he tried to hide his ugly mistake, which was only ferreted out by an extraordinary accident.

ⁿGreg has an uneasy paragraph (pp. 128f) saying: 'For the purposes of the play he accepted the Christian mythos and the Christian ethic . . . Behind the mask Marlowe remains inscrutable. There is, it is true, a change of tone in the Epilogue' but the lines are 'what Marlowe might be expected to write if constrained to furnish a conventional ending. Boas appears to assume that he would have refused to do so.' A warning to the audience at the end, with Wagner as the Chorus and words that may easily be made to sound pert, even Marlowe need not have refused. But does 'the Christian ethic' necessarily tell you to burn witches and wizards alive, and enjoy it? The final additions insinuate that it does. And what does the soliloquy say? Greg was right to feel that it made the tragedy real, because it surveys all the beliefs that men have ever held about the after-death – oblivion, reincarnation, an absorption into nature, a return to the World-soul. What confronts Faust is therefore remarkably bad. The words 'if my soul must suffer for my sin / Impose some end'[15] imply a doubt whether he has sinned at all, and we have to agree, except for his final act of exasperation with Old Man. To give him eternal punishment is plainly tyrannous. I will probably be told that this is typical 'reading in', the putting of modern thoughts into an old author (whether or not they were also

[15] B:2067f.

subliminally at work in Greg), but as it happened I had been keeping an eye open, in my reading, for several years, looking for any early occurrence of the idea that the soul at death is like a rain-drop returning to the sea, and finding it nowhere, when I belatedly read *The Pursuit of the Millenium* by Norman Cohn,[16] and found it had been standard among medieval pantheists and the Family of Love and Cromwell's Ranters, though not till the Ranters did it reach print. Marlowe used it right at the end of his list, with the coming of the thunder and the devils, and many of his audience must have known the distinctive slogans of the Family of Love.

°I ought to pause here a moment and thank the shade of Greg for restoring the text of these crucial lines:

> O soul, be changed to little water drops,
> And fall into the ocean, ne'er be found.
> (A:1503f; B:2086f)

The A-text had 'into little', and the editor of the B-text, whose source here, as so often, was a text of A3, corrected the scansion, giving 'into small'. This makes an ugly line, said Greg rightly, and he suspected 'that the reporter had anticipated *into* from the following line, and that Marlowe wrote *to*'.[17] This ought always to be printed, but I have never seen a later critic even mention the conjecture. (The good is oft interréd with their bones!)

PGreg regards Marlowe as an aesthete of the 1890s, whereas he was rather noisy about his advanced views; he was unlikely to fall into this pathetic situation. All the same, there is no other standard solution for the many problems about Marlowe's *Faust* beyond the grand design of Greg, and it should have received more attention on this point. There is supposed to be a firm rule among bibliographers that the final decision of an author must be accepted, whether he had gone mad or not, and however plainly bad his decision may be. Well then, surely this doctrine may be used for a bit of rescue work; if you agree with Greg, the play ought not to be reprinted with the dirty bits stuffed in, as is at present always done.

qIt makes a wonderful play, once allowed its full variety of incident, with the soggy weight of sanctimonious horror removed.

[16] London (Secker & Warburg) 1957; 3rd (revised) edn, London (Paladin), 1970, p. 172.
[17] Greg, p. 400.

One may rightly feel that it is still tragic; Faust dies just as he finds happiness, or believes himself to have found it. This gives a satisfactory moral: you had better not get mixed up with the spirits. But then again, if the reason why Faust cannot repent is that he cannot bring himself to love God (and the idea is already suggested early in the Faust-book, when Meph tells Faust he cannot back out because 'Thy heart's despair has brought thee there')[18] – if so, then it would be no kindness to send him to Heaven either; a pious member of the audience might well regard God as doing an act of un-covenanted mercy when he lets Faust die outright, like a cow. In thinking so he would be inventing a heresy which was already familiar to many of his neighbours. And a modern spectator, all the more, surely, if a Christian, is likely to feel that Faust does not deserve eternal torment, in spite of his one crime at the end; the injustice of the superstition is what makes a pretended acceptance of it in the theatre feel so disgusting. Clearly, then, the missing passages should be fudged; and this is possible because no imitation of exalted poetry by Marlowe is required, indeed hardly any poetry at all. The Chorus before act II needs to be in verse, to give it authority and consistency, but verse of a very sober kind. The two outraged magicians may just as well be reduced to prose, like the sinful comics. Perhaps Turkey may continue to forbid the scenes with the Sultan, but even if allowed they should be short, using the prose of the Faust-book as much as possible, and remembering the evident sympathy of Marlowe for Islam; the Sultan should point out to his wives, while ending the affair, that he can give absolute honour to his prophet without confounding the prophet with the Creator, as the Christians do. This could make a tolerably short play, and the pause for drinks should come at the end of Act II; at that point, the actor of Faust should convey with sufficient firmness that the apparently jolly meeting has reduced him to horror and despair. In a modern theatre there is no need to carry off the corpses; the rather puzzling question of how Meph and an accomplice removed the body of Faust at the end can be ignored. Probably the Epilogue was slightly fudged by the censor Tilney, before he allowed the first performances; he inserted the words 'hellish' and 'fiendfull' by way of reassurance for the public:

[18] Sp. 14.

> Faustus is gone, regard his hellish fall,
> Whose fiendful fortune may exhort the wise.
>> (A: 1513f; B: 2117f)

[I have not been able to find any MS continuation but we are clearly within sight of the end. Empson would have explained how easily the Epilogue could have been reconstructed. Fortunately, he discussed this point with me and dictated the necessary changes into his copy of Greg. There are only three: the two words he considered Tilney's, and 'burned' (amended to 'withered' in the second line):

> Cut is the branch that might have grown full straight,
> And *withered* is Apollo's laurel bough,
> That sometime grew within this learned man:
> Faustus is gone, regard his *fearful* fall,
> Whose *ghastly* fortune may exhort the wise,
> Only to wonder at unlawful things,
> Whose deepness doth intice such forward wits,
> To practise more than heavenly power permits.
>> (cf. A:1510–17; B:2114–21)

Empson had long planned to make a full restoration of the 'missing' parts but he was always too busy to engage upon it and death finally precluded the work.

> *Terminat hora diem, Terminat Author opus*]

Appendix 1
Additional Material

[The following MS sequences, while introducing new material, could not conveniently be intercalated in the main body of the essay without distortion and they are too long as footnotes.]

The necessary constraints

[a]Any theory that Marlowe's *Faust* was originally a good play needs to satisfy several rather stringent conditions:

1 Faust has invented a way to escape Hell, and at the end, to his surprise, it works. Few if any of the spectators would believe in this plan, but it must seem homely, made out of familiar materials, rather as in Gilbert and Sullivan (instead of being a deduction from a learned theory). Nothing less than this wildly improbable end to the play, and the discovery that it was already delighting the audiences, would produce the vehement and yet temporizing reaction of the censors.

2 There was nothing to warn a censor reading the text beforehand that a surprise would come at the end; it was 'all in the acting'.

3 However, the theory of the thing must have been spelled out to the audience in the course of the play; to get the required effect, at least half of them, though the end comes as a great surprise, must be confident of what has happened.

4 The tone must [b]be right; it is very remote from the 'savage farce' of *The Jew of Malta*. Faust is killed at the end, and the final Chorus gives us a warning not to get mixed up with spirits. Most spectators would feel, if not that he deserved to be killed, at least that he ought to expect his contract to be acted upon literally; but they would also feel that he did not deserve eternal torment. This is almost implied by the original Faust-book; such is the reason why it was so thrilling and so fishy, and remains an object of permanent regard. . . . [Here Empson discusses the two groups of Faust-legends, cf. pp. 46ff.] . . . Marlowe makes an effort to explain or at least present the toleration of Faust, for which he has been given no credit; his act IV has an indignation meeting of peasants who have suffered from his practical jokes, and they listen to a horse trader, who allowed a drink in the village horse-pond to a horse he had just that moment bought from Faust, and it melted into the pond. 'All' the company cry out 'O brave Doctor' (*Faust* IV. vi. [B: 1623]), forgetting their indignation for a moment, and this does at least establish the tone firmly. Probably the miracles of saints were often tiresome like that. And in the last act (of the A-text) the absolutes in conflict are merely given full statement, so that the characters hardly ever answer one another, any more than in Aeschylus. It is an exalted death, so this condition, though hard to satisfy, is already satisfied by the surviving A-text.

5   The final condition refers only to ourselves, not to the first audiences. Greg is very lively about the bits in the play where the grand rhetoric of Marlowe is used out of place, as if by Ancient Pistol; he picks out quite a number of them, using the term 'parody' at least once, and decorously presumes that they were all written by hired hacks. Marlowe could not have afforded to hire such men, and anyway could not have endured them; all the corruption of his text was done after he had been murdered. An adequate solution of the problem would clear up all these absurd bits (in the A-text, though indeed the B-text cannot give rise to any new ones), showing that they were not absurd in the situation Marlowe had planned for them.

Astronomy in the play [cf. p. 145]

'Marlowe is always enthusiastic about soaring, and one might expect the third act Chorus to be better. It has a courtly magnificence, but actually says very little. Probably Marlowe had taken advice from his friend Hariot, who would first say 'He couldn't discover anything by flying up; he would only see there what we see here.' Marlowe would say timidly: 'I have recommended the Copernican view by altering the direction of the flight. Of course, if he went straight up, he would think he saw the earth turning beneath him. So I put

> From East to West his dragons swiftly glide

– leaving the audience to deduce that the Chorus is a quite simple man'. Hariot would answer: 'What a curious thing it is that people cannot recognize the principle of inertia except when playing catch. Of course, he would go up retaining the speed of the part of the earth's surface ^dthat he left. The angular velocity of this, around the earth, would become smaller as he got further away, but it could hardly cause any delusion; if he went up slowly, he would just think the earth at rest for a considerable time; if he went up fast, he would see almost at once that the earth was revolving.' Marlowe would think stubbornly that his line was the right one for the audience, and make no reply. 'But then', Hariot would say, 'how fast can he be going? Where are the dragons bound? They could not go beyond the sphere of the moon, which is the limit for both devils and Middle Spirits. Now, that distance is the only tolerable number in astronomy. It is sixty times the radius of the earth, and the speed of the surface of the earth at the Equator is 1,000 miles an hour; familiar enough, as it is just about the speed of sound.[1] If the dragons went at 3,000 miles an hour, and they must be expected to give a bit extra, they could get Faust to the sphere of the moon and back in seven days, so that he had half a day or so to imagine he was seeing some novelty. Apparently he did not dare broach the moon, or speak to the angels on the other side of the barrier.' Marlowe still felt that, as it was all magic, the dragons could just as easily stop movement in one direction as start it in another; but he expressed warm gratitude, as the answer had simplified his work, and the Chorus if examined carefully does not say that Faust went beyond the sphere of the moon. If Hariot was right, Faust after his first hour of flight would be 3,000 miles up and over the Hook of Holland, but over Cardiff on the more liberal view of the poet. Surely this amount of shift would be noticeable. Also Iceland, Greenland and Newfoundland would be looming up, whereas eastward there was only the unending land mass. At 3,000 miles up, though the earth is plainly a ball, one still feels part of it, and the delusion might just be supposed to occur. But the chief effect of the line is a signal to part of the audience, that Marlowe knows about the rotation of the earth, and that Meph has shown himself quaintly ignorant of it.

The Chorus begins:

> Learned Faustus,
> To find the secrets of astronomy
> Graven in the book of Jove's high firmament,
> Did mount him up to scale Olympus' top
> ((A: 810–13); B: 778–80)

– very debunking really, as a mountain is nothing in astronomy, but Jove is a Middle Spirit, and his real top is the sphere of the moon.

---

[1] Empson's figures are, designedly, very rough but 'Hariot's' conclusion is correct (a dragon speed of 2,850 mph would suffice).

> He views the clouds, the Planets, and the Stars,
> The Tropics, Zones, and quarters of the sky,
> From the bright circle of the horned Moon.
>
> (B: 783–5)

This is plain. But the next line throws in a grammatical confusion:

> Even to the height of *Primum Mobile*.
>
> (B: 786)

So perhaps he may *view* from both places, though he makes no such claim.

> And whirling round with this circumference,
> Within the concave compass of the Pole,
> From East to West his dragons swiftly glide,
> And in eight days did bring him home again.
>
> (B: 787–90)

The circumference of the *primum mobile* is what makes us all turn, and to say that it made Faust turn does not prove (as Jump supposed) that he had been there.[2] The next line, about the Pole, seems deliberately empty; at least, no critic has made any sense of it.

Debunking[3]

e[Greg] carries his distaste to the point of rejecting *Tut* and *Tush*,[4] which he feels could not have been written by Marlowe. But these fterms are not low class, belonging rather to dons and schoolmasters: 'Come now, you ought not still to be making that mistake; remember, you are in the sixth form.' Comic primness attaches to them. So it is quite in order for Lucifer to say, in answer to 'O this feeds my soul', the panting admiration of Faust for the absurd Masque of Sins, 'Tut, Faustus, in Hell is all manner of delight.' He means that a man like Faust ought not to be impressed so easily (it feels to me extraordinary that this point has to be explained). Of course, the effect is to invite the audience to laugh, and it does seem surprising that the author did not want them to be terrified; but the intention is consistent all through the scene. To suppose that it was written to be impressive, but the actors chose to make fun of it, which would require quite large changes in

---

[2] Christopher Marlowe: *Doctor Faustus*, ed. John D. Jump (The Revels Plays), London (Methuen) 1962, p. 46n.

[3] Cognate with p. 134.

[4] Referring to 'Tush, Christ did call the thief upon the cross' (A: 1173; B: 1550).

the words, not written into the prompt-book, and that the result is all that survives in either of our two texts, would be a very bold hypothesis, much bolder than what I am proposing.

I think indeed that a certain amount of low-mindedness or debunking does explain a number of variations in the B-text, but these are variations that Greg supports and finds decorous. He does not care to have the blaspheming sinner presented as a Renaissance hero, and nor (one may readily believe) did the editor of the B-text, or some of the other writers along the chain which ended in that text. Thus Faust, in the A-text, after signing his name in his own blood, finds it has made letters on his arm:

> My senses are deceived, here's nothing writ.
> I see it plain, here in this place is writ
> *Homo Fuge*. Yet shall not Faustus fly.
>
> (A: 520–2)

He is like a rock. But the B-text makes him say: 'O yes, I see it plain, even here is writ',[5] and he has become a silly excitable little chap. Greg's note says: 'The actor or reporter, having omitted the *O yes* at the beginning of this line, was later forced by the metre to expand *even here* to the over-emphatic *here in this place*',[6] and he refers us to his introduction, where it is called 'over-precise'.[7] Too precise for what? I expect there was a good deal of blood smudging his arm (the Elizabethan stage was accustomed to supply plenty) so that he had to hunt for the right place, as on a map. Or take Faust begging to see Hell, after Lucifer has told him it has delights:

> O might I see Hell, and return again, how happy were I then.
>
> (A: 799f)

[8]Only one word need be added in B, making 'and return again safe',[8] to make him sound footling and neurotic; the effect comes chiefly from breaking the blank verse rhythm. Or take Meph asserting that Hell may be anywhere under the sphere of the moon:

> where we are is Hell
> And where Hell is [there] must we ever be.
> And, *to conclude*, when all the world dissolves,
> And every creature shall be purified,
> All places shall be Hell that is not Heaven.
>
> (A: 568–72)

[5] B: 468.
[6] Greg, p. 326.
[7] Greg, p. 56.
[8] B: 733.

The B-text makes this 'to be short',[9] thus letting us down with a bump. Greg recognizes the loss of grandeur, which comes chiefly from removing the idea of the end of the world, but says it is 'proved correct' by the EFB, chapter 11. But the whole passage is extremely different both in matter and tone. The case goes to show that the debunking of the style in the B-text is not aimed only at Faust, though he is the most prominent target.

Greg, to do him justice, revolts against the most shocking case of the procedure, the botching of the lyrical comments of the students upon Helen, as she passes over the stage.[10] B is committed to treating Helen as a devil, so the poetry about her must be spoiled, and it is done very efficiently, with the minimum of alteration. Greg makes her a devil too, but he recognizes the claims of poetry; so he invents a theory that Marlowe wrote the B-version in his manuscript and then was allowed to write his improved version, the A one, into the prompt copy. There is no evidence that authors were ever allowed to interfere with the prompt copy, but this need not be fatal; what is unlikely is that he would have made such a recovery from such a very bad first draft. But ideology comes back at the end; Greg cannot endure having the summoning of a devil called a 'glorious deed' – that must have been 'introduced by the reporter', probably so as to remove 'one of Marlowe's characteristic jingles'. Modern actors should therefore restore the jingle, and say:

> We'll take our leaves, and for this blessed sight
> Happy and blest be Faustus evermore
> (B: 1809f)

but immediately after, except for a speech in rebuke and a foiled attempt at suicide, he has her brought to him in private and says he will do glorious deeds for her; he will fight for her in the Trojan War. Ridiculous it may be, pathetically so, but the working to a [h]climax is consistent; this is the way he meets his end. There is an idea, however unreasonable, that to understand the ancient world would bring very important knowledge, as important as astronomy itself; and somehow the raising of Helen is a way to achieve it. Critics have been saying this for a long time, and the debunking procedure of Greg and his school has not even plausibility to offer. You may decide that Marlowe regards this delusion of Faust and the students with irony, but not that it does not occur to them. Perhaps one has to say rather more. Greg finds the phrase *glorious deed* 'singularly inept', and I can happily agree that it puts an excessive strain on the audience, whatever they do with their 'irony', if they have to feel sure all along that Helen is only a devil dressed up.

[9] B: 516.
[10] Greg, p. 80f.

Appendix 2
'Kill-Devil All the Parish Over'

[The following brief essay was found amongst the Empson papers after his death. It was attached to an autograph letter from him to Roma Gill, the text of which is as follows:

Studio House   8 Oct 79

Dear Roma,
    I plan to put this in my eventual book, and am keeping a carbon, so don't need it back. There is no need to mention your article as the enemy, since many other people are still misled by Greg. But please let me have your reaction.
    It seems to me that the play is well planned, if you allow the Benvolio and Pope Bruno additions to go, and make the 3rd Act normal by restoring Constantinople.
    Yours
            William

As the MS is the original, not a carbon copy, it seems that neither the letter nor the piece were sent. (This suggests he may have decided to revise the piece before sending it; the slight repetitions it contains indicate that it had not been fully reworked, although corrected by hand. He would have made it tighter.) The article referred to is Roma Gill's '"Such conceits as clownage keeps in pay" – Comedy and *Doctor Faustus*' in *The Fool and the Trickster*, ed. P. V. A. Williams, Cambridge (Brewer) 1979, pp. 55–63, notes pp. 133f; Roma Gill had sent Empson a preprint of her article (also present amongst his effects, liberally annotated) and this was clearly the immediate stimulation for the following piece. Roma Gill considers the clowning scene (act I, scene iv) as an example of memorial reconstruction in which there is a borrowing from Lodge and Greene's *A Looking-Glass for London*:

Lodge and Green owed a considerable debt to Marlowe, having taken much of Faustus's final soliloquy to give to their repentant Usurer in scene xvii of *Looking-Glass*. Now their comedian, variously called 'Clown' and 'Adam', makes some little repayment. (p. 60)

In the following essay Empson argues against this theory (and against memorial reconstruction here), holding that the borrowing was in the other direction.]

In the difficulty of dating the play of *Faust* by Marlowe, dreadfully short though his life was, so that the possible stretch is hardly more than 1590–2, there have been many attempts to argue from internal evidence, especially in the comic scenes. He may have been following an existing fashion for plays about magicians, or devils, or the plays may have followed *Faust*. If our two surviving sources, of 1604 and 1616, are both, even in part, 'memorial reconstructions' from the memories of actors, there is no hope of any conclusion from this method; the actors may have remembered a detail from any intervening date. But the text of such a prominent play is extremely unlikely to have been lost. The many confusions in this peculiar case are much more naturally explained by heavy trouble with the censorship; the first company sold the prompt copy to Henslowe, surprised that he would buy it, as the censor had cut out at least 500 lines, and soon after, they had to go on tour. Before handing over the prompt copy, they would have another copy made giving the parts which they were still allowed to act, which became our A-text of 1604. The only part Henslowe could win back, by negotiation with the censor, was the pub-and-castle affair at the end of act IV; probably the censor had said that this insulted a Protestant ally of the Queen, and Henslowe trumped him by getting permission from a visiting envoy of the Duke of Anhalt. The rest of the B-text contains additions by other hands, which might possibly include bits of 'memorial reconstruction' (and sometimes looks like it) but the A-text does not. One should realize that the quickest way to make a copy is to have one man read and another write, which can produce nearly all the evidence for 'memorial reconstruction', as in 'a dog so bade' for 'a dog's obeyed', in *Lear*.

It is useless to argue that the servant Wagner of Faust becomes in the play a kind of university student, like the Miles of *Friar Bacon*; he is said to be one in the English translation of the Faust-book, which Marlowe certainly used, and he did not need more. The German text realizes that twenty-four years are involved, and says that Wagner started working for Faust as a schoolboy, and probably did take some courses at the university. There is no evidence here.

The only strong detail, first used by Sir Walter Greg, is in Greene's *Looking-Glass for London*.¹ In *Faustus*, we are told, the lines do not arise naturally from the situation, as they do in the *Looking-Glass*; 'there is consequently no doubt where the lines originated'.² I think this is so plainly wrong that it is hard to imagine how the mistake arose. Devils are not normal in the situation in Nineveh; the Book of Jonah in the Bible says nothing about them at all. The play has only said that ghosts have appeared there; also of course portents, but they have been explained away by scientists. Even the Good Angel is never seen by the inhabitants. However, in this extremely flimsy play, some man who is never identified chooses to dress up as a devil (that is, presumably, as the devils had been dressed in the recent successful play of *Faust*; surely the audience were not all experts on medieval plays?), 'to make a clown afraid that passeth this way; for of late there have appeared many strange apparitions'. The clown Adam can easily be supposed to have made an enemy, but maybe this man just wants to frighten *any* clown. Adam covers the escape of his lady, and approaches the devil, planning to make him drink. The devil says he is the ghost of a man who was killed at a drinking-party with Adam, which has just happened, so he probably at least knows Adam; and this is perhaps an excuse for bringing in a bogus devil where only ghosts have been mentioned so far. He refuses drink and demands to carry Adam to Hell. Adam works in a smithy, shoeing horses, so he offers to attend to the devil's feet; but on finding no cloven hoof becomes certain that this is only a man dressed up, and the man after being cudgelled runs out saying 'Thou killest me'.

> Adam Then may I count myself, I think, a tall man, that am
> able to kill a devil. Now who dare deal with me in the
> parish, or what wench in Nineveh will not love me, when
> they say, there goes he that beat the devil? (*Exit*)³

¹ Ed. W. W. Greg, Malone Society Reprints (Oxford, 1932). Where Empson quotes, he has modernized the spelling.

² Gill, 'Comedy and *Faustus*', p. 61

³ Neither Gill nor Empson mention that here 'tall' means 'brave' (NED:Tall-3: Good at arms; stout or strong to combat; doughty, brave, bold valiant – 'If he can kill a man ... he is called a tall man, and a valiant man of his hands' – John Northbrooke: *A Treatise wherein dicing, dancing, etc. are reproved*, 1577 (1579; Shakespeare Soc., 1843), p. 8), and it is used precisely in the sense of the quotation in *The Jew of Malta*, act III, when Barabas, commenting on the mutual killings of Mathias and Ludovico, exclaims: 'So now they have show'd themselves to be tall fellows.' I had suspected a proverb, such as 'It takes a tall man to kill a devil', but none such is listed in Tilley's *Dictionary of the Proverbs in England in the Sixteenth and Seventeenth Centuries* Ann Arbor (University of Michigan Press) 1950. Gill's

As the play has no other joke, this one is used again; Adam goes and tells it, in loving detail, to the king and queen, who reward him with drink. But then the king repents and orders everyone to fast, and Adam carries round a secret supply of beef and beer in his 'slops', so he is led off to be hanged; it is part of the pious happy ending. As the loose trouser, the 'slop', was merely working-class clothes, it could not make a very powerful connection with the one brief mention of it by the Robin of Marlowe.

It is usually admitted that the repentance of the Usurer is derived from Marlowe's play, but the details here may have been an improvement added for the publication in 1594. The wicked Usurer comes in bearing two means of death, a dagger and a halter, because he feels tormented by guilt. He wants to hide from God, and presumably feels that death might be a way. But he accepts belief in Hell, so that his plan could only bring a greater torment more quickly. This contradiction never occurs to him; nor does it to Faust, but suicide from fear of Hell is certainly envisaged in Marlowe's play, echoed from the Faust-book, where Meph boasts that spirits such as himself have frequently driven people to it (perhaps not really believing in Hell, as when the Duchess of Malfi says 'any way, so I am out of your whispering'). I do not think the idea was otherwise familiar to English playgoers, so this is an unusually strong bit of evidence for borrowing. Here we get a real devil on the stage, dressed no doubt like Marlowe's devils, as the false one had been; perhaps he is not very real, but only a voice in the Usurer's ears, as he does not himself bring the weapons of death. Next the Usurer says:

> Methinks I hear a voice amidst mine ears
> That bids me stay,

because the Lord is merciful to those who repent, so like the others he turns to prayer and fasting. It seems plain that this is a very thin play, run up rapidly by a rival company to cash in on the success of Marlowe's *Faust*, and imitating it frankly in details, while at the same time claiming to be far more Christian and un-upsetting and sympathetic. It is not likely to have appeared before *Faust*. But Greene, one cannot deny, may have been exploiting his rather greasy vein of piety of his own accord, and then have made small alterations after the appearance of *Faust*, so the argument for a reverse borrowing among the clowns does call for attention.

I think it turns upon a complete misunderstanding of the sensibility of Marlowe. What is called his homosexuality is basically a political

---

suggestion that the same actor played Adam in *Looking-Glass* and the Clown in *Faustus* can therefore only be supported by the 'round slop' in the latter play, where it does seem gratuitous.

sentiment, though he was likely enough to act upon it personally. He admires young men who use their wits, and such strength as they have, against a society which appears closed to them; he wishes them luck. It is automatic for him to back Robin; and indeed, if the exploits of Robin had been told at greater length, by another author, he would seem a good deal of a hero. Probably the comic scenes would be much better if Marlowe had not been stopped in the middle of revising them. But we are chiefly concerned here with one echo, taken by the *Looking-Glass* from I. iv, the scene in which the servant Wagner, having stolen a magic book, attempts to enslave Robin; and that scene, in the A-text, is a finished piece of work. The struggle of Greg, in the notes to his grand edition (1950), to prove that the B-text is the better here makes a most entertaining piece of reading, and does partly explain how the B-text editor came to do such harmful work. He and Greg were totally out of sympathy with their author, and in just the same way.

347–8 The author accidentally and rather carelessly used the phrase *I know* twice over. In representation (possibly in the prompt-book) one of the occurrences (the first) was naturally and very properly omitted.[4]

Come now, if it had gone the other way round, we would be told that slipshod repetitions and actors' gags are an infallible proof of memorial reconstruction. The reason why Greg sounds more huffy than usual is that he has to silence opposition here.

350 The repetition of the last words of the previous speaker in A betrays the actor's anxiety to raise another laugh.[5]

But this is what the scene is supposed to do; it is standard music-hall technique to allow the audience to savour the accusation before they get the absurd reply. The only question here is why the B-text editor cut the repetition; and Greg lets us see the answer – that he felt tetchy, as Greg did, and did not want the audience to laugh.

353–4 It may seem surprising that the author should expect his Clown (or his audience) to recognise . . .

---

[4] Greg, p. 316.
[5] Greg is referring to A.368–70 (scene iv):

| Wagner | I know he would give his soul to the Devil for a shoulder of mutton, though it were blood raw. |
| Clown | How, my soul to the Devil for a shoulder of mutton though twere blood raw? |

a bit of grammar-school Latin. But it is a basic part of the story that Robin could manage to use the magic book, which of course was in Latin; and Greg always resents the idea bitterly. I hope these examples are enough.

The crucial sequence must now be presented:

Wagner   Well, I will cause two devils presently to fetch thee away, Baliol and Belcher.

Robin   Let your Balio and your Belcher come here, and I'll knock them, they were never so knocked since they were devils. Say I should kill one of them, what would folks say? Do you see yonder tall fellow in the round slop, he has killed the devil. So I should be called kill-devil all the parish over.
(Enter two devils, and the clown runs up and down crying)

Wagner   Baliol and Belcher, spirits away. *(Exeunt)*

Robin   What, are they gone? a vengeance on them, they have vile long nails. There was a he devil and a she devil. I'll tell you how you shall know them; all he devils has horns, and all she devils has clifts and cloven feet.

Wagner   Well sirrah, follow me.

Robin   But do you hear? If I should serve you, would you teach me to raise up Banios and Belchios?

(A 404–20)

He has no class duty of courage, but fright does not make him appeal to the tyrant, as the B-text editor makes him do. As soon as the fright is removed, he sees how to take advantage of the experience – he begins to lecture on devils, even to the man who fetched them. As the critics of the text are all lecturers by profession themselves, I think they might show more understanding here. But none of them seem even to know that Robin is wrong – whether or not it is 'obscene'[6] (as they like to say) to mention the sexual differences in a newly observed species, devils did not have any difference of sex; he has invented it on the spot. Readiness of this kind is his charm; he is unpuncturable. And he immediately sets out to get control of these devils himself; he goes off with Wagner willingly because he expects to do so. At no point does he even pretend to enslave himself. Wagner tells him, as he goes out, to pace behind, in Latin, and he leers at the audience:

God forgive me, he speaks Dutch fustian: well, I'll *follow* him, I'll *serve* him, that's flat.

(A: 435f)

The words I have italicized mean 'I will behave as badly as he does; I will serve him right'. Greg contemptuously points out that they are 'echoed'

---

[6] Gill, 'Comedy and *Faustus*', p. 60.

from a few lines before,[7] thus presuming that they are empty padding. But Robin is stating an intention; when we next see him he has a job as ostler, in the stable of an inn, and is struggling to read the Latin of a magic book which he has stolen from Wagner or Faust. He succeeds in this scholarly work, because when we see him again, in danger of arrest for theft, he can call up Meph from the harem of the Sultan in Constantinople. I think this an impressive achievement, but Greg calls it 'significant' that the spells are nonsense. The B-text omits the remark which gives a lively end to the scene, presumably because the B-text editor was operating with the same automatic contempt as Greg. But it is greatly needed, to prepare the audience for the next appearance of Robin, where he has done what he promised; he has escaped from slavery to Wagner with a stolen magic book.

Robin should report this (the scene begins: 'O this is admirable! Here I have stolen one of Doctor Faustus' conjuring books') in the gap between our present act II scenes i and ii, where ii begins with Faustus gazing out of the window and saying 'When I behold the heavens, then I repent.' Even the B-text editor realized that a lapse of time, say a month, is implied by the words that follow, and he shoved in an irrelevant bit of a Chorus. But the great textual expert Fredson Bowers went on record as considering there was no need for any gap at all;[8] this is instructive, as proving that such a man does not attend to the meaning of the words. Greg could do that much, so he puzzled about what to put in the gap, and invented a comic scene which would be mortally dull but patiently explained what happened to Robin next. It recalls Dover Wilson, who improved the play of *Macbeth* by supposing a series of debates during the first act, in the manner of Racine. *Macbeth* needs to begin very fast (even so quickly may one catch the plague), and the explanations can be left for guessing. The case of *Faust* is different; there are possible reflections about the comic scenes, but the obvious need for them is to divide the serious ones. They allow Faust to get off the stage for a few minutes, and when he comes back the time may be presumed to be later, perhaps by a month or two. The only other way to let Faust off the stage is to reach one of the Choruses which come between the five acts; indeed, the B-text editor offered a bit of a Chorus as a break before II.ii, though it is obviously out of place. What the mood of the play requires is a brief moment of triumph for Robin, after he has got away with his magic book, just when Faust feels triumphant too. Then the back curtain opens upon Faust gazing at the night sky and feeling suspicious about Meph, so that he threatens to repent, and has to be reduced to despair. If

---

[7] Greg, p. 316.
[8] See his edition of Marlowe's *Works* Cambridge (Cambridge University Press) 1973.

the brief comic scene beginning 'O this is admirable' is put here, where something needs to be put, the audience have (I grant) to wait a long time before they see the consequence, when Robin calls Meph from the Sultan's harem; but they had been alerted to wonder what would happen when he had mastered the Latin book, so would easily remember this part of the story though it pops up as a startling irrelevance. They are all agog now to see what Faust did in the harem, but the spectacle would be either indecent or inadequate, so the snatching away of Meph solves a problem. I assume that the original version presented the banquet of the Sultan, as in the Faust-book, using precisely the same equipment and persons as for the banquet of the Pope: it would be enough to pull on 'oriental robes'. Robin appears again in the pub-and-castle incident at the end of act IV, which is not in the A-text; the censors had cut it in their first fury, but it was won back by Henslowe in negotiation with the censors, arguing that otherwise his 1594 production would be impossible (and they desired the play as it had become, after adding a lot of Hell at the end). The story of Robin is then clear and well spaced out, and he does not even have to go on wearing an animal head, let alone be sent to Hell.

I do not know any other play in which the comic scenes got out of order, and were still out of order hundreds of years later; that is the chief thing which requires explanation in the case of *Faust*. 'Memorial reconstruction', that romantic darling of the modern expert, is no help here. The idea is that the assembled actors recited their parts to a copyist, thus evading some law of property; but the actors would be sure to know the order of the comic scenes. It is a grim thought that neither the editor of the A-text nor of the B-text (who realized that *some* break was needed before II. ii) had ever seen the play performed, or never when sober. But, after recognizing this, we have still to ask how their copy got out of order. I propose a theory which fits in with the other sides of the puzzle, and surely any rival theory must do as much. The original *Faust* had been performed several times, perhaps twice a week for three weeks, when the censors demanded to see the prompt copy, already licensed by Edmund Tilney; and it came back, not entirely forbidden, but marked with many savage cuts, amounting to five or six hundred lines, which made it unactable in London. As a first reaction to this blow, the manager of the company told the copyist to write out all the bits which were not forbidden; then they could more easily consider what could be done. The friendly Tilney would be willing to certify that none of this text had been forbidden, so it could be acted in the provinces. This, with minor modifications, became our A-text, which is almost entirely the work of Marlowe. The artful Henslowe bought the old prompt copy, with the censor's cuts on it, and negotiated the return of the two final comic scenes, closing act IV, in exchange for the addition of some dirty sadism about Hell in act V. This was for his production in 1594, and

Henslowe's *Diary* shows that the first crowded audiences soon fell off sharply. He thought it essential to have the comic scenes tidied up properly, whatever the betrayal of the central idea, because otherwise it would obviously not be a well-made play. We have no reason to doubt that he put the short comic scene beginning 'O this is admirable' in its right place. But we need to find some reason why the hurried work of the copyist, which became our A-text, had left the order wrong. In the A-text Robin has just started to spell out the magic book, and immediately after can raise Meph with it, which is absurd.

I propose that Marlowe, just before that fatal event [the censor's demand for the prompt copy], had called in the comic scenes to review and improve them. What was sent to the censor had these scenes huddled in at the end, and they were ignored as harmless, but the copyist had to fit them in somewhere, and made a clumsy attempt at it. Of course the large final scenes of act IV, involving the Duke of Anhalt as well as the sinful comics, did not require improvement; they were left in place, and could easily be forbidden on the excuse that they were an insult to a Protestant ally of the Queen. (Probably Henslowe secured an approval signed by a visiting envoy of the Duke.) But the earlier ones were much harder to do; they need to be brief, not felt as an interruption, and yet very hard hitting, making a point plain. Marlowe was quite right if he felt that this was the part of his masterpiece which needed improvement, and he had already done a good deal of it, judging from the fragments which remain. The idea that he despised writing about Robin too much to do it himself, but would hire a hack to do it, betrays ignorance both of his income and of his sexual interests. He would think he could make better jokes than a hired man, too. Surely this nonsense about his collaborators needs to be blown away; he would be an impossible man to collaborate with. But he was willing to learn; I agree that he began writing these prose comic scenes by imitating his old fellow-student Nashe. This does not mean that he hired Nashe to write them; a prologue written by Nashe in 1589 is distinctly unfriendly towards Marlowe, though of course they may have made it up later on. What these Victorian experts never realize, while spotting the 'styles' of the poets as if they were types of beetle, is that any group of young men working on a common project becomes skilled at imitating a prominent member, so that the others laugh; they are in fact all learning from each other, though it is tactfully hidden by a pretence of aggression. Now the first fact about the prose style of Nashe is that he makes the speaker appear drunk. This is just tolerable on the printed page if you have the patience to work out the satire (it becomes exasperating when the text is your only source for a bit of historical information) but it was no use for these comic scenes, which needed to tell an interesting story briefly. Marlowe soon realized this point, and it explains the only thing Leo Kirschbaum ever discovered, that the obscurity of the comic A-text is sometimes cleared up in the B-text. When Marlowe writes down 'Thou art an etc.' he does not mean that the actor may say anything he likes but that the rest of the speech is available in an earlier draft.

Such details seem to be needed, to show that my theory is consistent, but perhaps a more radical difference of attitude is what really matters. Modern literary critics delight in finding a 'privy nip', as if it were a lethal knife-stab, given from behind unobserved in a crowd; so they think the function of the comic scenes is to jeer at the hero. These poverty-struck lousy criminals are obviously loathsome, and plainly Robin does what Faust does; he is meant therefore to imply that Faust, whose familiar devils are his lice, is sickening too. But logically it is just as possible to argue the other way; plainly Robin, who is always fun, does not deserve eternal torture, and the play assures us that he is soon released from his animal head; therefore Faust, who has not really done anything worse, and has taken to a life of fun, does not deserve it either. I am not making the play trivial; his terrors deserve entire sympathy; but (until Henslowe got to work) we were permitted to suppose he is spared at the end.

Coming now to the small but crucial point about the parallel between *Faust* and the *Looking-Glass*, I deny that the words 'arise naturally from the situation'[9] in the *Looking-Glass*, but not in *Faust*, therefore it is 'certain' that *Faust* came later. The tacit assumption here is that a lousy low-class man can never be plucky. When Wagner threatens to bring devils, Robin says at once he will fight them, and then (as he doesn't much believe it) his imagination soars into how much he will be admired if he kills a devil. When they appear, he knows he can't fight them, but starts at once planning to get the same control of them as Wagner. Devils cannot be killed, and have no sex, so he is twice absurdly wrong, but from the start he is determined to keep his defence and to learn. Adam in the *Looking-Glass* also showed nerve, and did not deserve the Hell to which Greene apparently sent him, but he does not talk in this fanciful way until he knows he is safe. After he has found that the opponent is not a devil, since he has human feet, he beats him but lets him run away, though killing was presumably possible, and then he laughs, imagining how he could boast of having beaten a devil, but takes care not to say he has killed one. He lives in the great city of Nineveh, and so he knows about devils. What does he mention his parish for, and then hurriedly add the whole city? Because Greene was echoing a well-known passage in Marlowe. Greene has told us that the inhabitants of Nineveh are 'ethnics', who would not have parishes, and that to cross Nineveh is three days' journey; but the Robin of Marlowe is a country boy determined to make his way, who would easily consider the opinion of his whole parish. The sentence in Marlowe obviously arises

⁹ Gill, 'Comedy and *Faustus*', p. 61.

more naturally than the one in Greene, unless you ascribe to Marlowe a stubborn bitter contempt for his comic characters; but he is much more likely to have felt fond of them, in view of his known predilections. The scene becomes much more agreeable if you allow yourself to see this.

I had hoped for a substantial improvement in this field. When Fredson Bowers admitted almost without comment, in his pachydermal manner, that the entry in Henslowe's *Diary* was correct, and he really had paid for additions to *Faust* which survive in the B-text, I expected that the logs would begin to flow normally down the stream. Greg had also refused to believe another entry in Henslowe, paying Jonson for the Additions to *Hierynomo*, merely because Greg was an expert on style and knew that the additions were not in Jonson's style. Obviously Jonson when young could imitate the romantic style, but he had to be bribed to do it, and did not boast of it afterwards. Once the experts had broken away from the whimsical paradoxes of Greg, I thought, the road was free. But they are still contriving to tie themselves up.

Appendix 3
Concordance of Acts and Scenes

The dramatis personae and actions in the left-hand column are listed according to Empson's proposed reconstruction; * indicates scenes not present in the surviving play texts, a † indicates a scene transposed, and # indicates material which is redundant.

D. P./Action	Empson	A-text	B-text
Prologue: Chorus.	Prologue	Prologue	Prologue
Faust's study: Faust, Wagner, Good and Bad Angels. The Magicians.	I. i	sc. i	I. i
Wagner, Scholars.	I. ii	sc. ii	I. ii
Faust conjures Meph. Disputation. Faust triumphant.	I. iii	sc. iii	I. iii
Wagner, Clown, in front of curtain. Devils torment Clown.	I. iv	sc. iv	I. iv
*Chorus: Faust's plan.	*Act II Chorus	–	–
Faust's study: Faust, Good and Bad Angels, Meph. Agreement is reached; a show of devils. The Deed. Disputations; the devil-wife. Meph gives Faust a book.	II. i	sc. v	II. i

D. P./Action	Empson	A-text	B-text
			Chorus 1
*Faust as bookworm: Wagner announces the Magicians; Faust boasts to them of what he has done; they hurry away.	*II. ii	–	–
†Robin, Dick: The stolen book.	†II. iii	sc. viii	II. iii
Faust repentant: Angels, Meph. Astronomy: the quarrel. Lucifer et al.; seven deadly sins. The second book.	II. iv	sc. v	II. ii
Chorus: Faust's journey to the stars; his land tour.	Act III Chorus	Chorus 1	Chorus 2
Faust, Meph in 'dragon'. Guide book speeches by Meph; the 'City of Rome' (following A-text).	III. i	sc. vii (first guide book speeches by Faust)	III. i
	–	–	# First Bruno scene
Papal feast: Pope and train. Faust boxes Pope's ears; Papal malediction.	III. ii	(sc. vii)	III. ii # Second Bruno scene
*Faust, Meph in 'dragon': Constantinople described.	*III. iii	–	–
*Sultan's feast: Faust renders him immobile. Fog. Faust enters the harem.	*III. iv	–	–

D. P./Action	Empson	A-text	B-text
Dick, Robin, Vintner: Robin conjures Meph. Animal heads.	III. v	sc. viii	III. iii
*Faust and Meph leave the harem: the Sultan questions his wives.	*III. vi	–	–
†Chorus: Faust's return.	†Act IV Chorus	Chorus 2 (between sc. vii and sc. viii)	–
	–	–	# IV. i – First Benvolio scene
The Emperor's Court: Faust received. The Knight scorns Faust. Alexander and Consort. Knight with horns. Faust rewarded.	IV. i	sc. x	IV. ii (# Bruno)
	–	–	# IV. iii – Benvolio
	–	–	# IV. iv – Benvolio
Faust's walk across the green. Horse-courser. Faust sleeps. Horse-courser/Meph. False-leg. Wagner with invitation to Anhalt.	IV. ii "	(sc. xi) "	– –
Robin, Dick, Horse-courser, Carter, Hostess; the Inn (indignation meeting).	IV. iii	–	IV. vi
Anhalt: Duke, Duchess, Faust. Grapes for the Duchess. Indignation meeting arrives.	IV. iv	sc. xii	IV. vii

D. P./Action	Empson	A-text	B-text
Faust silences them, to the amusement of Duke and Duchess.			
Wagner as Chorus.	Act V Chorus	sc. xiii	V. i

Faust, Scholars, Helen.
   Old Man persuades Faust to
   repent. The second quarrel.
   Faust confirms his pact.
   Return of Helen; the kiss.
   Old Man tormented, dies.
	V. i		

	–	–	V. ii # Lucifer, etc.

Faust, scholars.
   Faust confesses; the scholars
   retire.
	V. ii	sc. xiv	"

	–	–	# Meph mocks Faust; Angels; Hell discovered.

Clock strikes 11.
   Faust's soliloquy.
   Midnight: 'Ah Mephastophilis'
   Faust dies in Meph's arms.
			# devils. 'Oh Mephosto-philis'
			# V. iii.
			Scholars find Faust's body.

Epilogue: Chorus	Epilogue	Epilogue	Epilogue

Postscript

This postscript is intended, not as a criticism or analysis of Empson's thesis, but rather as an addendum, providing elaboration on one or two points considered in the essay, and submitting my own findings for discussion within the context offered. It also mentions some of the more recent work which has appeared since the essay was written.

The translator

Empson's speculative profile of P. F. is very brave (I suspect he may have been influenced here by his knowledge of the business dealings of the Marvell family), and although plausible, it could be very wide of the mark. The trouble is, all we know is 'P. F. Gent.' and even this much is suspect, since the initials differ in some subsequent editions of the EFB: 'P. R. Gent.' in 1608 and 'P. K. Gent.' in 1648. These variants are usually assumed to be misprints, but their occurrence does undermine the security of our knowledge. Neil Brough ('Doctor Faustus and "P. F."', *Notes & Queries*, NS.32 (1985), no. 1, pp. 15f) has drawn attention to an 'R. F. Gent.' who appears as translator of Friedrich Dedekind's *Grobianus*, and has aired his possible identity with 'P. F.'. Latin and German editions of this work, originally published in 1549, were printed at Frankfurt in 1584 and 1586 respectively and certainly the place and dates are suggestive. The English translation, *'The Schoole of Slovenrie; or Cato turned wrong side outward* translated out of Latine into English verse, to the use of all English Christendome, except Court and Cittie. By R. F. Gent.', was published in 1605. A careful comparison of the style of this work with that of the EFB needs to be made, but even if supportive it could hardly be expected to provide proof. If both books are the work of the same man, proficient in both German and Latin, then, says Brough, 'this would point more toward a scholar with a sideline in translating foreign works of popular appeal into English, and who had some connection with the Frankfurt book market during the years 1584–7, than towards the idea, held by some scholars, that the German Faustbuch was brought to England by returning actors'.

The topographical detail and references to local lore which P. F. adds to Faust's Grand Tour, particularly in the journey through Silesia, have led to speculation that P. F. had travelled through these parts (see R. Rohde: 'Das Englische Faustbuch und Marlowes Tragödie', *Studien zur Englische Philologie*, Heft XLIII, 1910), though others have argued that his factual errors show that he cannot personally have seen some of the sights he describes. (One could, of course, say that these places were not on his personal itinerary, or that he always had his nose in a book.) Rohde goes so far as to suggest the identity with Dr Dee who was at Heidelberg and then at Prague during the relevant period, 1587/8. This hypothesis (which does not explain the initials 'P. F.', other than suggesting they are a cipher) is considered attractive by G. Silvani ('Faust in Inghilterra' in M. E. D'Agostini's *Analisi comparata delle fonti inglesi e tedesche des Faust dal Volksbuch a Marlowe*, Napoli (Tullio Pronti) 1978). We may agree that it would explain the impatient outburst of the translator in the cosmological chapters, his apparent piety, and, indeed, his interest in the subject, but while it is not to be doubted that Dee read the Faust-book one can hardly imagine he would have made the translation. If he was not well versed in German, however, he might well have induced someone to translate it for him, and an association between Dee and the Faust-book cannot be ruled out. Dee returned to England in December 1589 and was certainly closely associated with the Ralegh circle from that time, so here at least is a possible link with Marlowe at a critical period. (Some association with Marlowe becomes more likely when it is recalled that Dee was host to Ortelius, himself a member of the Family of Love, whom Marlowe might well have aspired to meet.) Such speculations are not much help in identifying P. F. but they do broaden the field of Marlowe's possible advisers.

However, the theory that P. F. made a continental journey in 1587 receives some support from his failure to translate certain moralistic asides of the Faust-book which are additions by Spies to the manuscript W. This could indicate a knowledge of W on the part of P. F., most readily gained first-hand through Spies himself in Frankfurt or Heidelberg. There are also indications of German help with the translation. Thus he writes (EFB, p. 44) 'we Germains call this towne Ofen, but in the Hungarian speech it is Start' (GFB: 'The Hungarian name for the city is Start, in German, Ofen') whereas he usually takes pains to dissociate himself from the German author and inserts 'in Germany' wherever he feels the explanation necessary to his English readers. Sometimes too there are literal translations which do not fit with P. F.'s customary fluency, such as 'gave the flight' (EFB, chapter 34) for *'gab die Flucht'* (= took to his heels).

These considerations aside, an early date for the translation (either as MS, or preferably, a published edition) is a major premise of Empson's theory. What tentative evidence there is for an early dating, I have given in the introduction (pp. 35–6). This question must remain open, although I agree with Empson that the statements in the Court Book of the Stationer's Company do not imply that Jeffe's edition must have appeared in May 1592, as Greg decrees. However, the Court Book testifies to Jeffe's involvement in printing a book (not named) without authority and his subsequent imprisonment for so doing. The entry for Monday 7 August 1592 (O.S.) reads:

> whereas Abell Ieffes about the [22nd] day of July last did resist the search which master Stirrop, warden, Tho[mas] Dawson and Tho[mas Rente] man, renters, were appointed to make and would have made of his printing house according to the ordinance and decrees, and for that he contemptuously proceeded in printing a book without authority contrary to our master, his commandment, and for that he refused to deliver the barre of his press neither would deliver any of the book to be brought to the hall according to the decrees, and also for that he used violence to our officer in the search, it is now therefore ordered by a full court held this day, that . . . he shall be committed to ward. (*Records of the Court of the Stationers' Company, 1576–1602*, ed. W. W. Greg and E. Boswell, London (Bibliographical Society) 1930, p. 42, where the original spelling is retained)

On Monday, 18 December (O.S.) of the same year:

> In full court held this day, Abel Ieffes, according to the direction of the lord archbishop of Canterbury, his grace, appeared and humbly acknowledged his former offence and undutifulness, craving pardon and favour for the same and promising hereafter to live as becometh an honest man, and to show himself obedient and dutiful in the Company and to the ordinances thereof. (Ibid. p. 44)

This is followed immediately by the notice of the complaint against Orwin, quoted in the essay. It is tantalizing evidence for the powers of the censorship: we know the action but we are not allowed to know the name of the book. But even if this were the EFB, it need not have been the first edition. Logeman ('The English Faust-book of 1592', *Recueil des Travaux Publiés par la Faculté de Philosophie et Lettres, Université de Gand*, Ghent and Amsterdam (Université de Gand) fasc. 24, 1900) has argued from the pagination errors of the 1592 EFB (Orwin) that the latter is a page-for-page copy of a preceding edition – in other words the amendments to the 'imperfect matter' must have been present in the precursor (Jeffes' edition). If so, Jeffes' pardon, followed immediately by reinstatement of copyright, is the more readily understood. (It may be noted that Orwin had had his press seized by the Stationers' Company in 1591 but the nature of his offence is unknown. See Greg, p. 4.) More importantly, this implies an earlier edition, containing the 'imperfect matter', of which we have no knowledge whatsoever. This can hardly have been printed much after late-1591, so probably earlier.

Mephostophiles

Empson has dwelt at length upon the different treatments of Mephosto-philes in the German and English Faust-books. 'P. F.' has chosen (or has been forced) to build on the original, making the spirit 'a Prince, ruler (under Lucifer) of all the circuit from Septentrio to the Meridian', so that Faust congratulates himself on having raised so potent a being. Many subtle changes in the translation render P. F.'s Mephostophiles more compelling and more terrible. Thus where in the GFB the spirit recounts the torments of the damned saying '*They* will complain ... *They* will suffer', etc., P. F. makes him use the second person pronoun: '*You* will complain', and the effect is much more intense and Mephostophiles more malicious. This characterization is retained in Marlowe, and as in the EFB, Faust names the spirit in his first conjuration, whereas in the GFB any spirit will do and Faust does not learn the name of the one he gets until chapter 5, when they have already concluded their deal. Now this is very strange and it surprises me that Empson did not consider it further.

The name Mephostophiles has its first occurrence in the GFB – at least, it does not occur amongst any of the lists of spirits given in Wier or in any of the known grimoires. We must conclude it was the invention of the original Faust-book author. Its derivation has puzzled many commentators. Butler (*The Myth of the Magus*, (Cambridge) 1948) sees it as a near miss for both '*Me-photo-philes*' ('No friend to light') and '*Me-Fausto-philes*' ('No friend to Faust'), but one exact derivation was provided by Ernst Zitelmann (*Germanisch-Romanisch Monatsschrift*, XIV, 1926, pp. 65f): by interchange of the middle two syllables of '*Me to phos philes*' (Greek: 'The light is not a friend'). This seems far-fetched until it is remembered that nouns in a Greek lexicon are always followed by their article: *phos*, *to*, and at once the interpretation becomes acceptable. If true, it imposes some limits on the Greek proficiency of the Faust-book author. Also, if the Mephastophilis of the A-text of *Doctor Faustus* is Marlowe's usage, then this derivation was not lost on Marlowe who has changed 'light' to 'right' or 'lawfulness' (*phas*) without bothering to correct for gender. Hence Mephastophilis is antinomian, whether the laws be divine or human.

However, the important point is the novelty of this spirit. The name cannot have been well known in England when P. F. made or published his translation and yet he is gratuitously introduced as Faust's chosen intermediary. And this sets a difficulty for P. F. when he comes to translate chapter 5 of the GFB; keeping now to his original, Faust asks the spirit his name. Mephostophiles answers 'My name is as thou sayest, Mephostophiles' (perhaps with a quizzical look); the 'as thou sayest' becomes a necessary interpolation in the circumstances. So why does P. F. do this? Marlowe's position would have been quite different. By the time of the play Mephostophiles would have acquired recognized status from the EFB. Besides, it is dramatically sensible of Marlowe to build Mephostophiles by having Faust call upon him directly: '*ut ... surgat Mephastophilis*'. Marlowe's Faust never asks the spirit his name, and since P. F. was bold enough to introduce the name in the conjuration, one might wonder at him timidly following the GFB when he reaches chapter 5. A possible explanation is that the 'amendments' of the 1592 EFB were made in the light of the play. Of course, there is no *proof* here of 'reverse borrowing', but the strong suggestion of it does at least enhance the theory of an early date for *Doctor Faustus*.

We might then ask whether the other main dramatic invention by P. F. – the quarrel as pretext for the introduction of the seven principal spirits – is not also Marlowe's. In the play the quarrel is a direct result of Faust's explicit vacillation when he is angry with Mephastophilis' refusal to tell him who made the world:

Faust	Villain, have I not bound thee to tell me any thing?
Mephastophilis	Aye, that is not against our kingdom, but this is,
	Think thou on hell Faustus, for thou are damned.
Faust	Think Faustus upon God that made the world.
Mephastophilis	Remember this. (*Exit*)

(A: 698–702)

But in the EFB the excuse for the quarrel is rather limp and the insertion patches up the exclusion of Mephostophiles' heretical creation myth (GFB, chapter 22). Having responded to Faust's complaints of poor service by promising to answer anything he asks, Mephostophiles bullies him. The question was: 'how and after what sorte God made the world, and all the creatures in them, and why man was made after the Image of God?' (The final clause is P. F.'s invention.) 'The spirit hearing this, answered, Faustus thou knowest that all this is in vaine for thee to aske, I knowe that thou art sory for that thou has done, but it availeth thee not, for I will teare thee in thousands of peeces, if thou change not thine opinions, and hereat hee vanished away.' We learn that he was 'in a rage' but it is scarcely apparent from the words (Marlowe's actor, of course, can supply any amount of rage to accompany 'Remember this'). Then the devil comes and 'spake in this sorte: Faustus, I have seene thy thoughtes, which are not as thou hast vowed vnto me . . . wherefore I am come to visite thee and to shew thee some of our hellish pastimes, in hope that will drawe and confirme thy minde a little more stedfast vnto vs' (EFB, chapter 19). The idea that the devil had looked at Faust's thoughts is in the GFB (chapter 23): 'when you awoke at midnight I took a look at your thoughts. You were thinking how you would like to see some of the principal spirits of hell. And so I have come', etc.

P. F. cannot keep wholly away from the original here, as he is well able to do in his other flights, and this leads one to suspect amendment of a draft. In the EFB, both the appearance of the devil and the pastimes are a punishment for Faust, whereas in Marlowe's play the devils are a sufficient threat and the subsequent Masque becomes an entertainment. Marlowe's device of the seven deadly sins relieves him of the difficulties of animal transformations besides providing opportunity for much ribald dialogue. Such invention is the stock in trade of the dramatist, likewise the quarrel, but hardly to be expected of a translator, especially if the occasion is gratuitous. But the idea, once observed, could be used to help him out of the difficulty caused by his need to omit the creation myth.

P. F.'s mistranslations

The EFB has a fair sprinkling of trivial mistranslations of individual words indicating that P. F. was by no means a complete master of the German language. These are sometimes funny, as for example, when he translates '*Sprosse*' (the rung of a ladder)(GFB, chapter 45) as 'holly wand'. (As it is the seat on which the students are transported to the cellars of the Bishop of Salzburg, they might have discovered some discomfort.) He is several times in difficulty with '*Schlafftrunck*' (a last drink before going to bed, a nightcap) and has to resort to paraphrase. For example, '*es wirt zum Schlaff Trunck besser werden*' (Sp. 165) becomes 'according to the vse of our Countrie wee must drink all this night, and so a draught of the best wine to bedward is commendable', and even in the tension of the final chapter, '*Als nu der Sclafftrunck auch vollendet ward*' (Sp. 218) is translated as 'and when they sleeped (for drinke was in their heads)'. Many of the mistranslations seem to be the result of misreading of the German text, implying poor light or poor eyesight or both. Thus, in the description of the Bishop's Palace at Trier, '*so fest, daß sie keinen feind zu fürchten haben*' (Sp. 100), P. F. appears to misread '*fürchten*' as '*Fürsten*' and translates the phrase: 'so strong that it was impossible for any prince's power to win it'. This trivial error has considerable significance, as it passes into *Doctor Faustus*: 'Not to be wonne by any conquering prince' (A: 826), thus helping to dispose of the one-time theory that Marlowe made the additions to the EFB.

However, the majority of these failings are inconsequential. What has to be considered is Empson's suggestion that P. F. made wilful mistranslations which could, if necessary, be construed as slips. Two important cases are considered in the essay and I certainly concede that the second of these ('Oh that I might bear the heavens upon my shoulders') could plausibly be so interpreted if only P. F. were not so prone to error. There are others equally debatable and it seemed important to examine them.

When, at their second meeting (chapter 3), Mephostophiles tells Faust of Lucifer's empire, he says that Lucifer 'established a Legion and a government of many devils. We call him the Prince of the Orient since he has his dominion in the East' (GFB) ('*hat diser ein Legion vnnd jhr viel der Teuffel ein Regiment auffgericht, den wir den Orientalischen Fürsten nennen, denn seine Herrschafft hatte er im Auffgang*') (Sp. 13). P. F. gives: 'yet he hath notwithstanding a Legion of Diuels at his commaundement, that we call the Oriental Princes; for his power is great and infinite'. Now, it is a very simple slip to mistake 'prince' for 'princes' and to consider the relative pronoun as referring to the devils rather than to Lucifer, and if the error were not compounded by what follows it could be ignored. But P. F.'s logic is impeccable and he refuses 'since he has his dominion in the East' as a reason for calling the devils Oriental Princes, and supplies something less limiting to the power of Lucifer. So he is certainly using his mistranslation to good purpose. Besides, he later bills Mephostophiles as ruler of 'all the circuit from Septentrio to the Meridian', under Lucifer, and an accurate translation of Spies here would not have allowed for this. But we still have to confess that the original mistranslation is probably a slip.

In the GFB (chapter 10) Faust wants to marry because 'he was constantly tormented by sexual desire' ('*stach ihn seine Aphrodisia Tag vnd Nacht*') (Sp. 31). This follows a sentence in which we learn that Faust 'believed neither in God, Hell, nor the Devil and supposed that the soul died with the body'. P. F. seems to read the text as '*stand in seine(m) Aphrodisia*' and translates, adding a preamble: 'and had quite forgotten Diuinitie or the immortalite of his soule, but stood in his damnable heresie day and night'. Are we to believe he thought '*Aphrodisia*' was a heresy, the worship of Aphrodite perhaps? He continues: 'And bethinking himself of a wife', a non-sequitur unless 'stood' is taken as a *double entendre*. This example is clearly unrewarding.

Finally there is one most curious misreading which deserves a mention.

It comes in the final lamentation (GFB, chapter 66; EFB, chapter 61) not long after the 'heavens on the shoulders' howler, in a passage which is a play on Luther's *'Eine feste Burg'*: 'Where is my refuge? Where is my protection, succour and retreat? Where is my stronghold? By whom should I seek to be consoled?' (Text of final sentence: *'Wessen darf ich mich trösten?'*) (Sp. 215). Instead of the last sentence P. F. gives: 'knowledge dare I not trust', so it would appear that he has misread the text as *'Wissen darf ich nicht trösten'*, which is nonsense but readily transformable to P. F.'s rendering. Yet there is some point in this emphasis since it was particularly Faust's pursuit of knowledge which brought him to this situation. Earlier (Sp. 208), P. F. mistranslates *'Vermessenheit'* ('presumptuousness') as 'forgetfulness' (*'Vergessenheit'*). Was he purblind or was he attempting to pinpoint Faust's failing more accurately? We shall never know.

Conclusion

As I have mentioned in the introduction, Empson had completed his working draft of the essay by early 1982. This makes it unlikely that he had fully covered the Marlowe literature much beyond 1980 and he may well have missed some earlier publications. In preparing the bibliography I have worked back to 1975 and I would like to draw attention here to work bearing upon the material of the essay. (To economize on space I cite here only the author's name and the date of publication; full details may be sought in the bibliography.)

Empson receives support for his arguments against Greg from Constance Brown Kuriyama (1975) and Nicholas Kiessling (1975). The problems of the A- and B-text were reconsidered by Michael J. Warren in 1981, who concluded that both texts are 'probably faulty in relation to any authorial original' which 'cannot be recovered with any confidence by any bibliographic tools currently available', but in the A-text Faust 'has the possibility of salvation open to him to the end'. Both John Norton Smith (1978) and Michael J. Keefer (1983) argue for the superiority of the A- as against the B-text; the former author shows that the A-text follows the orthodox astronomy of the time, the latter exposes what he considers to be the 'aesthetic weaknesses' of the B-text.

Roy T. Ericksen (1981) aired the view shared here by Empson that the clownage scene (B-text II.iii, 743–75) constitutes the scene lost following II.i, and transposition of this scene restores the structural order of the play. On Empson's reconstruction (see appendix 3: 'Concordance'), this scene becomes the new II.iii, following a 'lost' scene in which Faust boasts to the magicians. As Empson does not mention Ericksen's paper, we must assume he was not aware of it, as the relatively late date makes probable.

There is one other work devoted to a reconstruction of *Doctor Faustus* which deserves mention although I can make no evaluation since I have been unable to locate a copy. It is *A Tragical History of Doctor Faustus*, Melbourne (Australian National University Press), 1981, by the poet A. D. Hope. (I am indebted to Andrew Best of Curtis Brown for this information.)

Textual Notes

Chapter 1

a	270; ET		cc	15; E2
b	402; E7		dd	16; E3
c	270; ET		ee	278; E9
d	271; E2		ff	406; E10
e	276; E7		gg	407;E11
f	20; E5		hh	279; E10
g	403; E8		ii	262; E5
h	404; E8a		jj	21; E6
i	405; E9		kk	262; E5
j	272; E3		ll	280; E11
k	273; E4		mm	21; E6
l	274; E5		nn	262; E5
m	275; E6		oo	405; E9
n	183; E4		pp	262; E5
o	14; ET		qq	281; E12
p	275; E6		rr	21; E6
q	37; E2		ss	22; E7
r	195; E7		tt	281; E12
s	196; E8		uu	282; E12a
t	275; E6		vv	283; E13
u	276; E7		ww	22; E7
v	45; E4		xx	23; E7
w	14; ET		yy	407; E11
x	183; E4		zz	22; E7
y	194; E5		aaa	24; E8
z	15; E2		bbb	26; E9
aa	277; E8		ccc	22; E7
bb	278; E9		ddd	26; E9

Chapter 1 (*cont.*)

eee	22; E7
fff	26; E9
ggg	27; E10
hhh	29; E11
iii	30; E12
jjj	263; E6
kkk	405; E9
lll	31; E13

Chapter 2

a	431; ET
b	325; ET
c	431; ET
d	325; ET
e	129; E5
f	325; ET
g	201; E0
h	325; ET
i	326; E2
j	171; E0
k	326; E2
l	232; E2
m	326; E2
n	327; E3
o	129; E5
p	130; E6
q	328; E4
r	327; E3
s	329; E5
t	330; E6
u	331; E7
v	332; E8
w	430; E0
x	428; E0
y	240; E9
z	225; E0
aa	131; E7
bb	242; E11
cc	434; E0

dd	128; E4
ee	242; E11
ff	243; E12
gg	166; E0
hh	243; E12
ii	244; E13
jj	167; E0
kk	242; E13
ll	245; E14
mm	246; E15
nn	68; E24
oo	246; E15
pp	246; E15

Chapter 3

a	370; ET
b	371; E1–2
c	131; E7
d	132; E8
e	371; E1–2
f	372; E2
g	341; E3
h	132; E8
i	133; E9
j	374; E4
k	375; E5
l	376; E6
m	139; E15
n	376; E6
o	345; E7
p	378; E8
q	379; E8a
r	380; E9
s	381; E10
t	382; E11
u	383; E12
v	384; E13
w	133; E9
x	134; E10
y	384; E13

z	385; E14		ll	414; E18
aa	386; E15		mm	422; E19
			nn	415; E21
			oo	392; E0
Chapter 4			pp	392; E23
			qq	388; E24
a	191; ET			
b	398; E3			
c	398; E3		**Chapter 5**	
d	389; E0			
e	231; E2		a	60; E18
f	192; E0		b	279; E10
g	231; E2		c	280; E11
h	192; E0		d	283; E13
i	193; E3		e	60; E18
j	399; E4		f	119; E0
k	400; E5		g	125; E0
l	203; E2		h	70; E0
m	56; E3		i	71; E0
n	203; E2		j	71; E0
o	401; E7		k	72; E0
p	392; E0		l	73; E0
q	193; E3		m	74; E0
r	393; E0		n	75; E0
s	394; E0		o	76; E0
t	350; E8		p	17; E0
u	342; E8		q	18; E0
v	349; E8		r	76; E0
w	6; E0		s	77; E0
x	7; E0		t	78; E0
y	342; E8		u	79; E0
z	342; E8		v	352; E0
aa	184; E0		w	79; E0
bb	335; E0		x	81; E0
cc	140; E16		y	54; E0
dd	452; E11		z	81; E0
ee	453; E12		aa	82; E0
ff	409; E13		bb	83; E0
gg	410; E14		cc	353; E0
hh	410; E14		dd	83; E0
ii	411; E15		ee	353; E0
jj	412; E16		ff	336; E0
kk	413; E17		gg	83; E0

Chapter 5 (*cont.*)

hh	84; E0
ii	336; E0
jj	84; E0
kk	185; E0
ll	84; E0
mm	85; E0
nn	86; E0
oo	221; E0
pp	222; E0
qq	87; E0
rr	88; E0
ss	89; E0
tt	91; E0
uu	286; E5
vv	91; E0
ww	92; E0
xx	93; E0
yy	94; E0
zz	95; E0
aaa	408; E12
bbb	108; E0
ccc	109; E0
ddd	110; E0
eee	111; E0
fff	112; E0
ggg	113; E0
hhh	114; E0
iii	115; E0
jjj	117; E0
kkk	118; E0

Chapter 6

a	288; E0
b	290; E0
c	291; E0
d	292; E0
e	293; E0
f	108; E0
g	293; E0
h	294; E0
i	295; E0
j	296; E0
k	260; E3
l	296; E0
m	297; E0
n	104; E0
o	105; E0
p	297; E0
q	451; E29

Appendix 1

a	260; E3
b	261; E4
c	185; E0
d	186; E0
e	96; E0
f	97; E0
g	98; E0
h	99; E0

Select Bibliography

The scope of this bibliography is limited to (a) standard critical editions of Marlowe's works and important literature appearing pre-1975; (b) materials relevant to Marlowe's *Doctor Faustus* and general Marlowe scholarship, appearing from 1975 to December 1986. To facilitate usage it is divided into four sections: Texts and concordances; Bibliographies; Books; Papers.

Texts and concordances

Bowers, Fredson ed.: *The Complete Works of Christopher Marlowe* (2nd edn; previous edn: 1973) Cambridge (CUP) 1981 (2 vols).

Cookson, Linda ed.: *Doctor Faustus* (with an essay by Jan Koff), Harlow (Longman) 1984.

Cornell University: *A Concordance to the Plays, Poems and Translations of Christopher Marlowe* Ithaca, N.Y. & London (Cornell University Press) 1982.

Gill, Roma ed.: *Doctor Faustus* (The New Mermaids) London (Ernest Benn Ltd) 1965.

Gill, Roma ed.: *The Complete Works of Christopher Marlowe* Oxford (Clarendon Press), 1986–.

Greg, Walter W. ed.: *Marlowe's 'Doctor Faustus' 1604–1616: Parallel Texts* Oxford (Clarendon Press) 1950.

Jump, John D. ed.: *Doctor Faustus* (The Revels Plays) London (Methuen) 1962.

Male, David A. ed.: *Doctor Faustus* London (Macmillan) 1985.

Tydemann, William ed.: *Doctor Faustus* Basingstoke (Macmillan) 1984.

Ule, Louis: *A Concordance to the Works of Christopher Marlowe* Hildesheim (Olms) 1979.

Bibliographies

Chan, Los Mai: *Marlowe Criticism: A Bibliography* Boston, Mass. (G. K. Hall), London (Prior) 1978.

Friedenreich, Kenneth: *Christopher Marlowe: An Annotated Bibliography of Criticism since 1950* Metuchen & London (Scarecrow Press) 1979.

Palmer, D. J.: 'Marlowe' in *English Drama (Excluding Shakespeare): Select Bibliographical Guides*, ed. Stanley Wells, London (OUP) 1975.

Post, Jonathan F. S.: 'Bibliography of Recent Studies in Marlowe criticism from 1968–1976' *English Literary Renaissance*, vol. 7, 1977, pp. 382–99.

Books

Altman, Joel B.: *The Tudor Play of Mind* Berkeley, L.A. & London (California University Press) 1978.

Ando, Sadao: *A Descriptive Syntax of Christopher Marlowe's Language* Tokyo (University of Tokyo Press) 1976.

Asibong, Emmanuel B.: *Comic Sensibility in the Plays of Christopher Marlowe* Ilfracombe (Stockwell) 1979.

Bakeless, John: *The Tragicall History of Christopher Marlowe* Cambridge, Mass. (Harvard University Press) 1942.

Birringer, Johannes H.: *Marlowe's 'Dr Faustus' and 'Tamburlane': Theological and Theatrical Perspectives* Frankfurt am Main (Lang), 1984 (Trierer Studien zur Literatur: Bd. 10).

Boas, Frederick S.: *Christopher Marlowe* Oxford (Clarendon Press) 1940.

Borinski, L. & Uhlig, C.: *Literatur der Renaissance* Düsseldorf & Bern (Bagel & Francke) 1975.

Bosonnet, Felix: *The Function of Stage Properties in Christopher Marlowe's Plays* (The Cooper Monographs no. 27) Basel (Franke Verlag Bern) 1978.

Bradbrook, M. C.: *The School of Night* Cambridge (CUP) 1936.

Bradbrook, M. C.: *Themes and Conventions of Elizabethan Tragedy* 2nd edn (1st edn: 1952), Cambridge (CUP) 1980.

Bradbrook. M. C.: *The Collected Papers of Muriel Bradbrook: vol. I: The Artist and Society in Shakespeare's England* Brighton (Harvester Press), Totowa, N. J. (Barnes & Noble) 1982.

Brandt, Bruce Edwin: *Christopher Marlowe and the Metaphysical Problem Play* Salzburg (Institut für Anglistik und Amerikanistik, Universität Salzburg) 1985.

Breuer, Horst: *Vorgeschichte des Fortschritts: Studien zur Historizität und Aktualität des Dramas des Shakespearezeit. Marlowe, Shakespeare, Jonson* München (Fink) 1979.

Brockbank, J. P.: *Marlowe: 'Doctor Faustus'* London (Edwin Arnold) 1962 (Studies in English Literature no. 6).

Chaudhuri, Sukanta: *Infirm Glory: Shakespeare and the Renaissance Image of Man* Oxford (Clarendon Press) 1981.

Cook, Ann Jennalie: *The Privileged Playgoers of Shakespeare's London* Princeton, N.J. & Guildford (Princeton University Press) 1981.

Cutts, John P.: *The Left Hand of God: A Critical Interpretation of the Plays of Christopher Marlowe* Haddonfield (Haddonfield House) 1973.

D'Agostini, Nemi: *Teatro Elisabettiano: Marlowe–Webster–Ford* Vicenza (Accademia Olimpica) 1975.

de Bruyn, Lucy: *Woman and the Devil in Sixteenth-Century Literature* Tisbury (Compton Press) 1979.

Dollimore, Jonathan: *Radical Tragedy: Religion, Ideology and Power in the Drama of Shakespeare and his Contemporaries* Chicago (University of Chicago Press) 1984.

Dutta, Ujjal: *Rhetoric and Synthesis: A Study of Marlowe's Dramatic Imagery* Calcutta (Prayer) *c.* 1979.

Ellis-Fermor, Una: *Christopher Marlowe* London (Methuen) 1927.

Gardner, Helen Louise: *Religion and Literature* London (Faber & Faber) 1971.

Godshalk, W. L.: *The Marlovian World Picture* The Hague & Paris (Mouton) 1976.

Greenblatt, Stephen: *Renaissance Self-Fashioning from More to Shakespeare* Chicago & London (University of Chicago Press) 1981.

Hattaway, Michael: *Elizabethan Popular Theatre* London (RKP) 1982 (Theatre Productions Studies).

Hope, A. D.: *A Tragical History of Doctor Faustus* Melbourne (Australian National University Press) 1982.

Hotson, J. Leslie: *The Death of Christopher Marlowe* London (Nonesuch Press); Cambridge, Mass. (Harvard University Press) 1925.

Howe, James Robinson: *Marlowe, Tamburlane and Magic*, Athens, Ohio (Ohio University Press) 1976.

Hunter, G. K.: *Dramatic Identities and Cultural Tradition* Liverpool (Liverpool University Press) 1978.

Kelsall, Malcolm: *Christopher Marlowe* Leiden (Brill) 1981.

Kernam, Alvin ed.: *Two Renaissance Mythmakers: Christopher Marlowe and Ben Jonson* (Selected Papers of the English Institute, 1975–6) Baltimore and London (Johns Hopkins University Press) 1977.

Kiessling, Nicolas: *The Incubus in English Literature: Provenance and Progeny* Washington State University Press (Washington) 1977, pp. 61–4.

Kocher, P. H.: *Christopher Marlowe: A Study of his Thought, Learning and Character* New York (Russell & Russell) 1962.

Kuriyama, Constance Brown: *Hammer or Anvil: Psychological Patterns in*

Christopher Marlowe's Plays New Brunswick, N.J. (Rutgers University Press) 1980.

Levin, Harry: *Christopher Marlowe: The Overreacher* London (Faber & Faber) 1954 (2nd edn: 1965).

Levin, Harry: *Shakespeare and the Revolution of the Times: Perspectives and Commentaries* New York (OUP) 1976.

Massinton, Charles G.: *Christopher Marlowe's Tragic Vision: A Study in Damnation* Athens, Ohio (Ohio University Press) 1976.

Moffett, Valerie A.: *Notes on Christopher Marlowe's 'Doctor Faustus'* London (Methuen) 1978 (Study-aid series; Methuen notes).

Murray, Christopher: *Doctor Faustus: Notes* Harlow (Longman) 1981 (York Notes no. 127).

Patterson, A.: *Censorship and Interpretation: The Conditions of Writing and Reading in Early Modern England* Madison, Wisc. (University of Wisconsin Press) 1984.

Phillips, D. Z.: *Through a Darkening Glass: Philosophy and Literature in Cultural Change* Oxford (Blackwell) 1982.

Princiss, Gerald: *Christopher Marlowe* New York (Ungar) 1975.

Reiss, Timothy J.: *Tragedy and Truth: Studies in the Development of a Renaissance and Neoclassical Discourse* New Haven & London (Yale University Press), 1980.

Reynolds, James A.: *Repentance and Retribution in Early English Drama* Salzburg (Institut für Anglistik und Amerikanistik, Universität Salzburg) 1982 (Salzburg Studies in English Literature: Jacobean Drama Series, 96).

(Routledge and Kegan Paul): *Marlowe: The Critical Heritage, 1588–1896* London (RKP) 1979.

Rowse, A. L.: *Christopher Marlowe* London & Basingstoke (Macmillan) (Papermac edn) 1981.

Shepherd, Simon: *Marlowe and the Politics of Elizabethan Theatre* Brighton (Harvester) 1986.

Steane, J. B.: *Marlowe: A Critical Study* Cambridge (CUP) 1964.

Stevens, David: *English Renaissance Theatre History: A Reference Guide* Boston, Mass (G. K. Hall) 1982.

Weil, Judith: *Christopher Marlowe: Merlin's Prophet* Cambridge (CUP), 1977.

Wickham, Glynne: *Early English Stages 1300–1600* 3 vols, London (RKP) 1959–72.

Papers

Aggeler, Geoffrey D.: 'Marlowe and the Development of Tragical Satire' *English Studies*, vol. 58 (no. 3) 1977, pp. 209–20.

Barnes, Celia: 'Matthew Parker's Pastoral Training and Marlowe's *Doctor Faustus' Comparative Drama*, vol. 15 (no. 3) 1981, pp. 258–67.

Bradbrook, M. C.: 'Marlowe's *Doctor Faustus* and the Eldritch Tradition', in *Essays on Shakespeare and Elizabethan Drama in Honour of Hardin Craig* ed. R. Hosley, London (RKP) 1963.

Brandt, Bruce E.: 'Marlowe's Helen and the Soul-in-the-kiss Conceit' *Philological Quarterly*, 64 (1984), pp. 118–20.

Brooke, Nicholas: 'The Moral Tragedy of Doctor Faustus' *Cambridge Journal*, V, 11 (1952).

Brough, Neil: '"Dr Faustus" and "P. F."', *Notes & Queries*, 32 (no. 1), 1985, pp. 15f.

Burnett, Mark Thornton: 'Two Notes on Metre and Rhyme in *Doctor Faustus' Notes & Queries*, 33 (no. 3), 1986, pp. 337f.

Craik, T. W.: 'Faustus' Damnation Reconsidered' *Renaissance Drama* NS2 (1969), pp. 189–96.

Danson, Lawrence: 'Christopher Marlowe: The Questioner' *English Literary Renaissance*, vol. 12 (1982), pp. 3–29.

Deats, Sara Munson: 'Ironic Biblical Allusion in Marlowe's *Doctor Faustus' Medievalia et Humanistica* 10 (1981), pp. 203–16.

Eriksen, Roy T.: 'The Misplaced Clownage-scene in *The Tragedie of Doctor Faustus* (1616) and its Implications for the Play's Total Structure' *English Studies*, vol. 62 (no. 3) 1981, pp. 249–58.

Eriksen, Roy T.: 'Giordano Bruno and Marlowe's *Doctor Faustus' Notes & Queries*, 32 (no. 4), 1985, pp. 463–5.

Finkelpearl, Philip J.: '"The Comedian's Liberty": Censorship of the Jacobean Stage Reconsidered', *English Literary Renaissance*, 16 (1986), pp. 123–38.

Gill, Roma: '"Such Conceits as Clownage Keeps in Pay": Comedy and *Doctor Faustus'* in *The Fool and the Trickster*, ed. P. V. A. Williams, Cambridge (Brewer) 1979, pp. 55–63.

Hardin, Richard F.: 'Marlowe and the Fruits of Scholarism' *Philological Quarterly*, 63 (1984), pp. 387–400.

Henke, James T.: 'The devil within: a *Doctor Faustus* for the contemporary audience', *Elizabethan and Renaissance Studies*, 1977.

Keefer, Michael H.: 'Verbal Magic and the Problem of the A- and B-texts of *Doctor Faustus' Journal of English and Germanic Philology*, LXXXII (no. 3) 1983, pp. 324–46.

Kiessling, Nicolas: 'Doctor Faustus and the Sin of Demoniality' *Studies in English Literature* 15 (1975) pp. 205–11.

Kirschbaum, Leo: 'Mephostophilis and the lost "Dragon"' *Review of English Studies*, XVIII (1942) pp. 312–15.

Kirschbaum, Leo: 'Marlowe's Faustus: A Reconsideration' *Review of English Studies*, XIX (1943), pp. 225–41, esp. p. 229.

Kirschbaum, Leo: 'The Good and Bad Quartos of *Doctor Faustus*' *The Library* XXVI (1945–6), pp. 272–94.

Knights, L. C.: 'The Strange Case of Christopher Marlowe' in Knights's *Further Explorations*, London (Chatto & Windus) 1965, pp. 75–98.

Kocher, P. H.: 'The English Faust Book and the Date of Marlowe's *Faustus' Modern Language Notes*, LV (1940), pp. 95–101.

Kocher, P. H.: 'Nashe's Authorship of the Prose Scenes in *Faustus'*, *Modern Language Quarterly*, III (1942), pp. 17–44.

Kocher, P. H.: 'The Early Date for Marlowe's *Faustus' Modern Language Notes*, LVIII (1943), pp. 539–42.

Kuriyama, Constance Brown: 'Dr Greg and *Doctor Faustus*: The Supposed Originality of the 1616 Text' *English Literary Renaissance*, vol. 5 (1975), pp. 171–97.

Lake, D. J.: 'Three Seventeenth-Century Revisions: *Thomas of Woodstock, The Jew of Malta*, and *Faustus B' Notes & Queries*, 30 (1983), pp. 133–42.

Mahood, M. M.: 'Marlowe's Heroes' *Poetry and Humanism*, 1950, p. 85.

Maxwell, J. C.: 'The Sin of Faustus' *The Wind and the Rain*, IV, 1947, pp. 49–52.

McAlindon, T.: 'The Ironic Vision: Diction and Theme in Marlowe's *Doctor Faustus' Review of English Studies*, XXXIII, 1981, pp. 129–141.

McMillin, Scott: 'The Queen's Men in 1594: A Study of "Good" and "Bad" Quartos' *English Literary Renaissance*, 14 (1984), pp. 55–69.

Muir, Kenneth: 'The Chronology of Marlowe's Plays' *Proceedings of the Leeds Philosophical and Literary Society*, V (1943) pp. 345–56.

Norton-Smith, John: 'Marlowe's "Faustus" (I. iii, 1–4)' *Notes & Queries*, vol. 223, 1978, pp. 436f.

Okerlund, A. N.: 'The Intellectual Folly of Dr Faustus' *Studies in Philology*, LXXIV (no. 3) 1977, pp. 258–78.

Pettit, Thomas: 'The Folk Play in Marlowe's "Dr Faustus"' *Folklore*, vol. 91, 1980 (i), pp. 72–7.

Phillips, D. Z.: 'Knowledge, Patience, and Faust' *Yale Review*, LXIX (no. 3) 1980, pp. 321–41.

Pittock, M.: 'God's mercy is infinite: Faustus' last soliloquy' *English Studies* 65 (1984), pp. 302–11.

Praz, Mario: 'Christopher Marlowe' *English Studies*, XIII (1931), pp. 209–23.

Ricks, Christopher: 'Doctor Faustus and Hell on Earth' *Essays in Criticism* 35 (1985), pp. 101–20.

Sahel, Pierre: 'Les prisons politiques chez Marlowe et Shakespeare' *Société Française Shakespeare, Actes du Congrès 1980*, ed. M. T. Jones-Davies, Paris (Touzot) 1981.

Seaton, Ethel: 'Marlowe's Map' *Essays and Studies*, X (1924), pp. 13–35.

Smith, James: 'Marlowe's *Doctor Faustus' Scrutiny*, VIII, i (1939), pp. 36–55.
Smith, Robert: 'Note on *Doctor Faustus* and *A Shrew' Notes & Queries*, vol. 224, 1979, p. 116.
Smith, Robert: '"Faustus' End" and *The Wounds of Civil War' Notes & Queries*, 32 (no. 1) 1985, p. 16f.
Urry, William: 'Marlowe and Canterbury' *T.L.S.*, 13 February 1964.
Warren, Michael J.: '*Doctor Faustus*: The Old Man and the Text' *English Literary Renaissance*, vol. 11 (1981), pp. 111–47.
Wion, Philip K.: 'Marlowe's *Doctor Faustus*, the Oedipus Complex, and the Denial of Death' *Colby Library Quarterly*, XVI (no. 4) 1980, pp. 190–204.
Young, David: '"Where the Bee Sucks": A Triangular Study of *Doctor Faustus, The Alchemist*, and *The Tempest*' in *Shakespeare's Romances Reconsidered*, ed. Carol McGuinis Kay and Henry E. Jacobs, Lincoln, Neb. & London (Nebraska University Press) 1978, pp. 149–66, notes pp. 178–9.
Zimansky, Curt A.: 'Marlowe's *Faustus*: The Date Again' *Philological Quarterly*, XLI (1962), pp. 181–7.

Index